The GAPPSI Method: Problem-solving, Planning, and Communicating

Concepts and Strategies for Leadership in Education

Douglas
ARCHBALD

NCPEA Publications

National Council of Professors of Educational Administration
Ypsilanti, Michigan

Published by NCPEA Publications
The publications of the National Council of Professors of Educational Administration (NCPEA)
http://www.ncpeapublications.org

Printed in United States of America
Library of Congress Cataloging-in-Publication Data

Archbald,, Douglas

The GAPPSI method: Problem-solving, planning, and communicating - concepts and strategies for leadership in education ISBN 978-1-4675-6536- 3 (pbk)

How to order this book:

NCPEA Press, a book publisher for NCPEA Publications offers *The GAPPSI Method: Problem-solving, Planning, and Communicating - Concepts and Strategies for Leadership in Education* as a Print-on-Demand hard copy and as an eBook at: www.ncpeapublication.org Books are prepared in Perfect Bound binding and delivery is 3-5 business days. eBooks are available upon ordering and delivered electronically in minutes to one's computer.

The GAPPSI Method: Problem-solving, Planning, and Communicating - Concepts and Strategies for Leadership in Education has been peer reviewed, accepted, and endorsed by the National Council of Professors of Educational Administration as a significant contribution to the preparation and practice of school administration.

NCPEA Publications Director and Editor   Theodore B. Creighton
NCPEA Publications Associate Director and Cover Design   Brad E. Bizzell

Contents

ABOUT THE AUTHOR

Doug Archbald, Ph.D. (University of Wisconsin) is Associate Professor of Education Leadership and Policy in the College of Education and Human Development at the University of Delaware. His primary affiliation is with the Education Leadership doctoral program, teaching, mentoring doctoral students, and contributing to program administration and improvement. He served as program coordinator for eight years and has taught courses in education policy, school law, curriculum design and evaluation, management applications of research, organizational communications, and data-based decision making. Archbald has published widely in leading academic and professional journals and been a principal investigator or consultant on numerous research studies and projects, including with the Consortium for Policy Research in Education, American Institutes for Research, the Council of Chief State School Officers, the Delaware Department of Education, Pearson Education, the Delaware Education Governance and Accountability Commission, the National Education Goals Panel, Towers-Perrin, and others. His most recent project was in a school district partnership initiative to strengthen data-driven decision making and translate research into useful knowledge for district leaders and policymakers.

PREFACE

The GAPPSI Method: Problem-solving, Planning, and Communicating - Concepts and Strategies for Leadership in Education

WHAT IS THIS BOOK FOR?

"GAPPSI" stands for *Gap Analysis for Problem-solving, Planning, and School Improvement*. This book guides problem solving and problem analysis projects for education leaders with the aim of school improvement. Henceforth, I refer to this book as GAPPSI.

WHO IS THIS BOOK FOR?

GAPPSI is appropriate for graduate courses in education related to leadership, problem solving and decision making. The vast majority of graduate degree holders in education, including doctorates, are *not* academics, researchers, and university professors (Archbald, 2011; Thurgood, Golladay, & Hill, 2006); most work in education organizations and many in roles of leadership involving planning, decision making, and problem solving.[1] This book explores the theory and practice of problem solving aimed at organizational improvement.

This book is ideal for graduate courses in Education Leadership/Administration programs (doctoral and Master's). Seeking "relevance and rigor," more programs now require problem-based capstone projects, portfolios, and theses connected with leadership, practice, and improvement.[2] This book is intended to help in these efforts, especially if students can apply GAPPSI to planning and improvement initiatives in their school or district or other education setting. Because the book is a practical tool for leadership, GAPPSI also can help K-12 administration practitioners and professional developers.

---

[1] Figures on employment sectors of education doctorates can be found at the website of the National Center for Education Statistics from the Integrated Post-Secondary Education Data System. Specific data are scarce with respect to questions related to types of positions and career paths by degree type (e.g., Ph.D. versus Ed.D.) and specializations within education; most Ed.D. programs have a professional orientation and therefore most degree candidates are not aiming for academic research positions.

[2] For literature on innovation in graduate-level leadership education, see Archbald (2008), Archer (2005), Andrew and Grogan (2005), Darling-Hammond, LaPointe, Meyerson, Orr, and Cohen (2007, Gaetane and Normore (2010), Hale and Moorman (2003), Schulman et al. (2006), Murphy and Vriesenga (2005), Orr (2006). For literature on problem-based pedagogy for education leadership development, see, Brenninkmeyer and Spillane (2004), Copland (2000), Copland (2003), Fenwick (2002), Leithwood and Steinbach (1995), and Leithwood, Seashore, Anderson, and Wahlstrom (2004). See also references in Chapter 1.

WHAT IS "GAP ANALYSIS"?

A problem can be defined simply as a gap between our expectations and current conditions. Little problems or obvious problems are not complicated. The photo copier is broken and should be fixed; two students are fighting and should stop. Here the gap between conditions and expectations is simple and clear. Organizational problems are more complicated, sometimes breathtakingly complicated. You are a principal and want all students to be successful, but forty percent of your students read below grade level. You expect an anti-bullying campaign in your school to reduce bullying, but it seems to have no effect. You have invested heavily in a new mentoring initiative, but it seems not to be working. Gaps like these between expectations and actual conditions are complicated organizational problems, neither easy to understand or solve.

GAPPSI is a framework to "define a problem," formulate and investigate questions, and create knowledge to guide planning and decision making. GAPPSI formalizes what we often do automatically and intuitively.[3] Automatic and intuitive is fine for little and obvious problems. With more complicated organizational problems and the complex improvement initiatives they engender, it pays to be thoughtful and systematic. Like any framework, GAPPSI is just a tool – like research methods and methods for data-based decision making are tools. GAPPSI doesn't guarantee success, but it builds expertise and improves the odds of successful outcomes.

HOW IS GAPPSI DIFFERENT FROM OTHER SIMILAR BOOKS?

There are many books on action research and on data-based decision making, some targeted for education leaders. GAPPSI is of this type, but offers a new contribution. Action research literature encourages practitioners to conduct research within their own organization (Houff, 2008; Mills, 2007). A typical action research book explains principles of research design, research applications in school settings, and requirements for publishing results. Like action research, GAPPSI requires empirical inquiry, but unlike action research, GAPPSI does not assume the goal is to produce research findings and to try to "prove" something. Rather, GAPPSI is about trying to make good decisions in complicated situations – decisions that help improve a school, program, or organization.

In this respect GAPPSI shares similarities with literature on data-based decision making (DBDM) (e.g., Bernhardt, 2004; Boudett, City, & Murnane, 2005; Creighton, 2007; Latess, 2008). DBDM literature is not about doing research per se; nor does it generally advocate theory-building or publishing results. Rather, it focuses on using data more effectively for planning and decision-making. GAPPSI is not heavily focused on data uses and methods of empirical analysis. GAPPSI's focus is much more on the logic,

---

[3] The term "gap analysis" is not my invention. Gap analysis's main roots are in policy analysis and business, with Clark & Estes's (2008) *Turning Research into Results* being notable. For other literature exploring the nature problems in education and how we think about problem solving, see Cuban (2001) and Gaynor (1998).

process, and discourse of identifying gaps in performance and then planning inquiry and actions to bring about improvement. Action research and DBDM literature tend to reflect an "objectivist" epistemology; GAPPSI, as I discuss more in the next chapter, reflects more of an "interpretivist" perspective in recognizing the subjectivity (values and argumentation) in defining problems.

GAPPSI projects require writing. Writing is integral to GAPPSI because communicating is essential to leadership and problem solving. Leaders and collaborators must share complex ideas, including proposals, justifications, explanations, instructions, procedures, and recommendations. Problem solving, teamwork, and communications are intertwined (Timperly & Robinson, 1998; Spillane, 2006). The words we use; how we organize ideas; how we describe problems and purposes; how we assert claims; how we present evidence and defend positions; how we tailor messages for specific audiences – all of these communications shape how we and others think about and act on problems.

I favor the word "communications" over writing because it is a broader term and emphasizes audience, message, and purpose. Typical graduate coursework requires students to write a paper in scholarly style for an academic audience. The assignment is usually phrased like this: "write a 15 page paper on [topic]." The student then endeavors to "fill up" the required pages with academic content delivered in scholarly prose. This is fine for liberal arts education and for scholarly training, but not the best for professional training in leadership.

GAPPSI curriculum requires authentic products. Products of GAPPSI coursework should include papers, presentations, and other communications delivered through print and digital formats or "live" through simulations, and all communications assignments should specify a purpose and target audience. My point is to I emphasize communicating, not just ruminating.

OVERVIEW OF CHAPTERS

Chapter 1 introduces the idea of ill-structured problems and presents the perspective and broad goals of this book.

Chapter 2 presents the gap analysis framework – its logic and what it requires to identify a performance gap. It requires persuading an audience to view certain facts and conditions as falling short of a preferred goal state; successful, it motivates change to achieve new goals and improve organizational performance.

Chapter 3 discusses using gap analysis to formulate questions. These questions help identify information needed and tasks to complete – steps which lead toward plans and decisions.

Chapter 4 focuses on causal analysis, decision analysis tools, and organizing a proposal or plan. Thinking about causes of performance gaps builds your and others' understanding of a complex situation and helps develop improvement plans.

Chapter 5 is about communicating. Improvement requires motivating people and coordinating action and this requires communications.

References

Archbald, D. (2008). Research versus problem solving for education leadership doctoral preparation: Implications for form and function. *Educational Administration Quarterly, 44*(5), 704–739.

Archbald, D. (2011). The emergence of the nontraditional doctorate: A historical overview. In J. Pappas & J. Jerman (Eds.), *Meeting Adult Learner Needs through the Nontraditional Doctoral Degree* (Chapter 1). San Francisco: Jossey-Bass.

Archer, J. (2005). Some Ed.D. programs adopting practical approach. *Education Week*, December 14, p. 8.

Anderson, G. & Jones, F. (2000). Knowledge generation in educational administration from the inside out: The promise and perils of site-based, administrator research. *Educational Administration Quarterly, 36*(3), August, 428-464.

Andrews, R. & Grogan, M. (2005). Form should follow function: Removing the Ed.D. dissertation from the Ph.D. straight jacket. *UCEA Review*, Spring, 10-12.

Boudett,, K., City, E., & Murnane, R. (Eds.) (2005). Data wise: A step-by-step guide to using assessment results to improve teaching and learning. Cambridge, MA: Harvard University Press.

Brenninkmeyer, L.D. and Spillane, J.P. (2004). Instructional leadership: How expertise and subject matter influence problem solving strategy. Paper presented at the 2004 American Educational Research Association Annual Meeting, San Diego, CA.

Clark, R. & Estes, F. (2008). *Turning research into results: A guide to selecting the right performance solutions.* Greenwich, CT: Information Age Publishers.

Copland, M. (2000). Problem-based learning and prospective principals' problem-framing ability. *Educational Administration Quarterly, 36*(4), October, 585- 607.

Copland, M. (2003). Developing principals' problem-framing skills. *Journal of School Leadership, 13*, September, 539 – 548.

Cuban, L. (2001). *How can I fix it? Finding solutions and managing dilemmas.* NY: Teachers' College Press.

Creighton, T. (2007). *Schools and data: The educator's guide for using data to improve decision making.* Thousand Oaks, CA: Corwin Press.

Darling-Hammond, L., LaPointe, M., Meyerson, D., Orr. M. T., & Cohen, C. (2007). *Preparing school leaders for a changing world: Lessons from exemplary leadership development programs.* Stanford, CA: Stanford University, Stanford Educational Leadership Institute.

Fenwick T., J. (2002). Problem-based learning, group process and the mid-career professional: Implications for graduate education. *Higher Education Research & Development, 21*, May, 5-22.

Gaetane, J. & Normore, A. (Eds.) (2010). *Educational leadership preparation: Innovation and interdisciplinary approaches to the Ed.D. and graduate education.* NY: Palgrave Macmillan.

Gaynor, A. (1998). *Analyzing problems in schools and school systems: A theoretical approach.* Mawah, NJ: Lawrence Erlbaum Associates.

Grogan, M. & Andrews, R (2002). Defining preparation and professional development for the future. *Educational Administration Quarterly, 38*(2), April, 233-256.

Hale, E. & Moorman, H. (2003). *Preparing School Principals: A National Perspective on Policy and Program Innovations*. Institute for Educational Leadership, Washington, DC and Illinois Education Research Council, Edwardsville, IL.

Houff, S. (2008). *The classroom researcher*. Lanham, MD: Rowman and Littlefield.

Latess, J. (2008). *Focus-group research for school improvement*. Lanham, MA: Rowman & Littlefield Education.

Leithwood, K. & Steinbach, R. (1995). *Expert problem solving: Evidence from school and district leaders*. Albany: State University of New York Press.

Leithwood K., Seashore Louis, K, Anderson A., & Wahlstrom, K. (2004). *How leadership influences student learning*. New York: Wallace Foundation.

Mills, D. (2007). *Action research: A guide for the teacher researcher*. Upper Saddle River, NJ: Prentice-Hall.

Murphy, J. & Vriesenga, M. (2005). Developing professionally anchored dissertations. *School Leadership Review. 1*(1), 33-57.

Orr, M. (2006). Mapping innovation in leadership preparation in our nation's schools of education. *Phi Delta Kappan, 87*(7), 492-499.

Schulman, L., Golde, C., Bueschel, A., Garabedian, K. (2006). Reclaiming education's doctorates: A critique and a proposal. *Educational Researcher,* April, 25-32.

Sheckley, B., Donalson, M., Mayer, A., Lemons, R. (2010). An Ed. D. program based on principles of how adults learn best. In G. Jean-Marie & A. H. Normore, (Eds.), *Educational leadership preparation: Innovation and interdisciplinary approaches to the Ed.D. and graduate education* (pp. 173 – 202). NY: Palgrave MacMillan.

Spillane, J. (2006). *Distributed leadership*. San Francisco: Jossey-Bass.

Thurgood, L., Golladay, M. & Hill, S. (2006). *U.S. Doctorates in the 20th century (NSF 06-319)*. Arlington, VA: National Science Foundation, Division of Science Resources Statistics

Timperley, H. & Robinson, V. (1998). Collegiality in schools: Its nature and implications for problem solving. *Educational Administration Quarterly*, 34, December, 608-29.

Weick, K. (1995). *Sensemaking in organizations*. Thousand Oaks, CA: Sage.

Woods, P., Bennett, N., Harvey, J. & Wise, C. (2004). Variabilities and dualities in distributed leadership: Findings from a systematic literature review. *Educational Management Administration & Leadership, 32*(4), 439–457.

CHAPTER 1

GAPPSSI's RATIONALE AND ASSUMPTIONS

INTRODUCTION

This book presents a framework for organizational improvement projects I refer to as "GAPPSI" (Gap Analysis for Problem-solving, Planning, and School Improvement). GAPPSI is a framework to "define a problem," formulate and investigate questions, and create knowledge to guide planning and decision making. Like any framework, GAPPSI is based on theoretical assumptions, reflects certain values, and uses a terminology discussed in this chapter (Table 1). Subsequent chapters cover the "how to" with theory, guidelines, and examples.

Table 1
Key Terminology

Ill-structured problems
Uncertainty
Current conditions
Desired conditions
Goal states
Performance gaps
TLO/TMO claims
Problem definition
Problem-solving
Solutions
Rationality
Subjectivity
Interpretivist

THE CONCEPT OF ILL-STRUCTURED PROBLEMS

Leaders in organizations often face "ill-structured" problems. An ill-structured problem is a situation that raises concerns about performance, is complex, has multiple and uncertain causes and interpretations, and lacks ready solutions (Cuban, 2001; Jonassen & Hung, 2008; Middleton, 2002; Rittel & Webber, 1973; Savery, 2006; Simon, 1973). John Dewey, eminent philosopher and educator, referred to these as "indeterminate situations" and "problematic situations" (Dewey, 1938; O'Connor, 1953) stressing that the ambiguity and difficulties they pose motivate inquiry – that is, a search for answers or solutions.

Donald Schon, another scholar interested in problem solving and professional practice, writes:

> In real-world practice, problems do not present themselves to the practitioner as givens. They must be constructed from the materials of problematic situations which are puzzling, troubling, and uncertain. In order to convert a problematic situation to a problem, a practitioner must ...make sense of an uncertain situation that initially makes no sense. (Schon, 1983, p. 40)

Leithwood & Steinbach (1995) interviewed 52 school principals over the course of a school year and determined 17% of the problems encountered could be classified as "non-routine" (ill-structured). Education leaders are frequently confronted with problems calling for action – achievement results are too low, staff turnover is too high, morale is eroding, bullying is increasing, and so on – but exactly what the problem is and what is to be done are rarely clear.

When I use the term "problem," then, I do so in the sense that it is an indeterminate or problematic situation. It is complex with troubling elements, and we don't know exactly what to do about it.

PROBLEM SOLVING WITHOUT SOLUTIONS

The words "solving" and "solution" have a special meaning in discourse on ill-structured problems. We don't *solve* ill-structured problems in the final sense that a detective solves a crime or an engineer designs a solution to a construction problem.[4] In some fields a problem is a discrete "thing" with a solution eliminating the problem. In social service organizations like schools, a solution doesn't eliminate an ill-structured problem. A school confronting a bullying problem can engage in GAPPSI and reduce the prevalence of bullying, but it does not *solve* the problem – kids will continue to bully. A high school seeking to lower the percentage of students dropping out won't solve the drop out problem. However, a school can lessen bullying or lower its dropout rate. Problem "solving," then, is a misnomer in this context, because it is not really about "solving." Rather, think of problem-solving as a *process* of GAPPSI and solutions as decisions and actions resulting from GAPPSI. Improvement is the aim.

PROBLEM SOLVING AS GAP ANALYSIS

Fundamentally, a problem is a gap between an *existing* and a *preferred* organizational state (the "goal" state). It is a gap between "is" and "ought" – between current conditions or practices and desired conditions or practices. This is a simple idea in the abstract. It is more complicated when the problem definer must make the problem definition concrete, specific, persuasive, and easy to understand.

Problem statements initially start with, what I call, "too little of" or "too much of" (*TLO/TMO*) claims: e.g., "there is too little effective use of technology in our science curriculum;" or "our school's drop-out rate is too high." It is useful to identify and formulate "key" problem sentences this way. This is the work of problem definition as you reflect on conditions or performance in your organization and seek to clarify a core issue. For practitioners in schools, districts, or postsecondary institutions there is rarely a shortage of problems to tackle. The hard part is fully developing and persuasively communicating the problem definition.

A persuasive problem definition makes clear the gap between *current* and *desired* conditions, practices, or performance. The problem definition will be persuasive if the audience:

- understands the current state
- understands the goal state
- believes the goal state is desirable (the leader may believe this, but the aim is to persuade others to believe it)

---

[4] For a seminal article on this subject, see, "Dilemmas in a General Theory of Planning" by Rittel and Webber (1973).

2

- believes there is a gap between the current state and the goal state
- believes the goal state is possible to achieve
- believes the costs required to achieve the goal state are justified (i.e., worth the effort)

PROBLEM DEFINITION AS AN INTERPRETATION

Peter Berger and Thomas Luckman (1967) wrote an influential book, "The Social Construction of Reality." They wrote about "defining a situation" and analyzed how people in certain situations define their own reality or "negotiate" a definition in cases where people or groups have different interpretations. The reality of a situation, Berger and Luckman remind us, is what the people believe it to be. Problem definitions in the workplace have a subjective quality, and in this sense are "interpretations."[5]

Consider this scenario: a high school principal reviews a report showing percentages of students getting As and Bs over the last three years in 9th and 10th grade in English Language Arts courses. The report shows a pattern of students getting higher grades in 9th grade English than in 10th grade Literature. In 9th grade, 54% of students get As and Bs, while 36% get As and Bs in 10th grade. Principal Jones, seeing these figures, expresses concerns about "standards" in 9th grade. He says the 9th grade teachers need to "raise the bar" and challenge the students more.

Ms. Smith, the department chair, has a different interpretation. She believes the higher grades in 9th grade reflect good teaching. She believes the 9th grade English teachers are a dedicated and cohesive group and get great results from their students. She wants to congratulate them, and is concerned about the quality of instruction in the 10th grade classrooms.

Mr. Green, a 10th grade teacher, thinks that a larger portion of special education students are getting placed in regular education 10th grade classrooms, bringing down the 10th grade GPA. Mr. Green wants this issue discussed at the next faculty meeting because he thinks it makes teaching more difficult and shortchanges both special education and regular education students.

This scenario shows three different interpretations of a situation – a situation with some factual evidence, but with a great deal of incomplete information and room for sub-

---

[5] There is large literature on interpretivist perspectives in research. Most relevant are case studies of school reform and policy implementation showing how different actors have different understandings of their context, conceptions of reform or program aims, and interpretations of outcomes (see, for example, Coburn, 2006; Cohen, 1990; Cohen, Mofftti, & Goldin, 2007; Spillane, Reiser, & Reimer, 2002; Weick, 1976; and Weick, 1995). Bolman and Deal (1991, p12) write: "Organizations are filled with people who have different stories about what is happening and what should be happening. Each story contains a glimpse of the truth, but each is a product of the prejudices and blind spots of the viewer. None of these versions of the truth is comprehensive enough to make the organization truly understandable or manageable." Bolman and Deal seem, though may not intend, to assume there *is* an underlying "truth." I will leave to philosophers the debate as to whether a situation has an ultimate, underlying truth. What leaders in an organization have to worry about is building a productive consensus that moves the organization toward its performance goals.

jectivity. There are high school English courses (9th grade English and 10th grade Literature) with percentages of students getting As and Bs. Jones, Smith, and Green each see something different: 9th grade teachers' lax standards, inadequate instruction in 10th grade, and lower achievement of special education students lowering 10th grade GPAs. These different definitions of the situation reflect different values, perspectives, assumptions about causes, and implications for possible remedies. This is an indeterminate situation with problematic elements – a fuzzy problem – evoking multiple interpretations.

PROBLEM DEFINITION AS AN ARGUMENT

An interpretation may be a problem definition, but not all problem definitions (like not all interpretations) are equal; some have stronger rationales and more evidence. Some problem definitions lead to actions that improve organizational performance; others lead to decisions or actions, but no improvement. Some problem definitions, if they are based on false assumptions, bad information, or misguided principles, can make things worse. The expression, "jumping to a conclusion," reflects this and is a caution about the potential consequences of acting thoughtlessly. Gap analysis is the opposite: thinking deeply about a problem, being systematic in collecting evidence, and constructing a well thought-out, evidence-based plan.

In the scenario above, suppose Mr. Jones declares that the solution is a schoolwide policy requiring grading on a curve in each course, thereby limiting the percentage of students who can fall into each grade range (A, B, C, etc.) He asks four teachers to form a committee and decide what those percentages will be, and asserts that "the percentages of kids getting As and Bs can't continue to be in the 50s. It's got to be tougher than that."

Mr. Jones has a problem definition. How has he defined the problem? There are two parts to it. He believes (a) the percentages of As and Bs in 9th grade is too high and (b) that the percentage of As and Bs awarded in similar courses at different grade levels must not differ much. He has inferred a cause of problem (a) – that the 9th grade teachers are "soft" graders. He lacks evidence that the 9th grade teachers are soft graders or that their grading standards differ from the standards of other teacher. He does not specify what exactly constitutes "soft grading." These are assumptions that are part of his problem definition.

With respect to (b), Mr. Jones assumes an unstated principle: that it is inappropriate for different courses to have different distributions of grades. If asked for the rationale behind this principle Mr. Jones might answer that it is important for teachers to grade similarly. This however, is merely a rephrasing of the principle, not a justification. Pressed further, Mr. Jones might claim similar grade distributions would be evidence that different teachers have the same standards, and that it is important for standards to be consistent among different classrooms. The principle of consistent standards is theoretically defensible both on grounds of fairness and effectiveness, but can we assume, as Mr. Jones does, that similar grade distributions are evidence of similar standards? Studies show this assumption is questionable (Brookhart, 2011; Conley, 2000; Goodwin, 2011; Nye, Konstantopoulos, & Hedges, 2004; OERI, 1994).

Is Mr. Jones's problem definition valid? It is built on a number of assumptions that are unstated, unverified, and perhaps questionable, and on at least one concept ("soft grading") that is not clearly defined. If this problem definition prevails, but its assumptions are not valid, then it is unlikely anything will improve. Indeed, Mr. Jones's "solution" could very well create problems that previously did not exist.

As this example shows, decisions reflect problem definitions. Mr. Jones's "solution" reflects his definition of the problem. We all do this. We may not be fully aware of the logic of our assumptions, the evidence for our positions, and the ideas that shape our interpretations. This is OK much of the time – indeed it is necessary and functional. We encounter many routine problems and our responses are essentially automatic (Kahneman, 2012; Simon, 1993).

Some situations, however, are not routine. Quite the opposite: they are complicated, troubling, and difficult. Situations like these call for a more systematic problem-solving approach and that is where gap analysis is useful. It requires the problem-definer to build a case for their perspective. In this respect, a problem definition is an argument: you use facts, logic, and values to persuade others that a situation is a problem and that actions are needed.

WHAT IS THE RATIONALE FOR GAPPSI?

Developing Expertise: Knowledge, Thinking Skills, Communications

We often hear of problem solving referred to as a skill. To refer to GAPPSI this way would be like referring to a physician's ability to diagnose and treat illness as a skill or a lawyer's ability to analyze and resolve complex legal matters as a skill. Problem solving in professional practice cannot be narrowly construed as "skill." It is more properly viewed as a form of expertise. Expertise in education leadership, like expertise in any high level profession comes from discipline-based knowledge, critical thinking skills, and communications skills. Leadership expertise requires more than these domains, but these domains are an important part of leadership. These domains – knowledge, critical thinking, and communications – are what GAPPSI-based assignments and projects help develop.

Most of this book (chapters 2, 3, and 4) focuses on the knowledge and critical thinking domains – the conceptual and methodological aspects of GAPPSI. Chapter 5 focuses on professional communications – particularly on writing more effectively – because (a) expertise in leadership communications is crucial, (b) thinking and writing are mutually reinforcing, (c) many practitioners struggle with and avoid writing, and therefore lack an important tool for leadership, and (d) writing well is the key to success in graduate professional education. Writing well also advances professional and leadership success.

Communicating well is critical because *our best ideas and plans are of little worth if we communicate them.* A leader needs to be able to inform, motivate, and persuade, but will be ineffective if people do not understand or care about the message. **You** may understand your intentions and believe fervently in *your* interpretation of events, problems, or plans. Motivating others requires that *they* understand and accept your perspective. In *Words That Work*, communications expert Frank Luntz stresses: "It's not what you say, it's what people hear" (Luntz, 2007).

As a leader or a participant in collaborative leadership you may need to:

- persuade audiences to adopt your position or reject others' positions;
- present complex information in different ways for different audiences;
- assist others to clarify or strengthen their communications;
- propose policies, programs, or practices;
- inspire with motivating messages or inform with technical exposition.

Writing sharpens your thinking and helps you learn; indeed, writing better makes you smarter. Booth, Colomb, and Williams (2008, p. 12) express this idea. You should write:

> ...to get your thoughts out of your head and onto paper, where you'll see what you really *can* think. Just about all of us, students and professionals alike, believe our ideas are more compelling in the dark of our minds than they turn out to be in the cold light of print. You can't know how good your ideas are until you separate them from the swift and muddy flow of thought and fix them in an organized form that you – and your readers – can study. ... In short, we write to remember more accurately, understand better, and evaluate what we think more objectively.

A similar point is made by Paul and Elder (2007, p. 22), from the Foundation for Critical Thinking:

> The art of writing well forces us to make explicit what we do and do not understand. Often we have the illusion we understand an idea – until we try to express our understanding in written form. Suddenly, we see problems. We discover the subject is more complex than we thought. Writing to learn is a powerful tool in learning deeply and well. Get in the habit of writing as a tool in learning.

Graduate education generally emphasizes scholarly papers – reading, discussing, and writing them. Typical graduate course writing aligns with the scholarly world. GAPPSI writing aligns more with the world of education professionals and seeks to build needed expertise for leadership – critical thinking, analytical skills, data proficiency, communications. GAPPSI assignments require products relevant to leadership practice: problem statements, proposals, plans, and others artifacts involving writing and professional communication.

The form and content of products created should align with authentic organizational contexts and audiences. This reflects the essential inseparability of analysis and communications: the analytical tasks of GAPPSI – the thinking part – are intertwined with the communications tasks of GAPPSI – the design and construction of messages through writing, graphical representations, oral discourse, and formal presentations. Chapter 5, therefore, covers concepts and tips to improve writing and communications.

School Improvement

There are two ways GAPPSI work can contribute to school improvement. The first, as described above, is by building expertise. You build expertise through well designed and rigorous learning experiences. (Hopefully your GAPPSI experience is well designed and rigorous.) More expertise translates into improved leadership practice on the job. Since effective leadership matters in schools (Waters, Marzano, & McNulty, 2003; Seashore Louis, Leithwood, Wahlstrom, & Anderson, 2010), GAPPSI contributes to school improvement by building knowledge, skills, and dispositions of the leader.

The second mechanism is more direct: GAPPSI assignments and projects can be applied directly in organizational settings. GAPPSI is well suited for applied problem solving projects because assignments and projects can be connected with school or district based improvement initiatives. This is like doing action research situated in your own school, but connected with a university-based course and mentoring. With GAPPSI, you would focus on a need in your own organizational setting, such as student achievement or behavioral problems or problems of management or organizational culture. Assignments from class would aim at specific organizational improvements, such as altering a master schedule to create more common planning time for selected groups of teachers, or evaluating a behavior modification technique, or designing parent communications to generate support for an after school program.

A GAPPSI project designed and executed well is applied problem solving and learning. The project might be a month, a full semester, or extend over a year or more. Ideally, this application should seek to improve practices in your organization through your intellectual and leadership work.

LITERATURE ON PROBLEM-BASED CURRICULUM AND LEARNING

GAPPSI, as described here, is a form of curriculum referred to as "problem-based learning" (Bridges & Hallinger, 1995; Copland, 2000; Jonassen & Hung, 2008; Savery, 2006; Sheckley, Donalson, Mayer, Lemons, 2010). The learning theory undergirding GAPPSI assumes people learn best when pursuing personally or professionally relevant learning goals: when you seek information serving your *own* professional needs, you are more motivated to learn and you retain information better; using the information reinforces your understanding and retention.[6] Needless to say, good curriculum and mentoring are essential – mentoring that, like good coaching, is not just training and guiding but also motivating. Sometimes we all need some "pushing" to keep going forward. A good instructor and mentor serves that role.

Problem-based learning for leadership education is not a new idea. It is advocated in scholarly literature on leadership preparation. Grogan and Andrews (2002, p. 250), summarizing two research reviews of education leadership preparation judged most ef-

---

[6] For literature on the critical role of intrinsic motivation in learning, see Hmelo (1998), Ormrod (1995), Paris and Turner (1995), and Van Berkel & Schmidt (2000). For literature on cognitive development and contextualized problem solving, see Bransford (1993), Brown, Collins and Duguid (1989), Fenwick (2000), Gijselears (1996), Hung (2002), and Prawat (1991).

fective the programs that "provided authentic experiences, simulated the development of situated cognition, and fostered real-life problem-solving skills." Davis, Darling-Hammond, LaPointe, and Meyerson's (2005, p. 9) research review concludes that the best programs "apply curricular content in authentic settings and toward the resolution of real-world problems and dilemmas." They advocate curriculum to "simulate complex real-world problems and dilemmas, promote the blending of theoretical and practical knowledge, improve problem-solving capacity, and help enhance candidates' self-concepts as future school leaders." Leithwood, Seashore, Anderson, and Wahlstrom, (2004, p. 67) write:

> The work of district and school leaders can be conceptualized as practical problem-solving, a type of thinking embedded in activity. A significant part of the learning required for such leaders to further develop their practical problem-solving expertise is usefully conceptualized as "situated." Such learning is specific to the context in which it is learned and most likely to be learned in contexts exactly the same as or closely approximating the situation in which it is to be used.

Scholars and management experts in other disciplines also take this view.[7] There are other books similar in philosophy to GAPPSI, but only a few related to education leadership (Bridges & Hallinger, 1995; Gaynor, 1998).

The research base supporting the educational perspective of this book comes primarily from the literature just cited. This literature draws largely on learning theory and the testimony of academics and practitioners; several studies are noteworthy because they relate directly to problem solving in leadership preparation.

Evidence shows that cognitive processes of defining and analyzing a problem are more developed in expert leaders. Leithwood and Stager (1989) studied 22 principals – 6 of them classified as "expert" based on a two-stage screening procedure.[8] In an extensive set of interviews, the 22 principals described their thinking and responses to a large number of problem situations varying from "structured" to "unstructured." The expert principals were better at such things as problem interpretation, how they stated intentions and goals, their ability to explain and justify decisions, and the depth of their understanding about constraints shaping proposed solutions. Differences between the experts and non-experts *increased* as the problems became more ill-structured.

---

[7] See, for instance, Bell, Raiffa, & Tversky (1988); Buyukdamgaci (2003); Connoly, Arkes, & Hammond (2000); Hogarth (1980); Isenberg (1988); March (1994); Mintzberg, Raisinghari, & Theoret (1976); and Schwenk (1988).

[8] The designation of "expert" was made by a two-stage screening process, the second stage utilizing the *Principal Profile* instrument developed by Leithwood and others. The first stage was based on confidential interviews with district administrators in three districts, asking them to identify the most effective building principals in their districts. This interview process was guided by a protocol and district administrators were interviewed independently. Only principals receiving *two* independent nominations were considered for the second screening stage.

Brenninkmeyer and Spillane (2004, April) interviewed 33 principals. These principals had been previously identified as "expert" or "typical" based on surveys of their staff and measures of their schools' performance over the previous years – up to five years. "Principals whose schools revealed improving leadership and organizational measures during the tenure of the principal (over a 5 year period) were grouped as 'experts' whereas schools with flat or slightly declining performance over time were classified as 'typical' principals" (p. 11). The researchers interviewed the principals and recorded their responses to a variety of scenarios involving ill-structured problems. The responses were coded and analyzed. The results showed statistically significant differences between the two groups: "the principals who were identified as experts using the school measures were found to exhibit more of the classic expert problem solving strategies over the typical principals, who were found to have more of the typical problem solving strategies" (p. 14).

Research on leadership expertise in other fields is similar. Mumford, Friedrich, Caughron, and Byrne (2007, p 517), discussing research on business managers, write that in problem solving situations the role of experience and expertise grows as problem complexity grows (they define complexity on five dimensions: choice optimization; ambiguity; novelty; resource accessibility; lack of social/structural support). In a similar vein, Morrison and Zori (2009) and Robbins and Davidhizar (2007) examining research on leadership roles and responsibilities of health care professionals conclude the evidence calls for more emphasis on critical thinking and problem solving in advanced professional preparation programs.

Several studies involving principals explore the developmental benefits of problem-based curriculum. Copland (2003) found principals' "problem-framing" ability improved significantly in a principal preparation program (three consecutive summers of coursework) with a heavy focus on problem-based learning. The students showed a statistically significant gain from pre-test to post-test on a rubric-based assessment of the principals' written analyses of five problem scenarios drawn from administrative practice. In follow-up interviews with the cohort two years after the program, the principals reported using what they learned in the program and attested to the program improving their ability to conceptualize, communicate, and solve problems in their work.

Leithwood and Steinbach (1995: 304) conducted a study similar to Copland's, although the duration of instruction was shorter. The results were similar. They write:

> With respect to the components of our problem-solving model, the experimental group showed significantly greater expertise in their thinking related to the interpretation of the problem, the goals set for solving the problem, and their understanding of the importance of anticipating and planning for the handling of possible conflicts. The most striking example of growth occurred in the goals component; every measure showed significant gains for the experimental group.

Other studies of problem-based learning in graduate programs for professionals are consistent with these findings (Berliner, 1986; Bridges & Hallinger, 1995; Fenwick, 2002; Gaetane & Normore , 2010; Hart, 1993; Leithwood, Jantz, Coffin, & Wilson, 1996).

This book with gap analysis in its title is itself aimed at a gap – the gap between prevailing practice in leadership education and a widely endorsed goal of authentic, rigorous, and relevant leadership curriculum. That professional education graduate programs, particularly those in education leadership, are perennially criticized for insufficient relevance to practitioners[9] attests to this gap and the need for the perspective and curriculum of this book. Given the persuasive testimony and evidence endorsing problem-based learning for leadership education and the lack of a book on this subject, I believe this book fills a gap.

No book or curriculum can guarantee school improvement. In school systems, many problems are rooted in conditions beyond the control of educators; and problems with personnel, resource, and organizational roots are deeply complex and fraught with uncertainty: improvement goals are often fuzzy, information is sketchy, and decision outcomes are unpredictable. With ill-structured problems, some variables are beyond decision makers' control and others only partially controllable. The goal of GAPPSI is to help current and prospective leaders understand the complexity of problems, to be systematic and analytical in problem solving, and to improve the odds of success in improvement initiatives.

CONCLUDING COMMENTS: PROBLEMS AS OPPORTUNITIES FOR LEARNING AND IMPROVEMENT

I conclude by connecting problem solving with a concept called organizational learning (Argyris & Schon, 1996; Collinson & Cook, 2007; Kruse, 2001; Leithwood, 2000; Senge, 1990; Senge, 2000).

Consider the scenario starting this chapter: the differing interpretations about the pattern of higher grades in 9th grade English compared with 10th grade Literature. From Mr. Jones's perspective, the "problem" could be fixed by a quick decision and directive. His perspective was "raise the bar" in the 9th grade classes – tell the teachers to be less generous in awarding high grades, develop an agreement on appropriate percentages of As and Bs, and follow the guidelines they develop. "Each semester we will print out and review a classroom-by-classroom report of grade distributions." Follow the new guidelines; problem solved.

From Mr. Jones's perspective, this approach to problem solving has benefits. He believes he is displaying an important quality of leadership – being decisive. Also, this approach takes little time. We all value saving time. And he believes his decision will solve the problem – as he has defined it.

Mr. Jones's decision will produce a change, but does it solve the problem? Will it improve the organization? Probably not.

Just as important, it is a lost opportunity to cultivate skills and values conducive to organizational learning. Organizational learning is "the deliberate use of individual, group, and system learning to embed new thinking and practices that continuously renew and transform the organization in ways that support shared aims" (Collinson & Cook, 2007, p. 8).

---

[9] For examples, see Darling-Hammond, LaPointe, Meyerson, Orr, and Cohen (2007), Elmore (2006), Hale and Moorman (2003), Levine (2005), Levine and Dean (2007), Murphy (2006), Orr (2006), Rees, Petrilli, and Gore (2004), Stein (2006), Young, Crow, Ogawa, and Murphy (2009).

Organizational learning results from processes of reflection, investigation, and deliberation. Mr. Jones's approach to problem solving lacks these qualities. It is not reflective – he has spent little time analyzing the situation. There was no attempt to investigate the situation – to learn and become informed. His approach reveals no deliberation – he has not involved other participants in discussing different problem definitions and consequences of alternative solutions. Mr. Jones's approach is counter to best practice models from literature on leadership, problem solving, and decision-making.

Reflection, investigation, and deliberation – these processes force us to consider the complexity of ill-structured problems. Ill-structured problems have lots of variables interacting in complicated and unpredictable ways. If we do not try to understand this complexity, we run the risk of changing one variable, unaware of interactions with other variables that can create other more serious problems. Like nature's ecosystems and society's economic systems, organizations are complex systems; understanding this helps avoid simplistic assumptions about one-to-one connections among variables.

Through investigation – inquiry and data – we learn about how our organization works and about performance. We learn about procedures and practices; about organizational resources, data, and technical systems; and about performance outcomes.

Deliberation also produces learning – acquiring information from each other and clarifying beliefs and values. Deliberation among the teachers would help identify information they need and how to get it. Information needed would include data on grade distributions from different courses and sections as well as student test scores and the teachers' espoused grading criteria.

Information alone is not enough. It is interpreted through beliefs and values. The teachers reflect on their beliefs and values about grading. Why assign grades? What is the rationale for our grading criteria? Must we all grade in the same way? Is there evidence that uniform grading is better? And so on.

These processes – reflection, investigation, and deliberation – produce organizational learning. It may be more time-consuming and bumpy at times, but experts believe it is better for the organization in the long run. To make this happen, leaders must believe, model, and communicate these qualities.

REFERENCES

Argyris, C., & Schon, D. (1996). *Organizational learning II: Theory, method, and practice*. Reading, MA: Addison-Wesley.

Barnett, B. (1995). Developing reflection and expertise: Can mentors make the difference? *Journal of Educational Administration, 3*(5), 45 – 59.

Bell, D., Raiffa, H., & Tversky, A. (1988). *Decision making: Descriptive, normative, and prescriptive interactions*. Cambridge: Cambridge University Press.

Berger, P. & Luckman, T. (1967). *The social construction of reality: A treatise in the sociology of knowledge*. NY: Doubleday.

Bernhardt, V. (2004). *Data analysis for continuous school improvement*. Larchmont, NY: Eye on Education.

Bolman, L., & Deal, T. (2003). *Reframing organizations: Artistry, choice, and leadership*. San Francisco: Jossey-Bass.

Booth, W., Colomb, G., & Williams, J. (2008). *The craft of research*. Chicago: The University of Chicago Press.

Boudett, K., City, E., & Murnane, R. (Eds.) (2005). *Data wise: A step-by-step guide to using assessment results to improve teaching and learning*. Cambridge, MA: Harvard Education Press.

Braxton, J. (2005). Reflections on a scholarship of practice. *The Review of Higher Education, 28*(2), 285–293.

Bridges, E. & Hallinger, P. (1995). *Implementing problem-based learning in leadership development*. University of Oregon: ERIC Clearinghouse on Educational Management.

Brookhart, S. (2011). Starting the conversation about grading. *Educational Leadership, 6*(3), November, 10-14.

Buyukdamgaci, G. (2003). Process of organizational problem definition: How to evaluate and how to improve. *Omega, 31*(4), 327-239.

Coburn, C. (2006). Framing the problem of reading instruction: Using frame analysis to uncover the microprocesses of policy implementation. *American Educational Research Journal, 43*(3), 343-379.

Cohen, D. (1990). A revolution in one classroom: The case of Mrs. Oublier. *Educational Evaluation and Policy Analysis, 12*(3), 327-345

Cohen, D., Mofftti, S., & Goldin, S. (2007). Policy and practice: The dilemma. *American Journal of Education, 113*(4) August, 515 - 549.

Conley, D. (2000). Who is proficient: The relationship between proficiency scores and grades. Paper presented at the Annual Meeting of the American Educational Research Association (New Orleans, LA, April 24-28, 2000).

Connolly, T., Arkes, H. & Hammond, K. (Eds.) (2000). *Judgment and decision making: An interdisciplinary reader*. Cambridge: Cambridge University Press.

Copland, M. (2000). Problem-based learning and prospective principals' problem-framing ability. *Educational Administration Quarterly, 36*(4), October, 585- 607.

Cuban, L. (2001). *How can I fix it? Finding solutions and managing dilemmas*. NY: Teachers' College Press.

Cutshall, S. (2003). Is smaller better? When it comes to schools, size does matter. *Techniques, 78*(3), March, 22 - 26.

Darling-Hammond, L., LaPointe, M., Meyerson, D., Orr. M. T., & Cohen, C. (2007). *Preparing school leaders for a changing world: Lessons from exemplary leadership development programs*. Stanford, CA: Stanford University, Stanford Educational Leadership Institute.

Davis, S., Darling-Hammond, L., LaPointe, M. & Meyerson, D. (2005). *School leadership study: Developing successful principals (Review of Research)*. Stanford, CA: Stanford University, Stanford Educational Leadership Institute

Dewey, J. (1938). *Logic: The theory of inquiry*. NY: Henry Holt and Company

Dreeben, R. (1968). *On what is learned in school*. Reading, MA: Addison-Wesley.

Elmore, R. (1979-80). Backward mapping: Implementation research and policy design. *Political Science Quarterly, 4*, Winter, 601- 616.

Elmore, R. (2006). Breaking the cartel. *Phi Delta Kappan 87*(7), 517-18.

Epstein, N. (2004). (Ed.) *Who's In Charge Here?* Washington, D.C.: Brookings Institution Press.

Farrar, E., DeSanctis, J. & Cohen, D. (1980). The lawn party: The evolution of federal programs in local settings. *Phi Delta Kappan 62*, November, 167 - 172.

Fullan, M., & Miles, M. (1992). Getting reform right: What works and what doesn't. *Phi Delta Kappan,* 73(10), 745-752.

Fusarelli, B. & Boyd, W. (Eds.) (2004). *Curriculum politics in multicultural America.* Thousand Oaks, CA: Corwin Press.

Gaetane, J. & Normore, A. (Eds.) (2010). *Educational leadership preparation: Innovation and interdisciplinary approaches to the Ed.D. and graduate education.* NY: Palgrave Macmillan.

Gaynor, A. (1998). *Analyzing problems in schools and school systems: A theoretical approach.* Mawah, NJ: Lawrence Erlbaum Associates.

Goodwin, B. (2011). Grade inflation: Killing with kindness? *Educational Leadership, 69*(3), November, 80-1.

Hale, E. & Moorman, H. (2003). *Preparing school principals: A national perspective on policy and program innovations.* Institute for Educational Leadership, Washington, DC and Illinois Education Research Council, Edwardsville, IL.

Hawley, W. & Rollie, D. (2002). *The keys to effective schools: Educational reform as continuous improvement.* Thousand Oaks, CA: Corwin.

Hogarth, J. (1980). *Judgment and choice: The psychology of decision.* Chichester: Wiley.

Houff, S. (2008). *The classroom researcher: Using applied research to meet student needs.* Lanham, MD: Rowman & Littlefield.

Howell, W. (Ed.) (2005). *Besieged: School boards and the future of education politics.* Washington, DC: Brookings Institution Press.

Isenberg, D. (1988). How senior managers think. In D. Bell, H., Raiffa, & A., Tversky (Eds.), *Decision making: Descriptive, normative, and prescriptive interactions* (pp. 525 – 539). Cambridge: Cambridge University Press.

Jacoby, S. (2006). *The age of American unreason.* NY: Pantheon Books.

Jonassen, D. & Hung, W. (2008). All problems are not equal: Implications for problem-based learning. *Interdisciplinary Journal of Problem-based Learning, 2*(2), Fall, 6 - 28.

Kahneman, D. (2011). *Thinking: Fast and slow.* NY: Farrar, Straus, & Giroux.

Kerckhoff, A. (2000). *Generating social stratification: Toward a new research agenda.* Boulder, CO: Westview Press.

Kliebard, H. (2002). *Changing course: American curriculum reform in the 20th century.* NY: Teachers College Press.

Kruse S. (2001). Creating communities of reform: Continuous improvement planning teams. *Journal of Educational Administration, 39*(4), 359- 383.

Lanham, R. (2000). *Revising prose.* Boston: Allyn & Bacon.

Latess, J. (2008). *Focus-group research for school improvement: What are they thinking?* Lanham, MD: Rowman & Littlefield.

Leithwood, K. (2000). (Ed.). *Organizational learning and school improvement.* Greenwich, CT: JAI.

Levine, A. (2005). *Educating school leaders.* New York: Columbia University Teachers' College, The Education Schools Project.

Levine, A., & Dean, D. (2007). Deleting the doctorate (and other vestiges of outmoded preparation). *School Administrator 64*(7), 10-14.

Lucas, S. (1999). *Tracking inequality: Stratification and mobility in American high schools*. NY: Teachers College Press.

Luntz, F. (2007). *Words that work: It's not what you say, it's what people hear*. New York: Hyperion.

Madda, C., Halverson, R., & Gomez, L. (2007). Exploring coherence as an organizational resource for carrying out reform initiatives. *Teachers College Record, 109*(8), August, 1957-79.

Manna, P. (2006). *School's in: Federalism and the national education agenda.* Washington, D.C.: Georgetown University Press.

March, J. G. (1994). *A primer on decision making: How decisions happen.* NY: The Free Press (Division of Macmillan, Inc.)

Marcy, R. & Mumford, M. (2010). Leader cognition: Improving leader performance through causal analysis. *The Leadership Quarterly, 21*(1), February, 1-19.

Middleton, H. (2002). Complex problem solving in a workplace setting. *International Journal of Educational Research, 37*(1), 67-84.

Mills, G. (2007). *Action research: A guide for the teacher researcher.* Upper Saddle River, NJ: Pearson.

Mintzberg H, Raisinghari D, Theoret A. (1976). The structure of "Unstructured" decision processes. *Administrative Science Quarterly, 21*(2): 246-75.

Mumford, M. D., Friedrich, T. L., Caughron, J. J., & Byrne, C. L. (2007). Leader cognition in real-world settings: How do leaders think about crises? *The Leadership Quarterly, 18,* 515–543.

Munter, M. (2006). *Guide to managerial communication*, 7/E. Upper Saddle River, N.J.: Prentice Hall.

Murphy, J. (2006). *Preparing school leaders.* Lanham, MD: Rowman & Littlefield Education.

NCES (2003-03). Public secondary schools, by grade span, average school size, and state or jurisdiction: 2002-03. Table 98. From: U.S. Department of Education, National Center for Education Statistics, The NCES Common Core of Data (CCD), "Public Elementary/Secondary School Universe Survey."

Nye, B., Konstantopoulos, S., & Hedges, L. (2004). How large are teacher effects? *Educational Evaluation and Policy Analysis, 26*(3), Fall, 237-57.

O'Connor, J. (1953). Indeterminate situation and problem in Dewey's logical theory. *The Journal of Philosophy,50*(25), 753-770.

OERI (1994). *What do student grades mean? Differences across schools.* OERI Education Research Report #8. Office of Educational Research and Improvement, U.S. Department of Education, Washington DC.

Orr, M. (2006). Mapping innovation in leadership preparation in our nation's schools of education. *Phi Delta Kappan, 87* (7), 492-499.

Paul, R. & Elder, L. (2007). *A thinker's guide for students on how to study and learn.* Dillon Beach, CA: Foundation for Critical Thinking Press.

Pearsall, T. (2001). *The elements of technical writing.* Boston: Allyn & Bacon.

Rankin, E. (2001). *The work of writing: Insights and strategies for academics and professionals.* San Francisco: Jossey-Bass.

Rees, N., Petrilli, M., & Gore, P. (2004). *Innovations in education: Innovative pathways to school leadership.* U.S. Department of Education, Office of Innovation and Improvement, Washington, D.C.

Rittel H. & Webber, M. (1973). Dilemmas in a general theory of planning. *Policy Sciences, 4,* 155-169

Robbins, B., & Davidhizar, R. (2007). Transformational leadership in health care today. *The Health Care Manager, 26*(3), 234-239.

Rotondo, J. & Rotondo, M. (2002). *Presentation skills for managers.* NY: McGraw-Hill.

Rowan, B., Harrison, D. & Hayes, H. (2004). Using instructional logs to study mathematics curriculum and teaching in the early grades. *Elementary School Journal, 105*(1), 103-127.

Middleton, H. (2002). Complex problem solving in a workplace setting. *International Journal of Educational Research, 37*(1), 67-84.

Savery, J. (2006). Overview of problem-based learning: Definitions and distinctions. *Interdisciplinary Journal of Problem-based Learning, 1*(1), 9-20.

Schon, D. (1983). *The reflective practitioner.* NY: Basic Books.

Schwenk, C. R. (1988). The cognitive perspective on strategic decision-making. *Journal of Management Studies, 25,* (1), 45-56.

Seashore Louis, K. Leithwood, K., Wahlstrom, K., & Anderson, S. (2010). *Learning from leadership: Investigating the links to improved student learning.* Final Report of Research to the Wallace Foundation. NY: Wallace Foundation.

Senge, P. (1990). *The fifth discipline: The art and practice of the learning organization.* New York: Doubleday.

Senge, P. (2000). *Schools that learn: A fifth discipline fieldbook for educators, parents and everyone who cares about education.* New York: Doubleday.

Sergiovanni, T., Kelleher, P., McCarthy, M., & Wirt, F. (2004). Public values and school policy: The roots of conflict (Ch. 1, pp. 1 – 15). *Educational governance and administration.* Boston: Pearson.

Sheckley, B., Donalson, M., Mayer, A., Lemons, R. (2010). An Ed. D. program based on principles of how adults learn best. In G. Jean-Marie & A. H. Normore, (Eds.), *Educational leadership preparation: Innovation and interdisciplinary approaches to the Ed.D. and graduate education* (pp. 173 – 202). NY: Palgrave MacMillan.

Simon, H. (1973). The structure of ill-structured problems. *Artificial Intelligence, 4*(2), 181-201.

Simon, H. (1993). Decision making: Rational, nonrational, and irrational. *Educational Administration Quarterly, 29,* 392-411.

Smith, J., Lee, V., & Newmann, F. (2001). *Instruction and achievement in Chicago elementary schools.* Chicago: IL: Consortium for Chicago School Research

Spillane, J., Reiser, B., Reimer, T. (2002). Policy implementation and cognition: Reframing and refocusing implementation research. *Review of Educational Research, 72*(3), Fall, 387-431.

Stein, S. (2006). Transforming leadership programs: Design, pedagogy, and incentives. *Phi Delta Kappan, 87*(7), 522-524.

Waters, J. T., Marzano, R. J., & McNulty, B. A. (2003). *Balanced leadership: What 30 years of research tells us about the effect of leadership on student achievement.* Aurora, CO: Mid-continent Research for Education and Learning.

15

Williams, J. (2007). *Style: Lessons in clarity and grace*, 9/E.: NY: Longman.

Weick, K. (1976). Educational organizations as loosely coupled systems. *Administrative Science Quarterly, 21*(1), 1-19.

Weick, K. (1995). S*ensemaking in organizations*. Thousand Oaks, CA: Sage.

Young, M. D., Crow, G., Ogawa, R., & Murphy, J. (2009). *The handbook of research on leadership preparation*. New York: Taylor & Francis.

CHAPTER 2

THE LOGIC OF PROBLEM DEFINITIONS:
A GAP BETWEEN CURRENT AND DESIRED STATES

A problem definition is an interpretation and an argument. It is an interpretation in that it reflects your perspective on a problematic situation. It is an interpretation based on facts, logic, and values.

Table 2.1
Key Terminology

Systems model
Organizational Inputs
Organizational Conditions
Organizational Goals
Organizational Performance
Problem Definition
Problem Statement
Problem Sentence
TLO/TMO sentence
Simple TLO/TMO claim
Benchmarked TLO/TMO claim
Compared with past
Compared with others
Compared with expectations

A problem definition is an argument in that you are building a case. You use facts, logic, and values to persuade an audience that a problem exists and changes are needed. If there is no problem, then there is no reason to change, no reason to improve. In this logic, a problem definition is needed to justify change. (Sometimes change is mandated and there is no clear and logical problem definition.)

This chapter provides frameworks and terminology for thinking and writing about problems. I discuss the logic of problem definitions and terminology to communicate this logic (Table 2.1). This chapter will help you analyze, study, and communicate about organizational problems.

Defining terminology needs to come first. The first section below distinguishes between organizational performance, conditions, and inputs – distinctions useful for developing a clear and logical problem definition. The subsequent section, "The Logic of Problem Definitions," presents three comparative frames of reference for developing a problem definition: other organizations, prior states in your organization, or goals and standards.

DISTINCTION BETWEEN ORGANIZATIONAL
PERFORMANCE, CONDITIONS, AND INPUTS

Figure 2.1, referred to as a "systems model," diagrams organizational inputs, conditions, and outputs (i.e., performance). The terms in Figure 2.1 are useful for writing and communicating about problem statements. It is called a systems model because it views the organization as a dynamic system of inter-connected variables.

Organizational Goals and Performance

There is a difference between goals and performance. Goals are the intentions; performance is what happens. *Performance* is the degree to which an organization achieves its goals. It is important to understand that the word "performance" (as in "organizational performance") is a *variable*. A variable is a something that varies, that exists in greater or lesser amounts, levels, or degrees.

Figure 2.1
Systems Model of Educational Organization

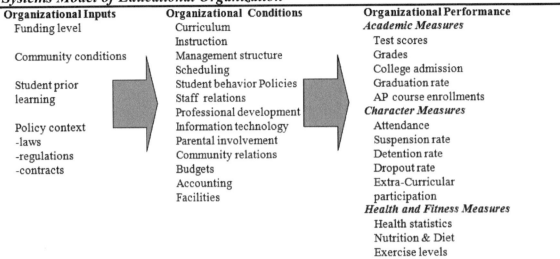

Organizational Inputs	Organizational Conditions	Organizational Performance
Funding level	Curriculum	*Academic Measures*
	Instruction	Test scores
Community conditions	Management structure	Grades
	Scheduling	College admission
Student prior	Student behavior Policies	Graduation rate
learning	Staff relations	AP course enrollments
	Professional development	*Character Measures*
Policy context	Information technology	Attendance
-laws	Parental involvement	Suspension rate
-regulations	Community relations	Detention rate
-contracts	Budgets	Dropout rate
	Accounting	Extra-Curricular
	Facilities	participation
		Health and Fitness Measures
		Health statistics
		Nutrition & Diet
		Exercise levels

Educational goals are commonly thought of in two categories – cognitive and affective. Terms also used are "academic goals" and "character goals." Many would add health and fitness as a third category.

Academic goals: developing students' academic knowledge and skills (basic skills, subject-matter knowledge, creativity, problem solving, and reasoning). There are many ways to express these types of goals. Written curriculum goals and standards are well known.[10] Another popular classification of education goals in the cognitive dimension is Bloom's (1956) Taxonomy.

Character goals: developing good citizens and good people. These goals include values, beliefs, and traits like honest, integrity, self-esteem, respect for others, punctuality, diligence, industriousness, and compassion (Table 2 shows additional examples).

Table 2.2
Behaviors Reflecting Character Goals

Character is a set of qualities, or values, that shape our thoughts, actions, reactions and feelings. People with strong character:

- show compassion,
- are honest and fair,
- display self-discipline in setting and meeting goals,
- make good judgments,
- show respect to others,
- show courage in standing up for beliefs,
- have a strong sense of responsibility,
- are good citizens who are concerned for their community, and
- maintain self-respect.

From *Helping your child become a responsible citizen.* U.S. Department of Education, Office of Communications and Outreach, Office of Safe and Drug-Free Schools, 2005.

---

[10] The website of the Council of Chief State School Officers (ccsso.org) has links to all states' curriculum standards.

Health and fitness goals: developing healthy and physically fit youth and developing values supporting healthy lifestyles.

Selected "measures" of organizational performance are shown in Figure 2.1. While achievement measures – test scores – come to mind first, school performance is much more than test scores. Many valued outcomes of education are not easily measured (e.g., intellectual curiosity) and some outcomes have no satisfactory measures. Test scores get most attention, but educators know that schools develop all the outcomes shown in Figure 2.1.

Organizational Inputs and Conditions

Inputs are thought of as "givens" – factors over which the organization has little or no control in the short term. Every school operates in a community with particular geographic and socio-economic characteristics, within an established framework of laws and policies, and with funding resources beyond the school's control for most problem solving purposes.[11] Most problem solving is concerned with organizational conditions, but if the fundamental problem is inadequate resources, then this is an input concern (discussed later in this chapter).

Organizational conditions are variables controlled by the system. These variables include local policies, management structures and procedures, curriculum, instructional practices, personnel training and physical infrastructures. "Conditions" refers both to *state* variables (e.g., morale) and to *process* variables (e.g., planning or collaborating). "Morale" is not a process; it is viewed as a state. Planning and collaborating are processes. Problem definitions can refer to states (morale is too low) or processes (planning is inadequate; instructional practices are ineffective). Other similar terms are procedures or practices.

Note that while resources like funding levels, as described above, are viewed as a given – an input – *how* resources are allocated and used are functions of management and staff decisions and practices (Odden & Archibald, 2001). Thus, resource use decisions and practices fall within "organizational conditions" in the systems model.

This framework is useful conceptually in thinking and writing about problems. The logic of problem statements assumes current conditions in an organization are caused both by inputs and other causally prior conditions. The logic assumes performance is a function of inputs and conditions. Since inputs are not immediately changeable, performance improvement in the short run can only be accomplished by changes in organizational conditions. For performance to change, conditions must change. As the saying

---

[11] The definition of what is or is not an input is theoretical. Resource levels, like revenue per pupil, are fixed over most problem solving timeframes. However, a five year plan might aim at changing certain inputs. Or, as another example, employment levels within a municipal area are generally considered an "input" – an economic variable affecting local schools and over which they have little control. However, a school district might be able to change the level of unemployment within its boundaries over a six or eight year timeframe with an effective vocational training program. In this scenario, an output from the school system – vocational skills of graduates – affects an input. Owings and Kaplan (2004) argue that principals and other education leaders can and should advocate more that school finance is an investment in human capital, because too often the public and legislators view schools simply as an expense.

19

goes, "If you do what you've always done, you'll get what you've always got." Improvement requires change.

THE LOGIC OF PROBLEM DEFINITIONS

A problem is defined as the gap between an existing state in the organization and a preferred state (goal state). It is a gap between "is" and "ought." The logic is simple; it is more complicated to operationalize this concept in an actual organizational setting.

Understand that "organizational setting," as used here, refers to whatever unit *you* are concerned with in your problem statement – a school, a department, a school district, a college, a state agency, a program within a larger organizational unit, a professional association, or other entities. An important part of a problem definition is making crystal clear the scope of your concern – the boundaries wherein the problem resides.

Attributes of Persuasive Problem Definition

A persuasive problem definition makes clear the gap between is and ought – the *current state* and the *goal state*. Making the gap clear is necessary, but not enough. You must help your audience:

- understand the current state
- understand the goal state (clear)
- believe the goal state is desirable (desirable)
- believe there is a gap between the current state and the goal state
- believe the goal state is possible to achieve (feasible)
- believe the costs required to achieve the goal state are worth it (justified)

In the following, I refer to the important problem definition attributes just described with shorthand words: clear, desirable, feasible, and justified. "Justified" summarizes a more complicated idea deriving from decision theory – the concept of a subjective expected utility function. It assumes individual action is motivated partly by a subjective benefit-cost calculation.[12] A positive value in a subjective expected utility analysis supports the individual decision to act to pursue expected benefits (e.g., "Although doing more to differentiate my instruction will take many hours of extra preparation time, it is worth it because I believe my students will benefit and that is good for them and gratifying for me.")

---

[12] This concept is rooted theory and inquiry in economics and management studies. It assumes decision making behavior can be explained at least in part by individuals' subject calculations of expected benefits in relation to expected costs. It does not presume the accuracy of these calculations or their consistency with norms of appropriate conduct – just that these calculations happen and influence the decisions people make. For more literature on this see, Bell, Raiffa, & Tversky (1988), Connolly, Arkes, & Hammond (2000), or Hogarth (1980).

The Kernel of the Problem Statement:
The "Too little of/Too much of" (TLO/TMO) Claim

"Thirty-five percent of our high schools seniors have applied to college."

Does this sentence state a problem? No. It is simply a statement of fact. Suppose the claim is:

"Too few of our high school seniors have applied to college."

This sentence implies a problem. The sentence has a **TLO/TMO** claim – there is "too little of…" or "too much of…" something. While problem sentences can be phrased in many different ways, at their core is usually a **TLO/TMO** claim. There is something that is deficient – too much of something or too little of something.

A *simple* TLO/TMO claim is required, but is not enough by itself. It identifies simply and succinctly what is wrong in your view. This is important for communications – if it is specific and succinct, it is easy to communicate and understand. *But*, it is only a start because you must make the case for the problem. This entails "benchmarking" the claim: answering the "compared to what?" question.

The claim – "Too few of our high school seniors have applied to college" – invites the question, "Too few, compared to what?" A persuasive problem definition answers this "compared to what" question. It *benchmarks* the TLO/TMO claim

Claiming "*Too few* of our seniors have applied to college" presupposes that more *should* apply to college. The gap between the current state and the goal state is implied, but the problem definition is not complete. That audience wants reasons; you must supply a warrant for your claim of "too few." You must give reasons that more seniors should apply to college. There must be reasons given that the "goal state" (more seniors applying) is both desirable and achievable. *Comparisons* help you do this.

"Too few of our seniors have applied to college. Three years ago, fifty-five percent applied. This year, thirty-five percent applied to college. "

This statement identifies a gap between a current state and a goal state – a 20% decline in the college application rate. Benchmarking it this way makes it harder for someone to reject the claim that the current application rate is too low. However, more needs to be done to develop the problem statement. The implied goal state, a 55% application rate, must appear both *achievable* and *desirable*. I pursue these ideas more in following sections. This example is just to introduce key elements of the problem statement.

A Few Words on Terminology and Language

This book uses these three terms: *problem definition*, *problem statement*, and *problem sentence*. Problem definition is like saying "interpretation" or "your logic." The other two terms are more literal: problem statement is the narrative describing and explaining the problem. It may include other information about the organization as well. Problem sentence is the single "TLO/TMO" sentence – the kernel of the problem statement that succinctly expressed it.

The concepts and terminology of constructing a problem definition are not the same as the language of leadership communications. Table 2.3 lists words useful for organizational communications about problems and improvement needs. These word choices have different nuances and connotations. Be deliberate in fitting your language to the expectations of the audience and the rhetorical context.

The next three sections elaborate on frames of reference for defining problems. Each section comprises brief vignette-like statements showing different kinds of problem definitions. They show problem definitions of different types, contexts, and connections to literature.

Table 2.3
Problem Statements: Commonly Used Words

deficient	ineffective
insufficient	inefficient
inadequate	unacceptable
inconsistent	excessive
substandard	unnecessary
subpar	disproportionate
shortfall	uneven
suboptimal	weak

Three Types of Comparisons to Benchmark TLO/TMO Claims

Benchmarking a problem statement requires developing a comparative frame of reference. In the example above, the fact – "35% of our high school seniors apply to college" – only becomes "too low" with the additional information that 55% of seniors used to apply. Thus, 35% only becomes too low when it is compared to something better. There are three logical types of comparisons to use. For simplicity, I will refer to them this way:

- *Compared with others* – compares levels of inputs, conditions, or performance with other similar organizations. The problem is the gap between your and the comparison organizations. The gap may be performance, or it may be conditions or inputs. "Our department gets lower levels of resources than other departments." The implied goal state is the level of inputs, conditions, or performance of the comparison organization(s).

- *Compared with past* – compares current inputs, conditions, or performance with past levels. Leaders should be informed about trends in their organization. The gap is between the way things are now and the way they used to be. If trends show a decline in some attribute – inputs, conditions, or performance – the implied goal state is earlier, more desirable levels. The comparative frame of reference is the past.

- *Compared with expectations* – compares current levels of inputs, conditions, or performance with a goal, theoretical ideal, expectations, or a model. These problem definitions are not based directly on empirical comparisons (as above), but rather on asserted inadequacies of current conditions or performance in relation to a preferred state.

22

These three comparative frames of reference – the column headers in Table 2.4 – are logically different. Table 2.4's rows identify the focus of the problem: on inputs, conditions, or performance. Thus, conceptually, there are nine categories of problem definitions. Table 2.4 is a heuristic – a tool to facilitate analysis and understanding and to think more critically about our own and others' logic when analyzing problems.

Table 2.4
Frames of Reference to Define Problems of Inputs, Conditions, and Performance

	Compared with other organizations	*Compared with past state*	*Compared with expectations*
TLO/TMO claim about *Inputs*	Gap between district's funding and other districts' funding.	Funding level over three years has remained constant in context of rising educational costs.	Gap between current funding and "adequacy" standards.
TLO/TMO claim about *Conditions*	Gap between staff turnover in our school compared with others in the district.	School spirit has declined.	Gap between current curriculum and ideal models of curriculum coherence.
TLO/TMO claim about *Performance*	Student academic growth gains lower in our school than other schools.	Our high school's dropout rate has increased over past five years	Gap between current achievement and grade-level achievement standards.

In real life, of course, organizational problems and problem definitions do not fall into neat categories. Problem definitions may draw on multiple frames of reference and usually are not just about inputs, conditions, or performance; rather, a problem statement may start with claims about performance shortfalls and include conjectures about causal conditions. Or a problem statement may start with claims about inputs or condition and then draw out implications for performance.

The problem statement examples in the next three sections are "textbook," so to speak. They illustrate the logic, use of evidence, and elements of narrative development. The examples are not intended to illustrate actual communications in an authentic context. In real organizational contexts, communications are tailored to the interests of particular stakeholders and shaped by time constraints, resource limitations (sometimes limiting access to evidence), and political considerations. More on this in Chapter 5.

Problem Statements About Organizational Performance

Organizational Performance: Compared With Others

The logic of the problem definition is based on comparing performance of two or more organizations (or units within) that have the same or similar inputs. The two most critical inputs are resource levels and student socio-economic status (SES).[13] If two schools have

---

[13] SES refers to "socio-economic status" – a term from sociological research on poverty and its effects on education, health, employment and other outcomes. Many research studies show how children growing up in poverty face enormous barriers to success in school. See, for instance, Duncan, Brooks-Gunn, and

the same resource levels and SES composition of the study body, but one has lower achievement scores, the gap in achievement between the two schools can be the basis of a problem definition.

Figure 2.2
Plot of Reading Scores by School % Free Lunch

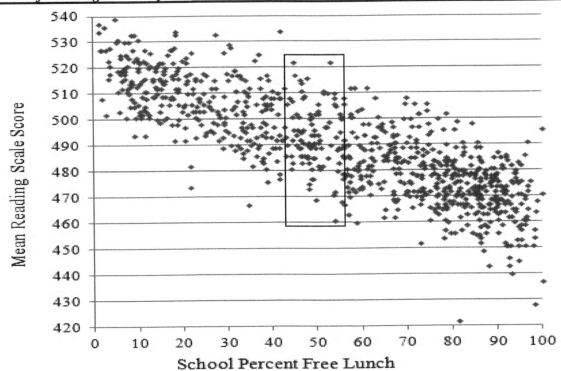

Figure 2.2 illustrates this logic. The chart is a plot of all elementary schools in a large state. The horizontal axis is "percent free lunch" and the vertical axis is the average 5th grade reading scores of the students in the school, using a scale unique to this state. On average, schools with higher percentages of poor children have lower test scores. Poverty takes a toll on academic performance. Schools serving large numbers of poor children have much greater challenges than schools serving more affluent populations. But, as the rectangle shows, you can identify many schools with similar percentages of free-lunch students, but with very different achievement levels.

The gaps in achievement among schools with similar SES composition indicate some schools are more effective; others less effective. The logic points to conditions in the lower achieving schools as the cause of the lower achievement because we can rule out differences among the schools' student bodies. However, we don't know anything about the resource levels of these schools, so we cannot be sure if resources are similar.

Klebanov (1994), Hart and Risley (1995), Hoff (2003), Klebanov, Brooks-Gunn, McCarton and McCormick (1998), Lesaux, Nonie, Vukovic, Hertzman, and Siegel (2007).

Possibly the schools with larger percentages of low-income students have less resources. If that is the case, then the cause of the lower achievement may be related to the resource input. On the other hand, if resource levels are similar among the schools, then input differences cannot explain the achievement differences. We therefore must focus on variables of management, curriculum, or teaching in the lower achieving schools.

The logic of this comparative perspective is creating "apples to apples" comparisons. This is the ideal – comparing performance of organizations with the same inputs – but the ideal is hard to achieve.[14] Notice that in Figure 2.2 there is no information on resource inputs and the student SES measure is based on the dichotomous "free lunch" classification.[15] Knowing a school's free lunch percentage is much better than having no SES information, but two schools with the same free lunch percentage do not have identical student bodies since the dichotomous categories, on free lunch versus not, encompass large ranges of family economic circumstances, especially the category "not eligible for free lunch."

Ideally, we should measure organizational performance as *productivity*. This requires knowing the organization's contribution to student growth over a unit of time. Most sensibly that unit of time is a school year. "Value added" measurement is the common name for this approach to measuring productivity.[16] Value-added measurement would answer a question like this: How much does the school raise reading achievement scores for 5th graders from September to May? Notice, this is very different from a "one point in time" measurement as the basis of comparing schools (like Figure 2.2 above).

Accountability testing, until very recently, has largely ignored productivity. Since school accountability testing began in the 70s, "one point in time" measurement has dominated. Consequently, schools with larger percentages of poor children have been much more likely to be reported as failing. How productive schools are – how much they help

---

[14] When American students' achievement levels are compared with achievement levels of students from other countries, we rarely have information on inputs. This information would make such comparisons more informative (Sen, Partelow, & Miller, 2005).

[15] Input-matched comparisons based on free-lunch percentages are widely used for three reasons free: (1) Free-lunch data are collected by all school districts and so it is a measure used nationally. (2) Free-lunch eligibility is a reasonably precise measure of low-income status, because it requires documented family income information, is calculated based on the federally defined income threshold for poverty, it takes account of family size. The eligibility requirement for free-lunch is at or below 130% of the federally defined income threshold for poverty ($30,000 for a family of four in 2012); reduced lunch eligibility is income ranging between 130% – 185% of the income threshold. (3) Family income is a reasonable proxy measure for a set of home-background variables that are correlated with student achievement, but that are largely beyond the school's control (Alexander, Entwisle, & Olson, 2001; Alexander, Entwisle, & Horsey, 1997; Berliner, 2006; Hart & Risley, 1995; Hoff, 2003; Klebanov, Brooks-Gunn, McCarton, & McCormick, 1998). Thus, for purposes of identifying under-performing schools it is reasonable to compare only those schools that are similar on these home-background variables, using percent free lunch as the measure of family income status.

[16] For more on measuring academic growth and school performance, see AERA (2004), Barton (2008), McCall, Kingsbury, & Olson (2004) or Meyer (1997).

25

students learn – has never been widely examined or reported. An example will illustrate how ignoring productivity can communicate false information and problem statements.

Imagine three schools in a district and every spring their test scores are reported ("May scores" in Figure 2.3). Assume all schools get equivalent resources, that the test covers the curriculum, and that a score of 48 is "at grade level." If the testing program is based on once-a-year reporting (in May), School A would be publicly identified as "the problem" – with a label like "Low Performing." But what does this mean? Does this mean School A's staff are less productive? (They are actually *most* productive.) The typical once-a-year testing program would mislabel not just School A, but also B and C.[17] Schools B and C, both would appear superior to School A, even though School C creates no academic gains. School A is most productive in true organizational performance – employee productivity.

Figure 2.3
Achievement Scores in Three Schools: A, B, and C

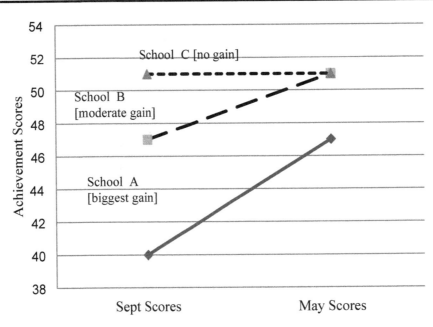

There is one obvious negative implication of the deficient measurement and mislabeling: School A is likely to receive the message "to improve," but if a staff's productivity is above-average, it is not clear that they *can* improve. Schools B and C need scrutiny and help to improve.

For School A's staff, the accurate message is: "Your productivity is above-average. Your students come to school far behind. Despite great gains, their skills remain below grade level."

What to do for School A is a different question. If anything, school A may deserve extra resources and assistance on grounds that its students start school far behind.

---

[17] An additional shortcoming of once-a-year testing is that summer learning gains or losses are attributed to schools even though students aren't in school.

If the legislated expectation is that these students catch up, then the school must have the resources to make this possible.[18]

All problem statements involving academic achievement make assumptions about the validity of output measures. Using test scores is appropriate, but there is no single perfect measure. Every measure has weaknesses and limitations. Test scores are not the full measure of a school's performance (see Figure 2.1). Test scores matter a lot, but are just one measure of academic outcomes.

Here are a few more examples of "comparison to other" problem statements.

(Comparison to other schools' ESL programs.) Students who remain for two years in our high school's English as a Second Language program average about 20% lower scores on the Language Attainment test as compared with students in the district's other two high schools. All three of these programs serve comparable students.

(Comparison to other schools' dropout rates.) Orchard high school has an unusually high dropout rate. Over the past five years our average dropout rate – 20% – has been higher than most other high schools in the state. Sixty percent of high schools in the state have lower dropout rates than Orchard's. However, Orchard's dropout rate is higher than 80% of high schools similar in size and demographic composition.

The above illustrates the logic and substantiation of "compared to other" problem definitions. To get the logic right, we try to compare organizations with the same or similar inputs and, of course, we want to be able to trust our performance measures. If, under these conditions we identify a gap between our organization and others, this is a problem (or a "concern" or "troubling evidence"), although we may not know the cause. Next, are "compared to past" problem statements.

Organizational Performance: Compared With Past

Performance declines always provoke concern. There is no "compared with others" because the "other" is our organization's past state. The gap generating concern is performance now compared with performance in the past.

Comparisons to the past are often the basis of reports urging education reform. The famous *Nation At Risk* report warned of a "rising tide of mediocrity" in America's schools. Unstated but implied is the decline: excellence is on the wane. We read of rising violence and bullying in schools (Astor, Benbenishty, & Meyer, 2004; Beaty & Alexeyev, 2008; Vail, 2004). Respect and tolerance, according to these perspectives, has waned. As with all problem definitions, the intent is to evoke concern and provoke action.

Here are a few examples more typical in the world of school leaders.

---

[18] For more on issues of equity and adequacy in school funding see, Ladd, Chalk, and Hansen (1999), Odden and Picus (2008), Odden, Goetz, and Picus (2008), or Picus (2004).

Orchard high school's dropout rate is increasing. Over the past five years our dropout rate has increased by 10%. Five years ago, our dropout rate was 9%. It has increased to 19%.

Over the last five years, 7th grade mathematics scores of Delta Middle School have trended downward, declining by about 12 percent overall.

In "compared to others" problem statements the gap is between one organization and others. In "compared to past," the gap is between current and past outcomes. The validity of the problem statement rests on the quality of the measures indicating decline. Causes of performance declines are assumed to be changes in organizational inputs or conditions (or both).

Organizational Performance: Compared With Expectations

Sometimes people want to create a problem statement, but there are no readily available comparison organizations and no evidence to show declining performance. What circumstances might motivate a "compared with expectations" problem statement situation? As pointed out in Chapter 1, someone can perceive a situation or learn information that contains "perplexing or troubling elements – situations that are complex and that raise concerns because they suggest performance shortfalls."

Imagine, for instance, Jane Reynolds, in May of her first year as high school principal, learns some troubling information. She learns that out of a senior class of 310 students, 34 have received notifications that they do not have enough credits to graduate. She learns that this happens every spring – they are called "nongraduating seniors" – and that many of these seniors and their parents are unaware they cannot graduate. They will be disappointed, and some angry. "Why were we not told of this earlier?" "How can this situation be allowed?"

Jane Reynolds does not know if her school's number of nongraduating seniors are worse compared with other high schools or if the numbers have grown in recent years – evidence of declining performance. From her perspective, 34 out of 310 is unacceptable – a performance shortfall compared to her expectation that the number should be much lower, although she does not know exactly what an "acceptable" number would be.

The above illustrates conditions that can motivate a "compared with expectations" problem statement. It is not unusual for people in leadership positions to (a) perceive conditions or learn information they view as troubling and problematic, (b) to lack comparisons to other similar organizations, and (c) to lack evidence of performance declines in their own organization, but (d) to want to draw attention to the situation because they think the situation is a problem needing attention and that performance should improve.

Here is another example, drawn from the literature.

"[A]veraged across disciplines, a 50% doctoral noncompletion rate exists in this country (Bowen & Rudenstine, 1992; Council of Graduate Schools, 2004; Lovitts, 2001). We believe that this noncompletion rate, a danger sign for higher education, is unacceptable" (Miller, 2006, p. 194).

In the above statement, the core TLO/TMO claim is "the noncompletion rate is too high." The gap creating the problem is between the current and a preferred completion rate. That half of doctoral students do not complete the degree is a problem from the author's perspective. The authors do not know if the noncompletion rate has gotten worse, or if it is worse in the U.S compared with other countries. To them, irrespective of what such comparisons might show, a 50% doctoral noncompletion rate is unacceptable – a problem.

Thus, when you write a "compared with expectations" problem statement, you identify a gap between how things are and how they should be – according to you. (Whether you are persuasive is a different matter, discussed below.) Since political and education leaders do not want purely subjective assertions of what performance "should be," they formalize expectations in many forms: organizational goals, grade level achievement standards, and achievement rubrics to name a few. State level standards documents are a commonly used frame of reference to identify under-performing school or groups of students. Some authors find problematic the gap between current skills of students and demands of the 21st century jobs or of a global economy (Rotherham & Willingham, 2010; Silva, 2009; Trilling & Fadel, 2009).

One more example: Schools sometimes use rubrics specifying grade-level expectations for student achievement and use curriculum-based assessments and scoring rubrics to define these expectations (Archbald & Newmann, 1988; Arter & McTighe, 2001; Herman, Aschbaker, & Winters, 1992; Squires, 2005). Table 2.5 is an example of a rubric created by teachers at an elementary school. It provides standards against which to compare student performance, individually or aggregated by groups. In this way, people in the school could clearly identify the literacy achievement gap between current performance and expectations.

Table 2.5
K-2 Literacy Scale: Children's Strategies For Making Sense Of Print

1 - EARLY EMERGENT - Displays an awareness of some conventions of writing, such as front/back of books, distinctions between print and pictures. See the construction of meaning from text as "magical" or exterior to the print. While the child may be interested in the contents of books, there is as yet little apparent attention to turning written marks into language. Is beginning to notice environmental print.

2 - ADVANCED EMERGENT - Engages in pretend reading and writing. Uses reading-like ways that clearly approxmimate book language. Demonstrates a sense of the story being "read," using picture clues and recall of story line. May draw upon predictable language patterns in anticipating [and recalling] the story. Attempts to use letters in writing, sometimes in random or scribble fashion.

3 - EARLY BEGINNING READER - Attempts to "really read." Indicates beginning sense of one-to-one correspondence and concept of word. Predicts actively in new material, using syntax and story line. Small stable sight vocabulary is becoming established. Evidence of initial awareness of beginning and ending sounds, especially in invented spelling.

4 - ADVANCED BEGINNING READER - Starts to draw on major cue system; self-corrects or identifies words through use of letter-sound patterns, sense of story, or syntax. Reading may be laborious especially with new material, requiring considerable effort and some support. Writing and spelling reveal awareness of letter patterns and conventions of writing such as capitalization and full stops.

5 - EARLY INDEPENDENT READER - Handles familiar material on own, but still needs some support

with unfamiliar material. Figures out words and self-corrects by drawing on a combination of letter-sound relationships, word structure, story line and syntax. Strategies of re-reading or of guessing from larger chunks of text are becoming well established. Has a large stable sight vocabulary. Conventions of writing are understood.

6 - ADVANCED INDEPENDENT READER - Reads independently, using multiple strategies flexibly. Monitors and self-corrects for meaning. Can read and understand most material when the content is appropriate. Conventions of writing and spelling are - for the most part - under control.

Note 1: The scale focuses on development of children's strategies for making sense of print. Evidence concerning children's strategies and knowledge about print may be revealed in both their reading and writing activities.
Note 2: The scale does not attempt to rate children's interests or attitudes regarding reading, nor does it attempt to summarize what literature may mean to the child. Such aspects of children's literacy development may be summarized in other forms.
Source: Rating scale developed by teachers at Cambridge Elementary School (South Brunswick NJ school district) and ETS staff - January, 1991.

Problem Statements About Organizational Inputs or Conditions

A problem statement may start with a performance gap, but solutions require a focus on organizational conditions or inputs. Thus, a problem statement paper that begins by showing a performance deficit, must shift to a focus on conditions or inputs.

On the other hand, a problem statement may start with concerns about inputs and conditions. This approach, after explaining the gap, must justify why it is a problem. Unlike a performance deficit, which is more readily interpreted as a problem, one cannot, logically, call inputs or conditions a problem without knowing how they affect performance – but, we often do not know precisely how inputs or conditions affect performance.

This reveals an interesting and challenging paradox: on the one hand, certain states of inputs or conditions must be shown to adversely affect performance before a problem can be defined; on the other hand, often we do not know precisely how certain inputs or conditions affect performance and we may never know because some cause and effect connections are hard or impossible to prove. We must act on the basis of theory, assumptions, values, and best available evidence. A problem definition is, after all, an interpretation – it is like a "working theory" guiding our inquiry and actions. And this implies we must always test the theory against evidence and revise it as warranted by new evidence, changing circumstances, or changing values.

The logic of comparisons – with others, the past, or expectations – applies to problem statements about organizational inputs and conditions. These problem statements target deficits in resources, infrastructure, management policies, staff support systems, organizational culture, or curriculum practices. Comparisons can be made with other organizations, with past inputs and conditions, or expectations (e.g., inputs that are needed, conditions that should exist).

Table 2.6 provides examples of variables reflecting organizational conditions. If an organization has measures of these variables, then leaders and stakeholders have a basis to understand conditions better, compare gaps between constituent organizational units, monitor conditions over time, analyze relationships among these measures, and explore connections with performance. This information enables systematic and evidence-based gap analysis and well substantiated problem definitions.

Table 2.6
Examples of Variables Reflecting Organizational Conditions

staff turnover	clarity of organizational goals
staff absenteeism	administrative overhead costs
staff training support	facility maintenance costs
staff attendance at meetings and events	coherence of curriculum policies
opportunities for professional development	consistency in staff evaluation
level of staff participation decision-making	rate of student disciplinary infractions
staff morale	student mobility (turnover of student population)
time on task in the classroom	student absenteeism
disorder in the classroom	student tardiness
curriculum coordination	student health
prevalence of rote learning	parental involvement or support
enrollments in advanced placement courses	parent attendance at school activities
administrative support for discipline	volunteer participation of parents in school support roles

Organizational Inputs or Conditions: Compared With Others

This problem definition framework is based on a gap between your organization (or the organization you're concerned with) and others in inputs or conditions. An example related to inputs would be a school district with significantly lower revenue than comparison districts. Documenting this is not that hard; more challenging, is making the case that the funding deficit is a problem.

Assume you are Superintendent of Binghamton School District (New York). One source of readily accessible data for comparing district funding is the National Center for Education Statistics' "Public School District Finance Peer Search" tool (nces.ed.gov). You use the Peer Search tool to determine your per-pupil-revenue compared with all the other districts in the state. Your analysis of your ranking shows that only about 16% of the K-12 districts have lower revenues. Is this a problem?

Most employees and parents of students in the district consider the district's relatively low revenue level as undesirable. In their view, there is a gap between current revenues and some more desirable revenue level. However, "lower taxes" advocates contend that the district's revenues are adequate, if higher revenues mean higher taxes. Other community members, even those who are not "lower taxes" advocates, assent to this view. Some believe schools and districts waste money, and so there is nothing wrong with the district's current revenue level.

To develop a more persuasive problem definition, you, as superintendent, must make the case there is a funding gap and it is a problem. Among other things, you must draw out implications for district performance. Here are possibilities.

Connecting inputs to conditions: Principals have expressed frustration at facility repairs that year by year are put off; high school teachers have complained about old and insufficient equipment and curriculum materials in science, art, and music; district instructional leaders say they can't provide needed support for important improvement initiatives because they are spread too thin; and coaches complain about inadequate protective gear for student athletes and outdated equipment for athletic training. Whether evidence is in the form of statements of belief, presentations, or district reports, all of these

31

concerns can be connected in a problem definition to organizational performance – to academic outcomes as well as health and fitness goals.

While it is hard to prove direct causal linkages between revenue and performance outcomes, theory and research can help. Crampton, Thompson, and Vesely (2004) identify adverse effects of funding disparities on schools' infrastructure and facilities; Greene, Huerta and Richards (2007) suggest teacher quality, which better funding purchases, is associated with better student outcomes like aspirations for college; Owings and Kaplan's (2004) research review makes the case for school funding as an investment in community socio-economic development. They urge school leaders to be informed advocates for public support of education:

> Using these data, principals can explain to the community how education acts as an economic stimulus. With increased earnings, wealthier individuals pay increased taxes. The enlarged tax revenues then finance increased education and related services that, in turn, further fuel economic growth. Education has a synergistic effect on the economy....

> Individuals with less education and fewer employable skills have difficulty finding employment in an information and service economy and difficulty keeping their jobs over time as the economy changes. ... Clearly this lack of employability seriously affects social service agencies, tax revenues, and overall economic spending. (p. 16, 18)

Does your district have large numbers of students from low-income families? If you are Binghamton's superintendent, you can add force to your case with the following logic: "Not only are our revenues lower than most, our enrollments of children in poverty are higher than most. Research shows unequivocally that schools face dramatically greater challenges in educating children who grow up poor." These challenges include, among other things, lower literacy rates in the community, lower levels of parental involvement, and greater parental transience. These disadvantages, according to some education economists, justify higher funding levels in the range of 150% to 300% to schools facing these input conditions relative to schools serving middle class communities (Alexander & Wall, 2006; Duncombe & Yinger, 2005; Picus, 2004; Verstegen, 2002).

Your problem definition, then, is built on facts, comparisons, inferences from theory and research, and, of course, values. All children, poor or not, should have equal access to an education that prepares them to be educated and productive citizens. Binghamton's superintendent could argue this district is falling short on these values.

Organizational Inputs or Conditions: Compared With Past

Sometimes the past furnishes a useful comparison – "there is more teasing and bullying now than there used to be," "parent attendance has dwindled at the annual academic fair," "student participation in extra-curriculars has declined," or "school spirit isn't what it used to be." These statements are about trends; the gap is between now and the past.

A strength of compared-with-past problem definitions is "apples to oranges" comparisons are less of a concern because the organization is being compared with itself

– only at an earlier time. You don't have the challenges of compared-with-other comparisons involving the appropriateness of comparative measures among multiple organizations or figuring out which organizations are appropriate comparisons. Consider, for example, student participation in extra-curriculars. A downward trending decline in participation in a school may be a cause for concern, and not particularly difficult to document because most high schools will have their own record-keeping system. Trends in participation are readily measureable. However, comparing your high school to others may not be so easy due to limited accessibility of this information and that different high schools have different configurations of extra-curriculars and different priorities in what they emphasize; also different schools may have different ways of keeping records, thus compromising the validity of comparisons. (This is not to say that having between-school comparative figures would not be helpful – indeed it would be informative.)

A trend showing changes in inputs or conditions is not by itself a problem definition. You must show the trend has adverse implications for organizational performance – student learning and development. Your audience must buy your logic, trust your evidence, and be moved by your message. Argue that values are at stake. In the example of declining extra-curricular participation, one would show how and why extra-curriculars are important. Information from parents, teachers, and students can support this and so, too, can literature with expert testimony, anecdotal accounts, and empirical research studies (Alfeld, Hansen, Aragon, & Stone, 2006; Braddock, Hua, & Dawkins, 2007; Cassel, Chow, & Demoulin, 2000; Demoulin, 2002; Leaver-Dunn, Turner, & Newman, 2007; Swedeen, Carter, & Molfenter, 2010; Turner, 2010).

Organizational Inputs or Conditions: Compared With Expectations

A gap between how things are and how we would like them to be can become a problem definition. It is a gap between a *current* and *desired* state (expectations). The desired state must be depicted in sufficient detail to contrast with current practice. The problem definition's persuasiveness depends on the degree to which audiences:

- understand the current state
- understand the goal state (clear)
- believe the goal state is desirable
- believe there is a gap between the current state and the goal state
- believe the goal state is possible to achieve (feasible)
- believe the costs required to achieve the goal state are worth it (justified)

Here is an example. A district science curriculum director is concerned about lack of curriculum coordination in the elementary schools. She bases her concerns on four sources of information: (1) observations revealing substantial classroom-to-classroom instructional variation; (2) discussions with teacher leaders; (3) reviews of annual school improvement plans; and (4) reviews of related literature (Fisher & Frey, 2007; Marzano & Kendall, 1996; Newmann, Smith, Allensworth, & Bryk, 2001; Rothman, 2009; Squires, 2005). The district has a curriculum guide, but she knows it is seldom used in schools to guide curriculum planning.

33

Teachers differ greatly in how much they teach science and how they teach it. In some classrooms, science class revolves around activity and materials – designing experiments; outdoor study; observing, hypothesizing, and testing. In other classrooms, science is mostly assigned readings, seatwork, and worksheets. In some classes, discussions connect science to current issues; in others, not much. Time allocation to science varies too. None of the teachers view their approach to science instruction as "a problem."[19]

These conditions in the view of the science director are a problem. She describes the current state with words like "fragmentation," "lack of coherence," and "inconsistency in standards." Asked to elaborate, she might provide an anecdotal description like mine in the previous paragraph, but with more detail. Her four sources of information substantiate her descriptions. (See Appendix 2-A for an example of an anecdotal description.)

If the director's conception of the preferred state for science is vague she will be less persuasive in her communications with others. If she is unable to connect the goal of "coherence" to achievement benefits for students, she will be less persuasive in her communications with others. Her communications must explain the logic and evidence for coherent, standards-based curriculum and create a clear and compelling picture of the goal.

Using Literature to Clarify "Desired State" Expectations

A problem definition presenting a gap between a current and desired state will be unpersuasive if audiences cannot envision the desired state or do not find it credible. Citing authoritative sources makes a desired state more compelling, which is why we often hear sentences starting with, "The research says..." Research and other forms of professional literature help clarify and justify the desired state. Two types of literature are important resources.

(1) Official statements of "Standards" are one type of literature to draw on for ideal models and standards.[20] When leaders in a field collaborate to write out models of practice, competence, or achievement in their subject or professional field, we call these "standards." For instance, the National Staff Development Council has standards for professional development. Organized into 12 categories, they present a vision of the management, objectives, and resources required for an optimal professional development system within a school or district. Standards documents like these serve as a guide for members of the field to determine how practice in their organization stacks up against the model – i.e., the desired state as envisioned by the experts. This is gap analysis.

(2) Prescriptions from research help establish authority for a desired state. "Best practice" syntheses are published by leading journals, R & D centers, and publishers. Use these. There is plenty of material available so avoid drawing on less credible sources. The U.S. Department of Education's website has a "Best Practice" link provid-

---

[19] For illuminating studies adopting perspectives similar to this vignette, see Newmann, Smith, Allensworth, and Bryk (2001) and Smith, Lee, and Newmann (2001).

[20] Appendix 2-B presents references to some prominent standards documents and websites.

ing access to a wealth of briefs, reports, and research syntheses. For more depth, to read the research behind prescriptive literature, several academic journals are devoted entirely to research reviews and syntheses. The best journals use a blind review process, only publishing articles meeting high standards of scholarship. *Review of Educational Research* and *Review of Research in Education* are two such journals; however, leading journals associated with subject areas in education (e.g., literacy, science, etc.) also publish informative syntheses as do professional journals in leadership, administration, evaluation, and policy. Remember the Latin expression "caveat lector" (reader beware). The literature on leadership, curriculum, and instruction is vast and of uneven quality; choose carefully and read critically.

SUMMING UP: THREE TYPES OF COMPARISONS TO DEFINE ORGANIZATIONAL IMPROVEMENT PROBLEMS

We can think of an organization as having inputs, conditions (practices), and performance outcomes. Inputs are what the organization is given to work with, conditions are what it does, and performance is what it produces.

Your problem definition should be clear about presumed connections among inputs, conditions, and performance – especially conditions and performance since inputs are by and large fixed. This is your theory. It is subject to revision with new information and changing circumstances, but it is better to have a theory than not have one.

Three types of comparative frames of reference were discussed. The first two (others, the past) draw on the logic of empirical comparisons: if we are doing worse than other organizations like us, that's a problem; if we are doing worse than before, that's also a problem.

Relevant and fair comparisons are essential. Relevant means compare organizations of the same type; fair assumes equivalent inputs among the organizations being compared. Input-adjusted comparisons may be necessary, but people must accept that the evidence is valid and the comparisons appropriate. Falling short of these principles reduces the credibility of the comparison and the persuasiveness of conclusions.

The third problem definition frame compares a current state to a desired state. Audiences must perceive the desired state as legitimate – backed up by research, authoritative sources, or direct observation.

The different comparative frames are not mutually exclusive. You can imagine an organization in which conditions have declined and are also worse than in other similar organizations. Efforts to improve must be guided by a clear and compelling vision of goals – the desired state.

"Compared with expectations" problem statements have special importance for leaders and leadership education. It is harder to lead improvement if you cannot articulate what "better" is. If you claim "our performance falls short" or "conditions are inadequate" – the logical question is, "compared to what?" If no one can answer this question, the problem definition is weak.

A clear goal state is not enough. The goal stated must also be viewed as desirable, feasible, and justified. A problem definition is weakened to the extent it falls short on these attributes. The most compelling conceptions of desired states draw on the authority of research, testimony of leading practitioners (experts), and input from participants.

Chapter 1 stressed the value of writing to improve our thinking and leadership communications – not just any kind of writing, but writing based on research, evidence, and disciplined reflection and writing tailored to specific audiences. Chapter 3 turns to practical suggestions and examples for writing problem definitions in graduate preparation courses or other professional contexts.

REFERENCES

AERA (2004). Teachers matter: Evidence from value-added assessments. *Research Points*, *2*(2), Summer, 1-4.

Alexander, K., Entwisle, D., & Horsey, C. (1997). From first grade forward: early foundations of high school dropout. *Sociology of Education*, *70*(2), April, 87 – 108.

Alexander, K., Entwisle, D., & Olson, L., (2001). Schools, achievement, and inequality: A seasonal perspective. *Educational Evaluation and Policy Analysis*, *23*(2), 171-191.

Alexander, K., & Wall, A. (2006). Adequate funding of education programs for at-risk children: An econometric application of research-based cost differentials. *Journal of Education Finance 31*(3), Winter, 297-319.

Alfeld, C., Hansen, D. M., Aragon, S. R., & Stone, J. R. I.,II. (2006). Inside the black box: Exploring the value added by career and technical student organizations to students' high school experience. *Career & Technical Education Research, 31*(3), 121-155.

Archbald, D. & Newmann, F. (1988). *Beyond standardized testing: Assessing authentic academic achievement in the secondary school*. Reston VA: NASSP.

Arter, J. & McTighe, J. (2001). *Scoring rubrics in the classroom: Using performance criteria for assessing and improving student performance*. Thousand Oaks, CA: Corwin Press.

Astor, R., Benbenishty, R., & Meyer, H. (2004). Monitoring and mapping student victimization in schools. *Theory Into Practice, 43*(1), 39-49.

Baker, E. L. (2003). Multiple measures: Toward tiered systems. *Educational Measurement, 22*(2), Summer, 13-17.

Barton, P. (2008). The right way to measure growth. *Educational Leadership, 65*(4), January, 70-3.

Beaty, L. & Alexeyev, E. (2008). The problem of school bullies: What the research tells us. *Adolescence, 43*(169), 1-11.

Bell, D., Raiffa, H., & Tversky, A. (1988). *Decision making: Descriptive, normative, and prescriptive interactions*. Cambridge: Cambridge University Press.

Berliner, D. (2006). Our impoverished view of educational reform. *Teachers College Record, 108*(6), 949-995

Bloom B. S. (1956). *Taxonomy of educational objectives, Handbook I: The cognitive domain*. New York: David McKay Co Inc.

Bowen, W. & Rudenstine, N. (1992). *In pursuit of the Ph.D.* Princeton NJ: Princeton University Press.

Braddock, J. H., Hua, L., & Dawkins, M. P. (2007). Effects of participation in high school sports and nonsport extracurricular activities on political engagement among black young adults. *Negro Educational Review, 58*(3), 201-215.

Cassel, R. N., Chow, P., & Demoulin, D. F. (2000). Extracurricular involvement in high school produces honesty and fair play needed to prevent delinquency and crime. *Education, 121*(2), 247-251.

Connolly, T., Arkes, H. & Hammond, K. (Eds.) (2000). *Judgment and decision making: An interdisciplinary reader.* Cambridge: Cambridge University Press.

Council of Graduate Schools. (2004). *Ph.D. completion and attrition: Policy, number, leadership, and next steps.* Washington, DC: Author.

Crampton, F. E., Thompson, D., & Vesely, R. (2004). The forgotten side of school finance equity: The role of infrastructure funding in student success. *NASSP Bulletin, 88*, September, 29-56.

Demoulin, D. F. (2002). Examining the impact of extra-curricular activities on the personal development of 149 high school seniors. *Journal of Instructional Psychology, 29*(4), 297-304.

Duncan, G., Brooks-Gunn, J., & Klebanov, P. (1994). Economic deprivation and early childhood development. *Child Development, 65*(2), 296-318.

Duncombe, W. & Yinger, J. (2005). How much more does a disadvantaged student cost? *Economics of Education Review*, 24 (5), October, 513-532.

Fisher, D. & Frey, N. (2007). A tale of two middle schools: The differences in structure and instruction. *Journal of Adolescent & Adult Literacy*, *51*(3), November, 204-11.

Frechtling, J. (2007). *Logic modeling methods in program evaluation.* San Francisco: Jossey-Bass.

Fuchs, L., Fuchs, D., Karns, K., Hamlett, C., Dutka, S. & Katzaroff, M. (2000). The importance of providing background information on the structure and scoring of performance assessments. *Applied Measurement In Education, 73*(1), 1-34.

Greene, G., Huerta, L., Richards, C., (2007). Getting real: A different perspective on the relationship between school resources and student outcomes. *Journal of Education Finance, 3*(1), Summer, 49-68.

Hart, B. & Risley, T. (1995). *Meaningful differences in the everyday experience of young American children.* Baltimore, MD: P.H. Brookes.

Hartman, C. (2006). Students on the move. *Educational Leadership 63*(5), February, 20-4.

Herman, J., Aschbacher, P., & Winters, L. (1992). *A practical guide to alternative assessment.* Alexandria, VA : Association for Supervision and Curriculum Development.

Hoff, E. (2003). The specificity of environmental influence: Socioeconomic status affects early vocabulary development via maternal speech. *Child Development, 74*(5), Sept-Oct, 1368 – 1379.

Hogarth, J. (1980). *Judgment and choice: The psychology of decision.* Chichester: Wiley.

Hosp, M., Hosp, J., & Howell, K. (2007). *The ABCs of CBM: A practical guide to curriculum-based measurement.* New York: Guilford.

Klebanov, P., Brooks-Gunn, J., McCarton, C., & McCormick, M. (1998). The contribution of neighborhood and family income to developmental test scores over the first three years of life. *Child Development, 69*(5), October, 1420 - 1436.

Ladd, H., Chalk, R., & Hansen, J. (1999). (Eds.) *Equity and adequacy in education finance: Issues and perspectives.* Washington, D.C.: National Academy Press.

Lesaux, N., Nonie, K., Vukovic, R., Hertzman, C., & Siegel, L. (2007). Context matters: The interrelatedness of early literacy skills, developmental health, and community demographics. *Early Education and Development, 18*(3), 497-518.

Leaver-Dunn, D., Turner, L., & Newman, B. M. (2007). Influence of sports' programs and club activities on alcohol use intentions and behaviors among adolescent males. *Journal of Alcohol & Drug Education, 51*(3), 57-72.

Marzano, R. & Kendall, D. (1996). *A comprehensive guide to designing standards-based districts, schools, and classrooms.* Alexandria, VA: Association for Supervision and Curriculum Development.

McCall, M., Kingsbury, G., & Olson, A. (2004). *Individual growth and school success.* A technical report from the NWEA Growth Research Database. Lake Oswego, OR: Northwest Evaluation Association.

Medeiros, L. C., Butkus. S., & Chipman, H. (2005). A logic model framework for community nutrition education. *Journal of Nutrition Education and Behavior, 37*(4), July/August, 197-202.

Meyer, R. (1997). Value-added indicators of school performance: A primer. *Economics of Education Review, 16*(3), June, 283-301.

Miller, C. (2006). Case study for making the implicit explicit. In Maki, P. & N. Borkowski (Eds.) *The assessment of doctoral education: Emerging criteria and new models for improving outcomes.* (pp. 188 – 196). Sterling, VA: Stylus.

Newmann, F., Smith, B., Allensworth, E. & Bryk, A. (2001). *School instructional program coherence: Benefits and challenges.* Chicago, IL: Consortium on Chicago School Research.

Odden, A. & Archibald, S. (2001). *Reallocating resources: How to boost student achievement without asking for more.* Thousand Oaks, CA: Corwin Press.

Odden, A. & Picus, L. (2008). *School finance: A policy perspective.* New York, NY: McGraw-Hill.

Odden, A., Goetz, M., & Picus, L. (2008). Using available evidence to estimate the cost of educational adequacy. *Education Finance and Policy, 3* (3), Summer, 374-397.

Owings, W. & Kaplan, L. (2004). School finance as investment in human capital. *NASSP Bulletin, 88*, September, 12-28.

Picus, L. O. (2004). School finance adequacy: Implications for school principals. *NASSP Bulletin, 88*, September, 3-11.

Rotherham, A. & Willingham, D. (2010). Not new: But a worthy challenge. *American Educator,* Spring, 17 – 20.

Rothman, R. (2009). Behind the classroom door: A rare glimpse indicates the extent – and persistence – of variation in teacher practice. *Harvard Education Letter, 25*(6), 4-6.

Silva, E. (2009). Measuring skills for 21st century learning. *Phi Delta Kappan, 90* (9), May, 630-634.

Smith, J., Lee, V., & Newmann, F. (2001). *Instruction and achievement in Chicago elementary schools.* Chicago: IL: Consortium for Chicago School Research

Squires, D. (2005). *Aligning and balancing the standards-based curriculum.* Thousand Oaks, CA: Corwin Press.

Swedeen, B. L., Carter, E. W., & Molfenter, N. (2010). Getting everyone involved: Identifying transition opportunities for youth with severe disabilities. *Teaching Exceptional Children, 43*(2), 38-49.

Trilling, B. & Fadel, C. (2009). *21st century skills: Learning for life in our times.* San Francisco: Jossey Bass.

Turner, S. (2010). The benefit of extracurricular activities in high school: Involvement enhances academic achievement and the way forward. *Academic Leadership, 8*(3), 239-244.

USDA (2008, January). Eligibility manual for school meals. Washington DC: Child Nutrition Programs, Food and Nutrition Service, US Department of Agriculture.

Vail, K. (2004). Troubling rise in school violence. *American School Board Journal, 191*(1), 9-10.

Verstegen, D. (2002). Financing the new adequacy: Towards new models of state education finance systems that support standards based reform. *Journal of Education Finance 27*(3), Winter, 749-81.

CHAPTER 3

FORMULATING A PROBLEM-BASED, ORGANIZATIONAL IMPROVEMENT STUDY: CONCEPTS AND MODELS

INTRODUCTION AND PURPOSE

GAPPSI's logic was the focus of last chapter. This chapter discusses the form and content of a paper proposing a GAPPSI project. I call it a problem statement paper.

A problem statement paper discloses your thinking – to yourself and to others. It helps you to be clear and specific about your ideas by justifying your claims, making your logic transparent, formulating precise questions and objectives, and explaining plans for inquiry and action. The paper presents the problem statement and plan. The GAPPSI project carries it out, which may include conducting a study, presenting results and recommendations, creating work products and tools, or actions to lead change.

A problem statement is not an academic paper like a journal article. However, it has scholarly qualities because it formulates a problem definition, uses literature, requires evidence, argues a position, and creates a framework for further inquiry and decision making.

A Few Words on Terminology

Table 3.1 list key terminology from this chapter; following are some definitions.

Information and evidence. All evidence is information, but not all information is evidence. Information builds general knowledge, but does not necessarily prove anything. The percent of teachers in a district certified in secondary mathematics is information. It is a fact, but not necessarily evidence of anything. Evidence is a subset of information, referring to information gathered systematically and intended to support or reject a specific claim and guide decision making.

Substantiation refers to backing up your claims with evidence. "Our school is big" is a claim, but without substantiation. Sometimes we refer to this as an assertion. Here is the claim with substantiation: "Our school is big, larger than 90% of the schools in the state." Now the claim is credible. It is not a problem statement because it lacks a TLO/TMO ("too little of/too much of") claim.

Study and research. Problem statement papers use the verb "study." This is not a synonym for research. Research is about theory – experimental or quasi-experimental design use to answer questions in the literature and develop generalized knowledge. Research in this sense is a theoretical project, separate from practice, separate from "deciding and acting." Problem-based study, in contrast, is closely integrated with practice, and as I use the term, refers to inquiry that is purposeful, systematic, and informed by data. In GAPPSI, a

Table 3.1
Key Terminology

Information	Consequence
Evidence	Factor
Substantiation	Prediction
Study	Outcome
Research	Goal
Analysis	Purpose
Cause	Key Questions

study is situated in a particular organization, focused on a problem, and intended to reduce or eliminate a gap between current and desired state.

Analysis: The separation of an intellectual or substantial whole into its constituent parts for individual study.

Cause: Something that produces an effect, result, or consequence. The person, event, or condition responsible for an action or result.

Factor communicates less certainty about causes. It can be plural, e.g., "We believe the following are factors in the community's waning support for the initiative."

Predictor communicates a low degree of certainty about something being a cause, and can be used to imply no causality at all – merely a correlation. "Research shows low self-efficacy is a predictor of job dissatisfaction among teachers."

Consequence: Something that logically or naturally follows from an action or condition; a synonym is "effect."[21]

Outcome is like consequence. "This outcome was a result of ..." or "If we neglect to consider public relations, the outcome will be ..."

Organization of Problem Statement (GAPPSI) Paper

Table 3.2 shows the main elements of a problem statement paper: the problem, the purpose, the improvement goal, the questions, and the study plan. This is not a fixed model – the format, length, and organization must ultimately depend on what your audience needs or expects. The format described in Table 3.2 is useful, but modifiable. The left side shows the heading structure; the right side provides explanations. Other examples follow.

---

[21] The definitions of analysis, cause, and consequence draw from *American Heritage Dictionary* (Boston: Houghton Mifflin, 1985).

Table 3.2
General Format for a Problem Statement Paper

Abstract	An abstract is optional. For a paper longer than a few pages, a one paragraph abstract can be useful. In a few sentences, explain the problem, purpose, and plan. An abstract generally is about 150 words or less. Write it last, after you have written the rest of the paper.
Introduction/Overview	An "Introduction/Overview" section provides background and context. Avoid superfluous information.
Problem	This is the problem statement. Avoid getting into material about possible solutions.
Purpose of Study/Project	It is useful to distinguish your study's or project's purpose from the "bottom line" goal – the ultimate improvement goal (discussed next). Goal statements are about organizational performance. The purpose statement expresses objectives of your project or study (for example, what information is sought and why).
Organizational Improvement Goal	This states the improved level of performance sought. What does "success" look like? If your project is successful how much will performance improve? If you could, how would you measure success? Can you specify an *amount* of improvement reasonable to expect?
Key Questions and Tasks (KQTs)	The KQTs section presents specifics of your "to do" plan. These are more specific objectives, consisting of the questions you want answers to and other tasks to move forward. Writing these helps organize your plan, inquiry, and other tasks. It is not enough just to list questions. Explain them. Each question has a rationale. Explain why you need the information, how it helps understand or solve the problem, what decisions it will support, and how you will get the information. Information needs are often expressed best in the form of questions, but writing questions is not the only way to describe information needs. Here, for instance, is a question: "Do our students think the in-school suspension policy effectively deters behavior code violations?" Alternatively, you could write: Objective #3: "We will determine students' beliefs about the effectiveness of the in-school suspension policy in deterring behavior code violations." These are different ways of saying the same thing.

EXAMPLES OF PROBLEM STATEMENT PAPERS
(SEE CHAPTER 3 APPENDICES)

Appendices 3-A, 3-B, and 3-C are examples of problem statement papers in a format for a graduate course. They follow the organization above, but are in different stages of development and vary in particulars – how the problem is introduced, purposes are stated, and a plan is presented. Papers differ because problems differ – in scope, clarity, information available, and manageability. Some problem statements are more about understanding a problem – they are more agnostic about the problem and the aim is to explore and understand; others are more about figuring how to implement a decision already made. Like any paper for coursework, there is flexibility in the specifications for length, depth, format, and content per instructor preferences.

WRITING PURPOSE AND GOAL STATEMENTS:
ADDITIONAL GUIDELINES AND EXAMPLES

Purpose Statements

The purpose statement focuses on your improvement initiative; the goal statement, on ultimate performance outcomes.

Purpose statements may have two components: your inquiry (information and learning) and your plan (decisions, actions, implementation).

The purpose statement should go beyond what the reader can infer from the problem statement, but be short enough to easily understand and remember.

Aim for a simple sentence with enough information to stand by itself. If someone reads only the purpose sentence they should understand what you are trying to do. Do *not* write, "The purpose is to study the problem and present an improvement plan." Make the sentence *specific to your problem*, but not long and complicated.

Table 3.3
Note on Verb Tense

Use future tense when referring to portions of a paper or report not yet written. If the purpose statement is part of a completed paper or report, use present tense with the paper as the subject of the sentence: "This paper recommends..." Or "Part 1 describes procedures..."

Here is a good test: after reading the purpose statement, can the reader restate it without having to reread the purpose statement? The key purpose sentence should present only a few main ideas and avoid unnecessary detail and distracting information.

Goal Statements

Aim for Precise and Measureable

Ideally, one sentence expresses the goal; make it stand out, then elaborate.

It is helpful to consider what measures would quantify *amounts* or *rates* of improvement. This aids precision in thinking about the desired organizational improvements. Hammond, Keeney, and Raiffa (1999, p. 73) recommend:

Select a meaningful scale that captures the essence of the corresponding objective. … Construct a subjective scale that directly measures your objective… To construct a scale yourself, you need to define concretely as many levels of [outcomes] as are needed... Trying as they may be, such struggles with difficult-to-measure objectives yield a significant benefit: determining how you would measure an objective forces you to clarify what you really mean by it.

In principle, you should be able to measure the organization's progress toward the goal. In practice, this is not always possible – some goals are challenging to measure.

Even if the improvement goal can be quantified, that doesn't settle the question of what *amount* of improvement to expect. You must estimate. In your professional judgment, what amount of improvement is ambitious but realistic given current organizational inputs and conditions? You must make assumptions about future staffing, resources, and policy conditions as well incoming students' academic preparedness. If you know the future will bring less favorable inputs or conditions, state this and adjust your goal estimates accordingly.

Here are three sources of guidance for goal statement estimates.

1) First, is your problem statement. A GAPPSI problem statement identifies a gap between current and desired conditions or performance. Therefore, the goal, logically, is to close the gap. For example, in the Valley High School example (Appendix 3-C) the improvement goal is to reduce suspension rates to match the levels of other schools in the district. Make sure your goal statement follows logically from your problem statement.

2) Second, consult colleagues for opinions, especially for more specific, short term improvement estimates. Closing the gap identified in your problem statement is the ultimate aim, but a "next year" or "in two years" goal statement can also be useful. To do this you have to decide what is achievable. Seek opinions from knowledgeable colleagues about levels of improvement they believe are reasonable.

3) Third, you can draw on research if relevant research is available. Here is more on this.

On Using Effect Sizes To Formulate Improvement Targets

Sometimes literature can help you estimate expected improvement. If there is appropriate research on a particular instructional strategy, program, or intervention, an "effect size" estimate can help. Some research reviews provide a specific estimate of impact, whether in a percentage, a correlation value, a probability or some other metric. Appendices 3-A and 3-B illustrate improvement targets informed by "effect size" estimates.

Review the U.S. Department of Education's online "What Works Clearinghouse" for one source of high quality reviews; many report how effective a program or intervention is in effect size metrics.

The best known effect size metric is "Cohen's D" based on the standard deviation statistic.[22]

> In educational research, the effect of an intervention on academic achievement is often expressed as an effect size. The most common effect size metric for this purpose is the standardized mean difference, which is defined as the difference between the mean outcome for the intervention group and that for the control or comparison group divided by the common within group standard deviation of that outcome. This effect size metric is a statistic and, as such, represents the magnitude of an intervention in statistical terms, specifically in terms of the number of standard deviation units by which the intervention group outperforms the control group. (Bloom, Hill, Black, & Lipsey, 2008, p. 290)

In a normal distribution, a score that is one standard deviation above the mean is at the 84th percentile (.5 of a standard deviation above the mean is 69th percentile). This is one benchmark to help think about the magnitude of a reported effect size. Imagine an intervention or instructional strategy designed for a particular student population, e.g., high school students with a learning disability. Now assume research shows an intervention *when implemented as designed* raises achievement scores on average by one standard deviation. Thus, if your school has this target population and you use this intervention as designed, you could expect an achievement gain that approximates the difference in achievement reflected in moving from the 50th to the 84th percentile. This is one frame of reference for interpreting the "Cohen's D" effect size.[23]

Here is another frame of reference. Bloom et al. (2008) write how it can be useful to compare a report of an effect size against the benchmark of typical grade-to-grade (one year) achievement gains. Their research indicates the typical level of gain in reading ability from 4th to 5th grade is about half (.5) of a standard deviation. Now imagine a reading intervention for upper elementary claims an effect size of .25; this boost in reading ability is equivalent to about half of a year of growth.[24]

Following are a few examples of purpose and goal statements. I have omitted material that would precede or elaborate on these purpose and goal statements.

---

[22] See also Chapter 6 of Vogt (2007) or Lipsey, Puzio, Yun, Hebert, Steinka-Fry, Cole, Roberts, Anthony, and Busick (2012); or do a web search on "effect size."

[23] See WWC (2013), available online, to see an example of a review of a study similar to the example described here.

[24] Note: .5 of a standard deviation is the level of the gain from spring of 4th grade to spring of 5th grade. As children get older, the amount of gain over the year in reading ability diminishes. It is largest in early elementary and diminishes to about .15 of a standard deviation per year by high school. Reading instruction is heavily stressed in elementary school; subject matter instruction grows in importance as students get older.

Example #1 – Purpose and Goal Statements:
Early Identification of Limited English Proficient Students
to Strengthen Language Support Services in Mayfair School District

Project Purpose

This project will recommend procedures for early identification of Limited English Proficient (LEP) students in Mayfair School District. Part 1 of the report will describe current procedures for identifying LEP students within the district. Part 2 synthesizes best practice literature on language assessment of LEP students. Part 3 reports beliefs of Mayfair teachers concerning needed changes in identification procedures for LEP students. Part 4 recommends an identification system and an implementation plan. This plan will specify a system to determine eligibility for ESL support services for students within an established timeframe following their matriculation in the district.

Improvement Goal

The primary goal is improved reading achievement: a 15% increase in the percentage of students achieving an expected one-year-gain on the District Literacy Assessment. The "expected one-year-gain" is a measure reflecting one year of growth in reading achievement for an average student. The goal is for the district to achieve this 15% improvement in performance for LEP students within three years of the implementation of the new LEP identification system.

Example #2 – Purpose and Goal Statements:
Supporting Data-driven Decision Making In Dover School District:
A Plan to Evaluate and Redesign Current Systems

Purpose Of The Study

This study will examine data systems in the district to improve their functionality for decision making. We will recommend modifications to improve data access and utility for administrators, school leadership teams, and teachers. The review will focus on these areas: school improvement planning, curriculum planning decisions, student placement for interventions, and professional evaluation. Recommendations will be based on needs identified by staff as well as best practice guidelines from professional literature.

Improvement Goal

The goal is to improve student learning by improving instructional planning and evaluation. Assuming inputs remain stable over the coming years, we believe it is reasonable to expect achievement gains over the long term, although the amount and timeline are difficult to specify because of the indirect connection between data systems, data use, and classroom instruction. Improvement will take time and hinges on other variables of leadership and policy, including leadership advocacy, resource allocations, staff training, and strengthened incentives for data use.

FORMULATING KEY QUESTIONS AND TASKS (KQTs): GUIDELINES, EXAMPLES, AND TOOLS

The main purpose of "Key Questions and Tasks" is to formulate and present a plan of inquiry and action. Writing and explaining this clarifies the logic of your inquiry; it disciplines your thinking; it helps you and others understand, evaluate, and if need be, critique, this logic. Here are some guidelines.

How Many KQTs?

Usually about three to five main KQTs are adequate. Too many KQTs and you risk a list that challenges comprehension – long, diffuse, and unfocused.

Use hierarchies. Place specific questions or tasks under *main* (hence, "key") KQTs – for instance, question #1 subsumes sub-questions 1a, 1b, and 1c. This approach, categorizing additional more specific questions under a smaller number of KQTs helps with coherence in your plan and helps you stay organized.

Formulate key questions carefully: they should be analytically distinct, non-overlapping questions. The questions should reveal coherently and comprehensively your information needs and other tasks as you presently understand them.

Explain the rationale for your KQTs. The rationale explains *why* a question or task is important – that is, how it contributes toward project purposes. The rationale is, "I need this information because…"

Explain your information sources. Information can come from organizational databases, surveys, interviews, reports, memos, policy statements, internal or external stakeholders, or from professional or scholarly literature. Chapter 4 is on this subject.

Three Categories of Questions

Problem solving involves uncertainty; information reduces uncertainty. That is why we try to learn about current conditions, investigating the problem to learn about what's going on, what are causes and consequences. We also want to learn what to do – information to guide planning and decision making, such as identifying obstacles or weighing tradeoffs of alternative solutions.

Figure 3.1 conceptualizes information needs. Problem solving is aided by knowledge about current conditions (what's going on?), about causes (what explains current conditions?), and about predictions (what will happen if we do X?).

1) Current State Questions/Claims

One category of questions is about the current organizational state of inputs, conditions, and performance. The goal is to understand better the current situation. For instance, perhaps there is a concern about morale. People claim it is low – implying it could and should be higher. How do you know what the current state of morale is? Unless you can divine it somehow, your only option is getting information. This is a "current state" (current conditions) question as shown in the top diagram in Figure 3.1.

This kind of current state question produces "descriptive" information – information that describes current conditions. It doesn't necessarily explain anything by itself.

Figure 3.1
Three Categories Of Questions in Organizational Improvement Problems

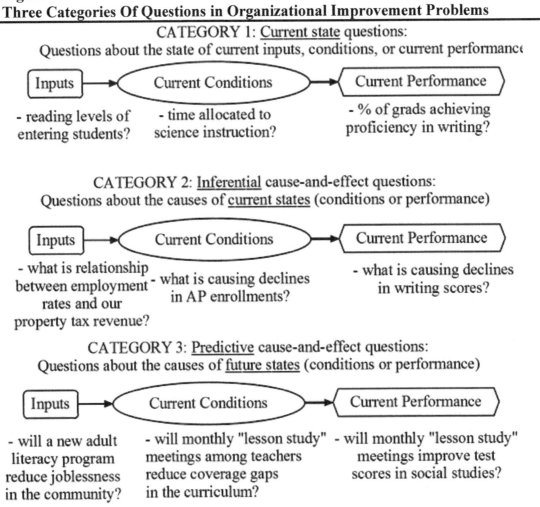

CATEGORY 1: Current state questions:
Questions about the state of current inputs, conditions, or current performance

Inputs → Current Conditions → Current Performance

- reading levels of entering students?   - time allocated to science instruction?   - % of grads achieving proficiency in writing?

CATEGORY 2: Inferential cause-and-effect questions:
Questions about the causes of current states (conditions or performance)

Inputs → Current Conditions → Current Performance

- what is relationship between employment rates and our property tax revenue?   - what is causing declines in AP enrollments?   - what is causing declines in writing scores?

CATEGORY 3: Predictive cause-and-effect questions:
Questions about the causes of future states (conditions or performance)

Inputs → Current Conditions → Current Performance

- will a new adult literacy program reduce joblessness in the community?   - will monthly "lesson study" meetings among teachers reduce coverage gaps in the curriculum?   - will monthly "lesson study" meetings improve test scores in social studies?

2) Inferential Cause-And-Effect Questions/Claims

Inferential cause-and-effect questions are about the past or present: what were or are the causes of this outcome (effect)? For example, why has parental attendance at monthly planning meetings declined? Why are more students getting into conflicts and fights? Has the termination of Friday pep rallies adversely affected school spirit? Why are so many sophomores and juniors ill-informed about college entrance requirements?

3) Predictive Cause-And-Effect Questions/Claims

Predictive cause-and-effect questions ask about future consequences: if we do X (or if X happens), then can we expect Y to result? For instance, if we eliminate pep rallies, will school spirit suffer? Or, if we improve the transition from our child-centered K-1 curriculum to our more academic 2nd grade curriculum, (a) can we expect more discipline problems and (b) will this improve students' performance on the 3rd grade reading assessment?

The distinctions among these categories of questions are useful to communicate about information needs. However, understand that: (1) Figure 3.1's framework should not be construed to imply rigidly linear planning and information gathering. It doesn't go like this: "first I will get descriptive information on organizational conditions; then I collect inferential evidence to ascertain causes; the last step will develop and evaluate predictive information." A single body of information, whether from a survey, interview, data set, or elsewhere can shed light on descriptive, inferential, and predictive questions. (2) Problems are not static "things," (as discussed more fully in Chapter 1). Organizational conditions and environments are fluid; what we view as problems and improvement priorities change. We may get information which changes how we think about a problem, raising new issues and new questions. (3) The framework does not suggest it is possible to answer all those questions. It is time-consuming to obtain good information and we never get complete information; 100% certainty never happens.

Causal Analysis to Generate Questions (Conjectures)

Causal analysis involves conjectures about causes of a certain outcome or condition. It is, in a sense, theorizing. Causal analysis is a good way to generate questions to investigate, "lines of inquiry." Consider the rising suspension rates at Valley High School (discussed in Appendix 3-C).

Recall that causes are unknown, but, like conversations that follow news of rising crime rates, we always wonder, is it really rising crime or are more people reporting it? Reasons for Valley High School's rising suspension rates fall logically in two categories (not mutually exclusive): (1) student behavior – suspension-eligible conduct violations – has in fact worsened and staff members are simply responding by issuing more referrals for suspension; or, (2) student behavior has not changed, but staff members are making more referrals for suspension. For each of these causal explanations, we can "backward analyze" causal processes and in doing so, generate more specific questions to pursue (hypotheses to investigate). Here is the analysis:

(1) Student behavior has deteriorated and so more students are violating the code of conduct rules and therefore teachers are reporting more students for suspension. (why has behavior worsened?)
- Proposition #1: VHS is getting larger numbers of students who more frequently behave in ways that violate the school's code of conduct (why?)
  ◆ there are more students now with norms of behavior that are out of line with the code of conduct
  ◆ there are more students now whose upbringing and circumstances at home contribute to growing conduct infractions within the school
  ◆ there are more students now with aggressive and "anti-establishment" personalities

• Proposition #2: the types of students are the same, but conditions *within* the school have changed causing more behavioral infractions of the code of conduct (why?)

    ♦ more students feeling alienated toward the school

    ♦ more students feeling provoked to "act out" toward teachers and administrators

        -classroom instruction has become less interesting and engaging

        -behaviors of teachers and/or administrators have changed in ways that students perceive as belittling or disrespectful

    ♦ more students feeling provoked to "act out" toward other students

    ♦ more incentives for students to commit behavioral infractions

    ♦ fewer disincentives for students to behave appropriately

    ♦ more students not knowing the conduct rules (therefore unwittingly violate them)

(2) Student behavior has not deteriorated, but teachers more frequently report infractions, issuing referrals they formerly did not report. (why more frequent referrals?)

    • staff members have become less tolerant of disruptive behaviors (why?)

        ♦ staff members have lost energy to deal with disruptive students

        ♦ staff members' morale has decreased

        ♦ organizational culture has changed to become more confrontational

    • staff members are more often inappropriately referring students for suspension (i.e., referrals for behaviors that are not really infractions of the rules) (why?)

        ♦ the code of conduct information is not being communicated effectively to staff

        ♦ new staff members are not getting the right information

        ♦ too much competing information (other memos, emails, and initiatives competing for staff attention)

This causal analysis does not exhaust all the possibilities, but it is a good, systematic start. Principal Smith can make more informed decisions if he has a better understanding of causes. Systematic causal analysis is feasible and practical and can help educate us to understand a complex problem better. Appendix 3-D shows a visual representation of a causal analysis exercise.

Stakeholder Analysis

What is Stakeholder Analysis?

Stakeholder analysis is another way to generate questions and gather information. Organizational improvement implies change and change affects people and the status quo. Since the status quo may be comfortable for many and since changing comfortable patterns and practices can be difficult, it aids in planning to consider the interests and potential actions – supporting, resisting, adapting, etc. – of stakeholders. Stakeholder analysis is a framework of questions about the interests and likely actions of stakeholders.

> A stakeholder is simply an individual or group with a reason to care about the decisions and with enough impact on the decision makers so that the reason should be taken seriously. Stakeholders are sources of value attributes. An attribute is something that the stakeholders, or some subset of them, care about enough so that failure to consider it in the decision would lead to a poor decision (Edwards & Newman, 2000, p. 21).

Doing Stakeholder Analysis

A summary of the process follows.
State your goal. What, specifically, is the change you envision? Be specific or the analysis will be less useful. These are examples of vague: "creating more personalized learning environments;" "writing across the curriculum;" "integrating technology in the curriculum;" "using formative assessment." Statements like these can be part of a vision and useful as value statements, but are too vague for stakeholder analysis.

Goal statements must be specific enough to contemplate specific consequences for specific groups. Suppose the proposed change is implementing block scheduling across the curriculum with 90 minute blocks and semester-length courses. The goal statement could contrast the old and new schedule and summarize key expectations for changes in curriculum. Illustrative schedules from published literature would help (Canady & Rettig, 1995; Edwards, 1993; Kramer & Keller, 2008).

List stakeholders (see Table 3.4). These can be groups or individuals. Examples of groups: pre-tenure elementary teachers in Orchard school; Valley High's Advanced Placement teachers; elderly community members; the football boosters; parents from a particular neighborhood. Examples of individuals: the school board president; the principal; Mrs. Jones, the influential community activist.

The stakeholder "unit of analysis" should be as small a unit as possible with a common perspective. Avoid lumping together groups that might actually have different interests in the proposed change.

Try to get answers to your stakeholder questions: Will they support or oppose the proposed changes? What can you do to gain support or reduce opposition? More specifically, you want answers to the kinds of questions shown in Table 3.4. A stakeholder analysis table is useful to organize your information.

Table 3.4
Stakeholder Analysis Table

List of Stake-holders	Interest/Stake in the Change	Support, Neutral or Oppose the Change	Consequences	Strategies
	What gains or losses (in their own eyes) will the stakeholder experience? (professional prestige? challenges to or affirmation of beliefs? quality of working conditions? monetary compensation? social amenities? other?)	What is the probability of stakeholder support? What is the probability of opposition?	How important is the stakeholder's support to the success of your plans? What are the consequences of opposition?	What are your options for gaining support? What kind of support do you want? What are your options for reducing opposition? Who are allies to help gain support or reduce opposition?
name				
name				
name				

Stakeholder analysis is not necessarily a "once and done" step. Circumstances change and plans evolve. As plans turn into decisions, policies, and practices, new challenges may arise, warranting additional stakeholder analyses. Stakeholder analysis can be a multi-step process, aiding design as well as implementation.

Consider the case of rising suspension rates at Valley High School (Appendix 3-C). Let's assume the principal's and planning team's work leads them to consider changes to implement more personalized learning environments. They believe a school-within-a-school model is worth considering and need to anticipate reactions and concerns among stakeholders likely to be affected by structural and scheduling changes. The planning team must ask, who are the specific stakeholder groups and what are their interests and likely actions? The team's deliberations must take account of the different stakeholders' positions.

Here are other examples where stakeholder analysis would be useful: policymakers are planning revisions in state testing or personnel certification; district officials are deliberating a new personnel evaluation policy or a restructuring of district governance or are planning a referendum to raise funds for capital improvements. At the school level, leaders could use stakeholder analysis to help plan for a major curriculum change, or a reallocation of resources, or a revised master schedule, or a new parent initiative.

Stakeholder analysis is a flexible tool.[25] It can be a 30 minute exercise, it can be part of a graduate thesis project with detailed explanations, justifications, and evidence, and it can be a lengthy, multi-stage analysis with data collection and many organizational participants (Miller, 2002; Mitchell, Agle, & Wood, 1997).[26]

---

[25] For additional literature, see Mitchell, Agle, & Wood (1997), Varvasovszky & Brugha (2000), and Welsh & McGinn (1997).

[26] For an example of district level decision-making informed by survey-based stakeholder input, see Miller's (2002) description of adopting and implementing a new reading curriculum. See also: "How to do (or not to do) . . . A stakeholder analysis" (Varvasovszky & Brugha, 2000).

Decision Criteria Tables

Two additional decision-making tools are decision criteria tables and decision charts. These require writing out objectives, criteria, and consequences and help identify information needs.

Decision Criteria Table In Theory

Dealing with a problem, you want to make the best decision, but best is not just one thing. Buying a car, for example, you consider multiple criteria: utility, cost, maintenance record, style, fuel efficiency, resale value, and so on. Each car has *attributes* and you have *criteria*. Your goal is choosing the car with the best overall set of attributes that meet your criteria.

A decision criteria table helps organize your analysis of attributes. It requires listing and rating the attributes of alternative paths to the goal and selecting the best of the alternatives.

Literature on this process explains this as a mathematical computation – adding the rating scores on each criterion for each alternative (Edwards & Norton, 2000; Kepner & Tregoe, 1997). However, this is only possible with some decisions, a point I address after a few examples.

Application of Decision Criteria Table

Simple decision: Candidate selection. Assume you have several candidates for a position. You have criteria for an ideal candidate; each candidate has attributes. Your criteria are (a) curriculum design expertise in mathematics, (b) proficiency with education technology, (c) effective in public communications, and (d) strong interpersonal skills. You will rate each candidate on these criteria.

Phrase each attribute so a high rating is positive for the attribute. In the candidate selection example you would likely do this naturally – it is taken for granted – but with more complex decisions and sets of attributes it is not so obvious. It is an important principle to remember.

You decide to rate the candidates on a 1-5 scale (1= unacceptable, 3=adequate, 5=excellent). Should each attribute be given equal weight?

If you weight each criterion equally, simply add the scores for each candidate – highest score wins.

However, weighting may be important. There is no reason to assume each attribute is equally important. You may decide that (b) (technology proficiency) is the lowest priority because the candidate can learn this on the job if need be, but the other attributes are essential at the start.

For sake of illustration, let's assume each criterion is *not* equally important. How do you take account of this in computing your ratings? Assume you have 100 points to allocate to the four criteria to signify their relative importance; the more points a criterion gets, the more important it is (but the total must be 100 points). You decide the criteria are weighted as shown in the second column in Table 3.5:

53

Table 3.5
Weighting For Candidate Selection

Criterion	Weight	Candidate #1's Ratings	#1's Weighted Ratings	Candidate #2's Ratings	#2's Weighted Ratings
(a) math curriculum expertise	40 pts	4	160	3	120
(b) technology proficiency	10 pts	4	40	2	20
(c) public communications skills	20 pts	3	60	5	100
(d) interpersonal skills	30 pts	3	90	3	90
			Total: 350		Total: 330

Table 3.5 shows the most weight (40 out of the 100 points) is allocated to "math curriculum design expertise." The remaining criteria have, respectively, the following weighting points: 10, 20, and 30. Each candidate's weighted rating on each criterion is determined by multiplying their initial rating by the points allocated to the criterion. Their total score is the sum of the four weighted ratings.[27] In this example, Candidate #1 comes out ahead of Candidate #2, 350 to 330.

More complex decision: Improving performance assessment capability. Some choices are among well-defined alternatives: choosing among several locations for a new school; evaluating competing bids for a building renovation contract; judging student science projects for a science and technology exhibition. These decisions lend themselves to numerical comparisons of tradeoffs. Many decisions do not.

Suppose you believe your school needs better assessment information to monitor student progress and plan instruction. You are considering three alternatives:

1) A system where students take reading comprehension tests on a computer which records their scores. The reading tests are linked with reading assignments in books you purchase as part of the package. The testing system produces individual and aggregate reports, including reports on individual and group progress based on the "Lexiles" measure of reading development.

2) A computer-adaptive testing system assessing general reading. Students are tested three times per year: at the beginning, middle, and end of the school year. The system produces a variety of individual and aggregate reports, including growth scores. The tests are said (by the vendor) to be aligned with your state's curriculum standards in reading.

3) A portfolio of performance assessments, including rubric-based assessments, designed by teachers with help from a consultant and literature on reading as-

---

[27] See Edwards and Norton (2000) for an explanation and examples of "multi-attribute evaluation." They illustrate complex weighting schemes.

sessment (Paratore & McCormack, 2007; Valencia, Hiebert, & Afflerbach, 1994; Vukelich, Christie, & Enz, 2008).

You want your group to review these alternatives and make recommendations. You identify and list the desired attributes of your assessment system – your "wish list," so to speak.

Then you review information on each of the three assessment systems and rate each system 1 to 5 on each of the attributes that are important:[28]

Scores can be aggregated for statistical analysis
Data can upload to district data warehouse
Produces classroom and group level reports
Scores comparable to national norms
Scores comparable to a validated proficiency scale

Items are aligned with state curriculum standards
System is easy to use:
- student assessment is easy to schedule
- student assessment is quick
- understandable reports for parents

Utility for:
- classroom grading
- special education screening

Utility for: (cont'd)
- Measuring student academic growth
- School accountability judgments
- Teacher accountability judgments
- Measuring 'value-added' of school program
- Instructional improvement planning:
  -information immediately available
  -information detailed enough for lesson planning
  -detailed enough for differentiated instruction
- Professional development planning

Annual cost is within prescribed budget limit

The preferred system is the one that scores highest overall on the attributes. In the above example, it is unlikely that each criterion is equally important, so a weighting system should be used, as described earlier in Table 3.5.

Decision Charts

Problem solving requires sequences of decisions; some decisions are possible only after others have been made. A decision criteria table does not represent this well. Sometimes a decision chart (also called a tree or map) is useful.[29] A chart helps people visualize options, tradeoffs, and uncertainties. A decision chart can be useful where different decision alternatives yield very different paths.

Assume you are in a district-level leadership position. Your state's 8th grade test has a cut score for "at standard." State policy requires accountability at the student,

---

[28] Note: Some attributes are "must haves" and need not be included in the tradeoffs list. The most obvious is "produces individual student reports." All the systems must have this feature or they will not be considered. Required attributes do not need to be added because they do not distinguish among alternatives being considered. However, the *kinds* of individual reports produced matter – their format, detail, and readability. These attributes affect a report's utility for communication to parents, classroom grading, and other purposes and should be included.

[29] For more elaboration and examples, see Hammond, Keeney, & Raiffa (1999, p. 123).

school, and district level. The district has an established policy that students who score "below standard" cannot matriculate in 9th grade Algebra I. Many of these students never get the math credits they need to be awarded a state-endorsed diploma; this, in turn, hurts their postsecondary opportunities. There are also stakes for the district: the state, as part of its education accountability policy, reports for each district the percentage of students enrolled in college prep courses and receiving a state-endorsed diploma.

Members of the district's executive committee and school board want action to improve middle school students' math performance. Some board members want to contract with a private education tutoring company; others want to convert a large, low scoring middle school to a charter school. Other proposals include developing a partnership with math faculty at a nearby college, purchasing a new curriculum series, and decentralizing control over professional development and school improvement budgets to the school level.

You collect information and determine that: (a) on average, over the last five years, 40% of 8th graders have scored below standard; (b) data-based projections indicate this percentage is unlikely to change in the absence of significant changes in the schools; (c) annually about 160 – 200 8th graders score within a quarter of a standard deviation below the cut score required to pass the test; (d) recent curriculum initiatives in literacy are occupying teachers' attention; and (e) allocating extra time to math during the school day will be hard given pressures for coverage of other subjects.

Thus, among other solutions, you contemplate a program of Saturday morning math sessions for students at risk of not passing the state's 8th grade math test. Should you do this? This is not a simple "yes" or "no" question. The decision depends on answers to other questions, many of which are not easily answered – there are unknowns and uncertainties. What are they? You need to have a better conception of the design, logistics, projected costs, and projected benefits of your contemplated plan. Then you can weigh your options more systematically.

A decision chart can help clarify the problem and plan solutions. Figure 3.2 shows a general model.

Figure 3.2
Decision Chart (Generic)

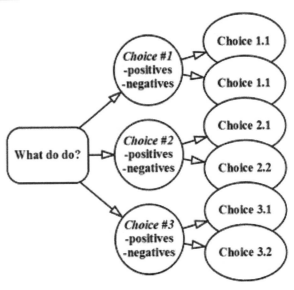

Appendix 3-E presents a larger and more detailed chart showing decision alternatives comparing a centralized to a decentralized management plan for implementing a Saturday math support program. It shows a map of alternatives ("Alt" in the chart), tradeoffs ("pros" and "cons"), and key uncertainties associated with different alternatives ("unknowns").

Analyzing the problem further, you establish a set of desired attributes based on discussions with colleagues – administrators, instructors, math specialists, and budget people; and you seek guidance from literature on similar programs implemented in other places.

Table 3.6 shows a result of planning discussions. Broader attributes (italicized) subsume more specific attributes listed underneath.

These attributes do not spring forth fully formed. Sometimes we think of broader attributes first, and these lead to more specific attributes, and sometimes the opposite. This process clarifies decision options, decision criteria, uncertainties, and questions needing answers.

Table 3.6
Planning for 8th grade math Saturday math program: Attributes and uncertainties

Cost efficient
- Operates within $$ budget (what is appropriate budget?)
- Low administrative overhead (how should the program be managed? how should the budget be managed?)

Effective program design
- Provides small-group instruction (~10:1 ratio; what is upper and lower limit?)
- 90 minutes of instruction (time on task; start & end times 9:30 – 11:30; incl lunch?)
- 10 class sessions
- Instruction targeted at identified academic gaps (how identified?)
- Instruction aligned with 8th grade content standards (who does this and how?)
- Best instructors selected (how? what criteria?)
- Best instructional practices used (who decides? how do we insure these are actually used?)

Select appropriate "in need" students
- How to identify targeted students (those who are predicted to fail, but not already receiving supplemental services)?
- How to encourage participation (must be voluntary, but incentives?)

Positive public relations
- Transportation for public (how? bus service or contract?)
- Convenient locations (where?)
- Communications emphasize support & enrichment (who will design these? web-info? newsletter? local media?)
- Certificate for completion (demonstrated improvement or just attendance [all sessions or most?]?)
- Positive atmosphere in instructional sessions (how to make these engaging? not 'more of the same old classroom instruction')

Good internal organizational relations
- Fair and open process for choosing instructors/contractors (symbolic function in addition to getting truly-committed instructors, not just people looking for extra pay)
- Appropriate compensation (what compensation amount is appropriate?)
- Not conflict with standard curriculum (Saturday instruction should supplement, not duplicate regular curriculum)

Evaluation of results
- Pre- and post- measurement of achievement on custom assessment (what assessments to use? design own custom assessment? off-the-shelf? other?)
- Analyze results on state test: compare participants to demographically-matched and prior-achievement-matched nonparticipants (identify person to do this in advance for technical guidance and buy-in)

The core problem – the TLO sentence – is "8th grade math achievement scores are too low." Here is a more specific problem statement: Annually, about 40% of 8th graders score below the "at standard" cut score on the state test. Using 7th grade test scores and math grades, we can identify with reasonable accuracy students likely to score below standard on the 8th grade test. If we provide extra support and instruction for these students prior to the 8th grade state test, we can improve their odds of passing. Extra instruction can *significantly* improve the odds for a subset of these students – the 160-200 students who annually are within a quarter of a standard deviation below the cut score.

There are different ways of framing the problem at this point. Our budget will support 18 teachers for 10 sessions (about 15 hours of on-task instructional time, assuming 90 minutes/session). There are different ways we can offer the extra instruction.

Selective enrollment. Should we concentrate resources on the 160 – 200 students "just below standard" to help most of them to pass? We can identify these 8th grade students early in December and send letters home to parents encouraging participation in the program. This approach will allow small class sizes with targeted instruction likely to help many of these students pass. They can then start high school in Algebra 1. This outcome will also significantly raise the district's 8th grade pass rate and aimporve the district's accountability report to the public.

Open enrollment. Should the Saturday morning sessions be open to anyone? The December letter would go to *all* 8th grade parents, announcing the Saturday program, describing its intent, and inviting participation. Compared with the selective plan, open enrollment will likely yield more participants, produce larger class sizes, and create more heterogeneous classes. There will be more students participating who have no chance of making the cut score and there will be students participating already likely to pass. This approach will raise the district average on the 8th grade test (relative to prior years), but will have a much smaller effect on the pass rate compared with the first approach.

This dilemma – selective versus open – illustrates different problem definitions. If the problem is narrowly defined as "8th grade passing rates are too low" then the selective enrollment plan makes sense by concentrating resources where they will have the biggest impact in increasing passing *rates*. If the problem is "average achievement in 8th grade math is too low," then the open enrollment plan is sensible because it allocates' the Saturday morning instructional resources to a broader number of students.

There is another benefit to the open enrollment plan. It is inclusive. The selective enrollment plan creates a public relations issue. Parents of ineligible students may complain. "Equal access" is a powerful norm in public schools. A program offered to some, but not all, must have a strong rationale and public relations.

The open enrollment plan presents less risk of complaints, but likely creates larger classes, thereby undercutting a key program design principle. The open enrollment plan will likely produce a smaller improvement in passing rates.

The two plans above are not the only options. The different ideas mentioned at the beginning of this section show other options for selecting and inviting students, for organizing the instruction, and for managing the program. Each option presents a unique set of costs, benefits, and uncertainties – these can be presented in a decision criteria table and a decision chart to aid decision-making. The goal is making the best decision under the circumstances.[30]

---

[30] In an interesting article, Goens (2001) explains "scenario planning" for addressing ill-structured problems. This process requires planners to map out and weight the consequences of different scenarios that could unfold following alternative decision paths.

SUMMARY AND CONCLUDING COMMENTS

This chapter discussed the form and content of a paper reflecting GAPPSI. I call it a paper out of convention, but it is not a traditional academic paper because it has elements of a proposal or plan and is action oriented – planning, inquiry, problem solving, and organizational improvement. At the same time, the paper has academic qualities in that, as Chapter's 1 and 2 discuss, it constructs an argument – it takes a position and justifies it.

The GAPPSI paper begins with a problem definition and typically ends with key questions and tasks. This chapter presented a framework for the paper and examples, drawing on problems related to discipline, student assessment, failing to graduate, and other examples.

The last portion of the chapter discussed analytic and decision-making tools.[31] These include causal analysis, stakeholder analysis, decision criteria tables, and decision charts. Appendices 3-D and 3-E show additional examples of charts to aid planning and decision-making.

Charts, tables, and other schematics help you think through a problem and communicate your thinking to relevant audiences. They are thinking tools and may be a produced in one sitting, like a meeting to be used once; on the other hand, multiple drafts can be appended to a GAPPSI paper showing how thinking and planning evolve over time.

These tools help clarify factors to consider in making decisions and plans, identifying information needs, and formulating a path to improvement objectives.

REFERENCES

Bell, D., Raiffa, H., & Tversky, A. (1988). *Decision making: Descriptive, normative, and prescriptive interactions*. Cambridge: Cambridge University Press.

Bloom, H., Hill, C., Black, A., & Lipsey, M. (2008). Performance trajectories and performance gaps as achievement effect-size benchmarks for educational interventions. *Journal of Research on Educational Effectiveness, 1*(4), 289-328.

Canady, R. & Rettig, M. (1995). *Block scheduling: A catalyst for change in high schools*. Princeton, NJ.: Eye on Education.

Connolly, T., Arkes, H. & Hammond, K. (Eds.) (2000). *Judgment and decision making: An interdisciplinary reader*. Cambridge: Cambridge University Press.

Edwards, C.M. (1993). The four-period day: Restructuring to improve student performance. *NASSP Bulletin 77*(553), 77-88.

Edwards, W. & Newman, J. (2000). Multiattribute evaluation. In Connolly, T., Arkes, H. & K. Hammond (Eds.), *Judgment and decision making: An interdisciplinary reader* (pp. 17-34). Cambridge: Cambridge University Press.

Facione, P. & Facione, N. (2007). *Thinking and reasoning in human decision making: The method of argument and heuristic analysis*. The California Academic Press.

---

[31] For more theory and research on rationality, decision-making, and choice see Bell, Raiffa, and Tversky (1988), Connolly, Arkes, and Hammond (2000), Facione & Facione (2007), Hammond, Keeney, and Raiffa (1999), Hogarth (1980), Kahneman (2011), Kepner & Tregoe (1997), March (1994), and Simon (1993).

Hammond, J., Keeney, R., & Raiffa, H. (1999). *Smart choices: A practical guide for making better decisions.* Boston, MA: Harvard Business School Press.

Hogarth, J. (1980). *Judgment and choice: The psychology of decision.* Chichester: Wiley.

Kahneman, D. (2011). *Thinking: Fast and slow.* NY: Farrar, Straus, & Giroux.

Kepner, C. & Tregoe, B. (1997). *The new rational manager.* Princeton, NJ: Princeton Research Press.

Kramer, S. & Keller, R. (2008). An existence proof: Successful joint implementation of the IMP curriculum and a 4 x 4 block schedule at a suburban U.S. high school. *Journal for Research in Mathematics Education 39*(1), January, 2-8.

Lipsey, M., Puzio, K., Yun, C., Hebert, M., Steinka-Fry, K., Cole, M., Roberts, M., Anthony, K., Busick, M. (2012). *Translating the statistical representation of the effects of education interventions into more readily interpretable forms.* (NCSER 2013-3000). Washington, DC: National Center for Special Education Research, Institute of Education Sciences, U.S. Department of Education. This report is available on the IES website at http://ies.ed.gov/ncser/.

March, J. (1994). *A primer on decision making: How decisions happen.* NY: The Free Press (Division of Macmillan, Inc.)

McCall, W. & Craig, C. (2009). Same-Language-Subtitling (SLS): Using subtitled music video for reading growth. In G. Siemens & C. Fulford (Eds.), *Proceedings of World Conference on Educational Multimedia, Hypermedia and Telecommunications* (pp. 3983-3992). Chesapeake, VA: AACE. [Available online from http://www.editlib.org/p/32055]

Miller, J. (2002). Adopting a districtwide reading program. *School Administrator, 59*(1), January, 16-19.

Mitchell, R. Agle, B., & Wood, D. (1997). Toward a theory of stakeholder identification and salience: Defining the principle of who and what really counts. *The Academy of Management Review, 22*(4), October, 853-886.

Paratore, J. & McCormack, R. (Eds.) (2007). *Classroom literacy assessment: Making sense of what students know and do.* New York: The Guilford Press.

Simon, H. (1993). Decision making: Rational, nonrational, and irrational. *Educational Administration Quarterly*, 29, 392-411.

Welsh, T. & McGinn, N. (1997). Toward a methodology of stakeholder analysis. *Educational Planning, 11*(3), 28-53.

Valencia, S., Hiebert, E., & Afflerbach, P. (Eds.) (1994). *Authentic reading assessment: Practices and possibilities.* Newark, DE: International Reading Association.

Varvasovszky, Z. & Brugha, R. (2000). How to do (or not to do) a stakeholder analysis. *Health Policy and Planning, 15*(3): 338-345.

Vogt, P. (2007). *Quantitative research methods for professionals in education and other fields.* Upper Saddle River, N.J.: Prentice Hall.

Vukelich, C., Christie, J., & Enz, B. (2008). *Helping young children learn language and literacy: Birth through kindergarten.* Boston: Pearson/Allyn and Bacon.

WWC (2013). Same-Language-Subtitling (SLS): Using subtitled music video for reading growth. *WWC Single Study Review.* U.S. Department of Education, Institute of Education Sciences, What Works Clearinghouse [available online at http://whatworks.ed.gov].

CHAPTER 4

GATHERING INFORMATION TO INVESTIGATE QUESTIONS AND SUBSTANTIATE CLAIMS

INTRODUCTION

Oak Street Performing Art Middle School is a specialty school, with choice-based enrollment. Teachers complain that many students in the school have limited talent and interest in the performing arts disciplines. Teachers in music, dance, and drama have at various times expressed frustration with students' misbehavior in their classes.

Oak Street's principal brings this up at a district office meeting, saying, "I think we need more specific admissions criteria. Teachers are telling me too many students are admitted without demonstrated qualifications or interest in the arts. I think a lot of parents choose Oak Street just because it's close. A lot of them probably don't know we have a performing arts theme."

Often, like the principal, we *think* we understand a problem and by intuition or habit, gravitate toward a particular solution. However, we risk taking actions that accomplish little, or worse, have unintended adverse consequences, because we misunderstood the problem.

At Oak Street, perhaps the complaining teachers' expectations are unrealistic, or perhaps the discipline problems lie not with the students – they are typical middle school kids – but from ineffective behavior management by certain teachers, or inconsistent policies at the school level. Maybe the school doesn't attract applicants interested in its theme due to poor advertising or the school's appearance is uninviting? Without getting more information on this situation – without examining the assumptions and claims people are making – no one really knows what the problem is, or even if there is a significant problem. Jumping to a change in admissions processes could waste time and effort and possibly create new problems.

This chapter discusses information-gathering to support a GAPPSI project. This book assumes that being more informed is better and that literature and local data can help you better understand a problem and devise better responses than you would in the absence of information.

In a widely cited *Harvard Business Review* article, management experts Hammond, Keeney, and Raiffa (1998) write about "The Hidden Traps in Decision Making."[32] Seven of their twenty recommendations concern seeking and using information.

- Never think of the status quo as your only alternative. Identify other options and use them as counter-balances, *carefully evaluating all the pluses and minuses.*

---

[32] Italics in the Hammond et al. excerpt are added. Another famous article is "Judgment under uncertainty: Heuristics and biases," by Tversky & Kahneman (2000). See also Kahneman (2011). For more on the role of biases and other distorting influences on decision-making, see Hammond, Keeney, and Raiffa (1998) or Hogarth (1980), especially Chapter 7.

Ask yourself whether you would choose the status-quo alternative if, in fact, it weren't the status quo.

• *Seek out and listen carefully* to the views of people who were uninvolved with the earlier decisions and who are hence unlikely to be committed to them.

• Always check to see whether you are *examining all the evidence with equal rigor.* Avoid the tendency to accept confirming evidence without question.

• Get someone you respect to *play devil's advocate, to argue against the decision* you're contemplating. Better yet, build the counterarguments yourself. What's the strongest reason to do something else? The second strongest reason? The third? Consider the position with an open mind.

• Be honest with yourself about your motives. *Are you really gathering information to help you make a smart choice*, or are you just looking for evidence confirming what you think you'd like to do?

• In seeking the advice of others, *don't ask leading questions that invite confirming evidence.* And if you find that an adviser always seems to support your point of view, find a new adviser. Don't surround yourself with yes-men.

• To minimize the distortion caused by variations in recallability [memory of recent salient events], carefully examine all your assumptions to ensure that they're not unduly influence by your memory. *Get actual statistics whenever possible.* Try not to be guided by impressions.

This chapter is not about conducting research motivated by theoretical questions and scholarly knowledge. GAPPSI inquiry supports decision making in a particular setting. GAPPSI inquiry does not revolve around a single research question; decisions don't hinge on a single unit of evidence. Rather, decision-oriented inquiry is about supporting professional judgment with literature and local data. This may or may not benefit scholarly knowledge, but it does build the local expertise – yours and colleagues' – what organizational theorists describe as "organizational learning" (Leithwood, Leonard, & Sharratt, 1998; Newcomb, 2003; Schechter, 2008; Silins, Mulford, & Zarins, 2002).

The main sections of this chapter are:

• Part 1: Using Literature In A GAPPSI Paper
• Part 2: Belief and Attitude Data: Surveys, Focus Groups, and Survey-Interview Hybrids
• Part 3: Information From Organizational Data

PART 1
USING LITERATURE IN A GAPPSI PAPER

Literature sources are divided into two categories: primary and secondary. *Primary source literature* consists of research studies and original work like a new instrument (e.g., a new assessment tool), invention (e.g., a new instructional technology), framework (Bloom's Taxonomy) or theory or conceptual framework (authentic assessment). *Secondary sources* are publications that draw on primary sources such as literature reviews, policy briefs, and books or articles that use primary sources and advocate a position or cause.

Literature should be part of a GAPPSI paper or project. Using literature, you learn from the research, experience, and ideas of others. You build expertise and credibility when you draw on the work and ideas of others.

This section discusses using literature:

- as a source of terms and definitions:
- as a source of examples
- to illustrate a principle or make a point to substantiate your claim that problems you identify are important (i.e., the condition you identify is a significant problem – something people should address)
- to organize an argument or analysis
- to substantiate predictions

Literature as a Source of Terms and Definitions:

Every professional field's discourse is filled with specialized terminology. Understanding and using this terminology appropriately is part of the process of building expertise.

In a GAPPSI paper – in any leadership communications for that matter:

(1) *be specific* about key terms you use (using a definition or several is helpful – or create the define yourself), and
(2) *use appropriate terminology* (this means picking the right terms, or at terms commonly accepted)

Assume, for instance, a special education coordinator is concerned about challenges experienced by English Language Learners; schools in her district are adopting "Response to Intervention" (RTI) to be more successful with struggling learners and to reduce special education placements. Her GAPPSI paper starts with a problem statement. A few paragraphs defining RTI are essential.

We are adopting a system called "Response to Intervention" (RTI) to design instruction more effectively around students' learning needs. One definition RTI is "the practice of providing high-quality instruction and interventions matched to student need, monitoring progress frequently to make decisions about changes in instruction or goals, and applying child response data to important educational decisions" (NASDSE and CASE, 2006, p. 2).

Here is another definition, from The National Center on Response to Intervention (NCRTI, 2010, p. 2). "Response to intervention integrates assessment and intervention within a multi-level prevention system to maximize student achievement and to reduce behavioral problems. With RTI, schools use data to identify students at risk for poor learning outcomes, monitor student progress, provide evidence-based interventions and adjust the intensity and nature of those interventions depending on a student's responsiveness, and identify students with learning disabilities or other disabilities."

Her paper needs these paragraphs; otherwise the reader may be unclear about what exactly RTI means. Here is another example:

> One strategy we will try is "Lesson Study." In Lesson Study, "teachers collaboratively plan, observe, and analyze classroom lessons, drawing out implications both for the design of specific lessons and for teaching and learning more broadly" (Lewis, Perry, Hurd, & O'Connell, 2006, p. 273).

It is essential not just to be clear and accurate with key technical terms, but also *consistent* in usage across your narrative – don't use "formative assessment" in one place and later call it "formative evaluation." Or "instructional technology" in one paragraph and "education technology," later.

Also understand that the field of education is rife with murky terminology and jargon. For some audiences, a term's meaning may not be self-evident. Or in other cases a term may be widely used, but people have different understandings of the term.

Here are examples of common words in the education field that are, in a sense, technical, but that can mean different things to different people.

- instructional technology
- professional development
- summative versus formative assessment
- professional learning community
- spiral curriculum
- academic engagement
- inclusion
- school culture

Literature helps you use key terms appropriately and clearly; decide on key terms carefully, and be consistent in you usage.

Literature To Establish That a Problem Is Important – Something People Should Care About

There are two elements to this. The first is persuading that the conditions or practices you identify actually exist (you're not just imagining things or concocting a problem); the second is persuading that the conditions or practices you identify need fixing – i.e., are a problem. It is possible to achieve the first goal, but not the second. Your audience may agree that the conditions or practices you identify exist, but may not agree there is a problem. "It's nothing to worry about" or "So what" are possible responses.

Literature can help establish that a condition or practice exists *and* is a problem. For example:

At Addison High School teachers in different academic departments rarely interact. Each department functions autonomously; rarely are there attempts to coordinate curriculum between different academic subjects. Research shows this is a relatively common situation in schools and a barrier to achieving a standards-based curriculum (references).

> This part of the passage states two facts – one about Addison and one about research findings; but it is not until the end of the passage that the author relies on theory and research to argue that the observed conditions – what exists at Adddison – are *a problem*.

Why is a standards-based curriculum desirable? Consider two schools, one in which teachers do a lot of joint curriculum planning and where the curriculum is carefully designed to align with standards in each subject and grade level. In a second school teachers operate more independently, planning each course on their own and rarely discussing or attempting to coordinate course curriculum. Even if we assume teachers in both schools are equally dedicated and talented, students in the first school students will be more likely to experience connections between courses and have lessons that build sequentially across courses and from one grade level to the next. Students in a school like this will learn more than in one where the curriculum is not aligned with any unifying set of standards, even if teachers in both schools individually teach effectively. Following, I present research supporting this principle (references).

As another example, suppose you work in a high school. Newmann and Associates (1996) studied curriculum and instruction in 24 high schools and found considerable variability among teachers in academic rigor. The study used a conceptual framework to collect and interpret its data, so the reader knows clearly the authors' perspective, such as what they mean by rigor and how they measured it. If you accept their framework and trust their findings, and if your school is similar in size and composition to the schools in their sample, then this study could help in at least three ways: (a) a framework to think about the concept and measurement of "rigor;" (b) reason to believe similar levels of variability across teachers my exist in your school; and (c) an estimate of the possible magnitude of this variability and its consequences.

Here is a third example. Research can help explain causes of a current state. Suppose you work in a district and are concerned about the achievement gains of low-income students falling short of their middle income peers. You suspect summer learning might be a factor – possibly its greater for low-income students. You might be able to examine this empirically on your own if you have the time, capability, and the needed local data. Or, you could turn to the literature.

Studies have measured summer learning loss (Alexander, Entwisle, & Olson, 2001; McCall, Kingsbury, & Olson, 2004). They give precise measures and strong evidence of differential achievement trends over summer of students in different demographic categories. On average, lower-income students fall further behind their more advantaged peers each summer. The cumulative effect over the years is an ever-widening achievement gap as the students get older. This is a generalization – it is a relationship of a certain type and magnitude that is generally true. Does this generalization apply to students in your district?

Chances are the size of the achievement gap in your district is similar, unless you believe the students in your district are unlike the students in the study samples.

Information like this can be useful in two ways: an estimate of the percentage of the achievement gap attributable to nonschool environments and information to argue for remedies – perhaps a year-round academic calendar or establishing a summer school program.

These examples illustrate drawing on literature to establish the significance of a problem you perceive and want others to know and care about.

Literature as a Source of Examples
To Illustrate a Principle or Make a Point

You may want an example to make a point. Literature can be a source. For instance, if you are explaining what a goal state or optimal practice looks like, an article can provide a description. When a researcher publishes a case study it may include descriptions of organizational conditions or professional practice (whether exemplary, ordinary, or deficient). Studies based on interviews sometimes quote respondents' descriptions about conditions or practices in their organization. Here is an example from a study.

Public Agenda's (2007) study of school leadership, based on site visits and interviews, found examples of leadership of two types, transformer and copers.

The "transformers" had an explicit vision of what they wanted their school to be like, and they talked about specific changes they were making now or planned to make in the near future. This year, introduce the new reading curriculum. Next year, get a teaching coach for math. Some had scanned their teacher rosters and pinpointed the teachers they wanted to move out. Maybe it couldn't be done in one fell swoop, but they had their plans. (p. 02)

The "copers," on the other hand, allocated almost all of their time to keeping the school running and generally felt they had nothing to give beyond this. This was their full-time job; their total commitment. It is not that these principals were not working hard; rather, they were preoccupied with day-to-day organizational maintenance and uninvolved in instruction. These principals did not see how they could do things differently, as illustrated in one's comment: 'I find myself wearing so many hats... it's unbelievable. I just cannot free myself up'

As another example, a study by Hampel (1995) offers conclusions and terminology useful for writing about challenges in leading change in a "school restructuring" initiative. His case studies of eight schools led him to place teachers in four categories:

- "Vanguard" – actively committed, always involved; volunteer and commit extra time; provide leadership for others.
- "Yes, but..." – supportive in word and spirit; occasionally on committees; help when convenient; sometimes participate, but prone to sit out periodically.

66

- "Sleepy" –uninvolved; privately skeptical; passively oppose by not participating.
- "Cynical" – actively resist change; unspoken criticism of change philosophy and goals.

These labels are shorthand. They condense complex information – detailed descriptions, quotes, and anecdotes that define and distinguish the four categories of teachers. Labels, quotes, and vivid descriptions from literature add richness and detail to flesh out a GAPPSI paper.

Literature Used To Organize an Argument or Analysis

A conceptual framework organizes an expository narrative around a small number of ideas. You can usually find a framework within the literature on your topic. Consider, for instance, a paper concerned with school-site staff lacking access to data for instructional planning and decision making. The problem statement might have a section in its narrative on barriers to data use. This paper and proposed analysis should be informed by prior theory and research. For example, a study of data use in schools examined districts' data systems and staff practices involving data-driven decision making. The authors conclude:

> School staffs' perceptions of barriers to greater use of data include a sense of lack of time, system usability issues, the perception that the data in the system are not useful, and district policies around curriculum coverage or pacing that prohibit modifying learning time to match student needs (Means, Padilla, and Gallagher, 2010, p. xvii).

The four barriers Means et al. identify could help organize an analysis presented in a GAPPSI paper. Key questions would be about how staff currently use data, their perceptions of the quality and utility of existing data systems, and needs they identify with respect to improving instruction and student learning. The paper should be informed by work like the Means et al. study. It would be informative to know how these researchers defined and operationalized the four barriers, and, possibly use their framework to organize a portion of the paper.

Here are a few other examples. If a problem definition relates to poor academic motivation in your school, an article discussing "academic enablers" is relevant (Diperna, 2006). Diperna (2006) draws on other literature and distinguishes four factors influencing students' academic work.

> Academic enablers have been defined as attitudes and behaviors that facilitate students' participation in, and benefit from, academic instruction in the classroom (DiPerna & Elliott, 2000). The purpose of this article is to provide practitioners with an overview of specific academic enablers (motivation, study skills, engagement, and social skills) and their relationships with academic achievement. In addition, a practical framework is provided for considering academic enablers within assessment and intervention practices in the schools (p. 7).

Diperna's framework could help organize a problem definition as well as frame an empirical inquiry.

Another subject is organizational change – promoting and managing it is a key role of leadership. "Moving Forward: A Guide for Implementing Comprehensive School Reform and Improvement Strategies" (AIR, 2007) is a framework for implementing school reform. This guide presents a seven-stage "change cycle" based on national research. The model "is intended to help educators think about the varying aspects of identifying, selecting, and implementing school improvement strategies suited to the characteristics of their own environment" (p. 4). For a GAPPSI paper, the framework could organize a problem statement or a "key questions/tasks" narrative on organizational change.

A GAPPSI project on high school drop outs may seek empirical data to understand causal factors. Since data collection requires questions and questions should derive from a theory of causes, a well-designed inquiry would draw on drop out research. If this was your concern, literature shows how researchers have conceptualized and measured causes of dropping out. If your concern is with students in one school, then your focus would be individual-level causes and measures such as family background, academic history, academic ability, self-esteem, self-efficacy, and other psychological or personality variables as well as variables within the school that may be contributors. If your concern is at the district level, then your purview expands to include school-level causes because conditions differ among schools (e.g., staff composition, school size, culture, etc.).

Literature To Substantiate Predictions

Educators want to know, if I do "X," then what is the probability that "Y" will happen? A good best practice synthesis or research study provides estimates to make evidence-based predictions.

For example, Vadasy, Jenkins, and Pool (2000) examined effects of tutoring by trained aides – 30 minute tutoring sessions for 1st graders in reading, about 4 times a week, over 27 weeks. They randomly assigned students into two groups: one sample received the tutoring for 27 weeks on a pull-out basis and the other sample remained in their regular classroom getting their regular reading instruction from their teacher.[33]

The tutoring procedures boosted achievement. Tutored students scored significantly better on a battery of reading assessments one year later, with effect sizes ranging from .4 to 1.2 standard deviations. The researchers provided demographic information on the sample of students and explained how the students were selected into the treatment and control groups (random assignment); they described in detail the tutoring procedures, the characteristics of the tutors, and the types of reading assessments.

An elementary school leader might wonder: If we institute a tutoring program, what achievement gains can we expect? The Vadasy et al. study above is one guide. Recognize that it provides estimates, not certainties. Your students may differ somewhat from those in the Vadasy sample; or your tutors may be different; or your tutoring meth-

---

[33] See Chapter 3, "On Using Effect Sizes To Formulate Improvement Targets" for more on the concept of "effect size" and its use in predicting outcomes.

ods may be different; or the amount of time available for tutoring may be different. Still, the study helps for deliberating strategies. It describes (a) one way of doing tutoring; (b) the likely achievement effects of this approach; and (c) an estimate of the costs of this approach (to weigh benefits against costs). You may conclude the benefits do not justify the costs or you may conclude otherwise. Either way, it is an informed decision.

Much literature, of course, recommends programs or practices, but without specific estimates of an effect. Much literature is like this:

> Teachers may find useful "benchmarking" as a method to improve instruction in writing. This requires comparing and discussing their grading criteria for assessing students' writing. According to Andrade, Buff, Terry, Erano, and Paolino (2009), collaborative grading of papers can be a productive activity if well planned, organized, and led by an experienced workshop leader with expertise in writing instruction and assessment. The activity involves reading and discussing a range of student papers, discussing the paper's strengths and weaknesses, comparing the attributes of weak papers to better ones, and individual participants explaining to others their grading criteria with examples from papers illustrating these criteria.

For "advice giving" literature like this, *you* assess the merits of the prescriptions. Consider the reputation of the author(s), the selectivity and prestige of the publishing source, the rigor of the argument, the quality of the evidence, and the consistency of the prescriptions with other literature and with your own professional experience – all of this must be weighed in judging and using literature-based prescriptions. Formulas guaranteeing success would be great, but education isn't reducible to formulas. Personality, communications skills, background knowledge, emotions, relationships and resources are all ingredients of the effectiveness of practice.

Still, a professional must know "best practice." Examples above are from books and journals. Another source is the *What Works Clearinghouse (WWC)*[34], maintained by the U.S Department of Education. The WWC states: "Our goal is to provide educators with the information they need to make evidence-based decisions." The WWC reports the strength of evidence on the effectiveness of a large number of recognized educational interventions (programs, products, practices, and policies). WWC explains in detail its research review process – the literature search process, standards of evidence, and how studies are rated. For additional guidance, Appendix 4-A provides a checklist of questions to consider in assessing the quality of a quantitative research study.

Next, Part 2 discusses opinion and attitude data from surveys, focus groups, and survey-interview hybrids. Later, Part 3 focuses on organizational data. For more depth I suggest these books.[35] The next two sections are on collecting and using decision-oriented data from people (part 2) and organizational databases (part 3).

---

[34] http://ies.ed.gov/ncee/wwc/

[35] For books on research and data analysis, see Boudett, City, and Murnane (2005), Briggs and Coleman (2000), Creighton (2007), Gall, Gall, and Borg (2003), Latess (2008), and Vogt (2006).

PART 2
BELIEF AND ATTITUDE DATA:
SURVEYS, FOCUS GROUPS, AND SURVEY-INTERVIEW HYBRIDS

Introduction

There are many words referring to the mental constructs disclosed by surveys and interviews – opinions, values, attitudes, perceptions, beliefs, feelings, convictions, for example – but the most used categorization is beliefs and attitudes. This is what I use below.

Another term is "stakeholder groups," which I use to refer to any group you target for gathering belief and attitude data for decision making purposes. This can be as small as "the department chairs in my high school" or much larger, like "all parents" or "all teachers in the district." Who you survey or interview reflects the group or groups you want to know about.

In GAPPSI, belief and attitude data are for decision making. Knowing how key stakeholder groups think about something can guide decision making. Belief and attitude data can help decide (a) *whether* improvement is needed, because groups believe something is satisfactory or not, or (b) *how* to improve by providing improvement suggestions directly (advice-giving) or by helping you understand how groups think or behave so *you* can develop improvement ideas.

Terminology: Beliefs and Attitudes

Belief Questions

The online Oxford Dictionary defines belief as: "an acceptance that something exists or is true, especially one without proof." Beliefs are expressed as verbal statements of assumptions, interpretations, suppositions, explanations, and predictions. If a survey asks a child – "About how many times in the last week have you been teased by someone?" – the child's answer will reflect his interpretation of what constitutes being teased and how many times this has occurred. The statement, "I have learned a lot in this course," reflects a belief as does, "high ability students learn more in ability grouped classroom than in heterogeneous classrooms."

Attitude Questions

The online Oxford Dictionary defines attitude as: "a settled way of thinking or feeling about something." Merriam-Webster adds, "a feeling or emotion toward a fact or state." Attitudes are how we feel about something; what we like and do not like; what we think of as good and bad; what we value, are indifferent to, or dislike. A similar term is "values." Attitudes and values can be measured using ranking scales, as in the following examples: "Rank the following attributes of your job from most important to least important." "Of the following list of leadership traits, which three do you admire most in a school leader?" Attitudes and values can be disclosed by statements like "I wish I were more socially popular in my school," "I don't like attending parent-teacher conferences," or "Teachers should be paid more." Words like "should," "ought," "like," or "good" are commonly found in attitude statements.

Distinction Between Beliefs and Attitudes

While the distinction between beliefs and attitudes is sometimes blurry, the two terms are useful nonetheless. Understanding the distinction between beliefs and attitudes is not just for academic knowledge; it helps to understand the range of questions that can be asked and to be precise in identifying the information sought.[36] Of course, not every survey or interview question must be one or the other type; some questions are factual in nature: What was your college major? How many nights last week did you do homework? How many walk-through classroom observations do you conduct in an average week?

Eight Guidelines for Better Surveys[37]

1) Know exactly what you want to find out and what the survey will prove.

"Prove" is a strong word. I use it to stress being clear about the survey's objectives and decision implications. Writing your survey's purpose is important.

> Objective: to learn whether K-6 teachers from Davenport School District are satisfied with last year's professional development opportunities, how they benefited, what they recommend for improving access to professional development, and what staff development needs they identify.

Think carefully about what *each survey item* will tell you. For each item, imagine the range of responses and for different values of the response, ask yourself: What decision(s) will this support? For instance, "A mean score of 4.5 indicates about half of the students would volunteer up to two hours a week to raise money for the spring field trip." As another example, a set of items[38] could let staff know about school spirit among the student body or specific subgroups and whether spirit is appropriately healthy or needs

---

[36] For additional readings on attitudes and beliefs and psychological measurement, see Albarracin, Johnson and Zanna (2005); Himmelfarb (1993); or Ostrom, Bond, Krosnick, and Sedikides (1994); or browse the journal, *Public Opinion Quarterly*.

[37] The following books are practical guides for survey design, analysis, and reporting: Bradburn, Sudman, and Wansink (2004); Cox and Cox (2007); Orcher (2007); Thomas (2007); and Willis (2005). A handy web-based resource on survey design is at *www.howto.gov* – a website hosted by the federal government's General Services Administration. See the web page called "Basics of Survey and Question Design."

[38] Researchers often use the word "scale" to refer to a group of items (usually about three to five) that are similar, but not inter-changeable and that therefore produce multiple measures of a single broader construct like school spirit; the scores on the items are combined to produce a single score and this, then, creates a more reliable estimate than would a single survey item trying to measure the same construct. This meaning of "scale" is different from referring to the numbers or categories as the "scale" allowing the respondent to provide a rating responding to an individual survey question.

attention. Having a clear purpose, then, means survey results support specific decision-oriented conclusions.

2) *Who Is Your Target Population?*

Who exactly do you need information from? Who do you want to know about? Think carefully about these questions and write out the defining characteristics of your target population. Here are three examples illustrating specific target populations: (a) *Teachers employed in the district who graduated from state teacher education programs in the last ten years.* (b) *Parents of elementary age children in the district who do not have health insurance.* (c) *The high school freshmen in the district.*

Writing down your target group forces you to be specific. This guideline relates closely to (#1) above and helps insure you are targeting the right respondents.

3) *Survey Everyone, Or Get A Good Cross-Section.*

Sometimes it is feasible to survey all members of the target population. For students and staff, this can be feasible. For parents or other community members, it is much more difficult, or impossible. Because most surveys use an anonymous response system (see #8, below), even with a staff survey it can be hard to get everyone to respond. This is why your survey should be as short as possible and why your cover letter (#7, below) should motivate people to respond.

Often, only a portion of those surveyed, respond. Therefore, you must think hard about these three questions:

- How might the people who did *not* return the survey differ from my respondents?
- Are there reasons to believe the nonrespondents would have answered any of the survey items differently (i.e., on average, as a pattern)?
- If so, how might the nonrespondents' answers be different, on the whole?

Imagine, for instance, a high school uses the homeroom period to survey all students about homework and study habits. On that day 10% of the students are absent. How might this 10% be different from the group as a whole? Some students are chronically absent, and members of the "chronically absent" category of students are more likely to be part of the 10% on the day the survey is administered, or any given day. This group probably has poorer study habits and does less homework, so survey results are likely to be biased in the direction of painting a more positive picture than is true. (Always be vigilant about biasing effects of missing data, whether or not it is survey day.)

Figuring out effects of and directions of bias is not easy.[39] Always be aware of the possibility, mindful about its effects, and cautious in data analysis and reporting; and take all feasible measures in advance to have a representative sample (minimize missing data).

---

[39] For more reading on this, review a statistics or research methods textbook (e.g., Gall, Gall, & Borg, 2003) or do an Internet search for content on "random sampling methods."

The survey itself can answer some questions about whether or not the respondents are representative of the target population. Items can ask respondents their age, race, gender, grade level, or other relevant personal characteristics. When computing results, determine how the sample matches up with population characteristics. For instance, if employment records show 25% of the teaching staff in a district has worked over 20 years, but a survey shows only 10% reported "more than 20 years," then this more senior category of teachers was less likely to respond. Now there is a possibility of bias in results (beliefs of senior teachers less represented).

4) *Appropriate Item Format: The Right Format For The Right Question.*

"I look forward to work" (strongly agree, agree, disagree, strongly disagree). The Likert format for survey items is oft-used, but not the only option. Likert items/scales were developed to measure beliefs and attitudes and are most useful to compare groups – e.g., males vs. females, racial groups, old vs. young, income classes, etc. If this is what you're after – comparing groups on beliefs/attitudes – then the Likert scale is appropriate. Likert items and scales are familiar and simple, so a survey can contain a lot of items that the respondent can answer relatively quickly.

But, as #1 above stressed, think *first* about what data you need and *then* about the most useful item and scale. The item below, for instance, could be in a Likert format, asking for agreement or disagreement (e.g., "I am informed about...."), but the following format gives more specific answers.

How informed are you about the APEX leadership development program?
_____ I have not heard of it.
_____ I have heard of the program, but know little about it.
_____ I know the basics (when it takes place, courses offered).
_____ I know quite a bit about the program (living arrangements, costs, application process, credits, course offerings).

This is not a recommendation against using Likert items – just consider alternatives before deciding. Here are a few examples showing different alternatives for items and scales (the scales are in parentheses).

How many teachers in this school: (scale: None, Some, About Half, Most, Nearly All). [40]
- Help maintain discipline in the entire school, not just their classroom
- Take responsibility for improving the school
- Are really trying to improve their teaching
- Are eager to try new ideas
- Feel responsible when students in this school fail
- Feel good about parents' support for their work

---

[40] From Herman (1993).

73

Circle the position on the scale that describes your attitude toward the workshop.[41]

```
|-----|-----|-----|-----|-----|-----|
interesting                    boring
|-----|-----|-----|-----|-----|-----|
challenging                    easy
|-----|-----|-----|-----|-----|-----|
useful                         unuseful
```

How important is it for you to:
(scale: Not Important, A Little Important, Important, Very Important)
- Stay physically fit
- Be informed about national politics
- Attend church regularly
- Support charities
- Participating in service activities or volunteer work
- Get good grades in school

How would you rate the *responsiveness* and the *quality of service* you received from each of the following units of the central office.

(Scale: Excellent=E, Good=G, Fair=F, Poor=P)

	Responsive-ness				*Quality of Service*			
Personnel	E	G	F	P	E	G	F	P
Technology	E	G	F	P	E	G	F	P
Facilities	E	G	F	P	E	G	F	P
Curriculum	E	G	F	P	E	G	F	P

Here are several Likert items from the "Teacher Follow-up Questionnaire" administered from the National Center for Education Statistics.[42]

(Scale: Strongly Agree, Somewhat Agree, Somewhat Disagree, Strongly Disagree)

- Rules for student behavior are consistently enforced by teachers in this school, even for students who are not in their classes.
- Most of my colleagues share my beliefs and values about what the central mission of the school should be.
- The principal or school head knows what kind of school he/she wants and has communicated it to the staff.

---

[41] This type of scale is called "semantic differential." See Helwig & Avitable (2004).

[42] See "Survey and Programs" webpage at *www.nces.ed.gov*.

5) Clear Questions: Concise, One-idea, Familiar Language

Always test your survey on a few people similar to your respondents. Get their feedback on how they interpret particular items or words and any confusing or unclear items. Three attributes of item construction are important:

- *Concise.* Make sure survey items are simple and concise questions. The following are *not*:

    - Often, changes in assignments must be given consideration to assist students who need improvement of their behavior in classrooms.

        Rarely- Occasionally - More often than not - Consistently

    - Students do not take illegal drugs because they want to participate in sports activities and illegal drugs are not allowed.

        Strongly Agree – Agree – Disagree – Strongly Disagree

- *Single idea questions.* Items should not contain multiple ideas. Here is an example: "I think the new expulsion policy has improved discipline and should be continued." The respondent may agree with the first part, but for different reasons disagree with the second part. An item should focus on *one idea*.

- *Familiar language.* Use words familiar to respondents. Avoid jargon, vogue expressions, and technical language unless you know the language is familiar to your respondents: "Leaders in our school emphasize power through people rather than power over people." What does this mean? "We should strive for more collegial interaction." Do people know what collegial means? If a particular term is important in a survey, define it in advance.

6) Constructing Appropriate Scales: Scale Metrics Reflect Your Purpose.

For measurement precision, an item's scale should capture the full range of responses in useful gradations. If you are measuring how often something happens or the frequency of a practice, the scale must reflect the full range of possible amounts or frequencies.

Suppose as part of a curriculum mapping project you use an on-line survey and ask K-5 teachers to report time allocated to each curriculum subject. What would be a good scale? "Minutes/per month" would be too hard to estimate; "minutes/day" might be hard for the respondent to answer if they think "it depends upon the day of the week." I would favor "minutes/week" and add the qualifier "typical week" to the survey question.

What would be a good range for this scale? If the curriculum subject is relatively specific (e.g., "spelling," "grammar"), then the scale range will be smaller; if the curriculum subject is defined more broadly (e.g., "language arts") then the scale range will be larger. If the subject is stated as "math," then perhaps 20 or 30 minute intervals would be sufficient with the maximum around 450 minutes (90 minutes/day X 5 days).

Another option is to give the respondents a blank and let them write in the number of minutes.[43]

A scale measuring how many hours per week students play video games would start at zero, but could be scaled in different ways depending upon measurement precision needed. If you need precision – perhaps you want to correlate hours of use with some other numerical variable – then use small increments (e.g., measuring in hours: 0, 1-2, 3-4, 5-6, ... 19-20, more than 20); on the other hand, if your main interest is estimating the prevalence of excessive use, then big categories are fine (e.g., measuring in hours: 0-10, 11-19, 20 or more).

The same principle applies to Likert scales, although measuring beliefs and attitudes is more subjective, less easily quantifiable. The usual question here is how many points on the scale to give respondents – it can range from 2 (agree vs. disagree) on up, although 7 is usually the maximum (strongly agree, agree, mildly agree, unsure, mildly disagree, disagree, strongly disagree). There is no single best scale because it depends on what you're asking and what you're after.

Gradations within the scale should be determined by your purposes. If you are only interested in the prevalence of one category, e.g., "definitely not going to college" then you don't need 7 point scale.

7) *Explain Your Purpose.*

Respondents should have an explanation of the survey's purpose. The explanation need not be lengthy, but it should communicate the survey's value and why the respondent's participation is sought. For instance, surveying teachers in its own district, the Office of Professional Development (OPD) does not need to provide a lot of explanation. *This survey seeks your ideas to help improve OPD services to teachers. Please rate the quality of workshops and other training experiences we have supported and recommend ways we may serve better your professional development needs. This survey is anonymous.* On the other hand, a survey of community respondents coming from a district office probably needs more explanation since some respondents may be unfamiliar with the district and the survey topics.

8) *Anonymous*

Most surveys are anonymous for the obvious reason that anonymity allows for candor; if respondents fear no risk of identity disclosure they more honestly disclose beliefs, attitudes, or practices. For most purposes there is no need to know respondents' identities, so anonymous surveying is preferred.

However, anonymous surveying prevents linking survey results with other individual level data on respondents. For instance, the results of a student survey on their

---

[43] For an interesting survey project to measure curriculum and instruction, do a web search on, "Surveys of Enacted Curriculum."

peer relationships cannot be linked at the individual level with other data on the respondents because there is no personal identifier information on the survey. Thus, if a study's purpose requires linking individual achievement and behavior records with individual responses on a survey, then the priority of anonymity may be subordinated to the priority of answering study questions. Under these circumstances, a higher level of justification for the study and more permissions and approvals are required – not least of which is prior parental consent and approval (if respondents are not adults).

High quality surveys are readily available. You can find surveys in research literature (e.g., Furlong, Greif, Bates, Whipple, Jimenez, & Morrison, 2005) and in books for educators (Thomas, 2004). Another source is the U.S. Department of Education's National Center for Education Statistics. Using your web browser click on "Surveys and Programs" and then "Elementary/ Secondary." You will find many types of surveys (see especially "Schools and Staffing Survey"), all publicly available and downloadable.[44]

Focus Group Interviews

While all focus groups involve interviews, not all interviews are focus groups. Ethnographic research is usually based on individual interviews. I discuss focus groups here because this method is more common for management and decision making purposes, although much below applies also to interview methods.[45]

The Moderator and a Group

When you interview people in groups, it is called a focus group. Group size is typically 6 to 10 people. There is no prescribed length of time, but 30 minutes to an hour is typical. Here are the basics.

The interviewer is called the moderator. Having a second person available to take notes is helpful, so the moderator can concentrate on questions and answers, nonverbal cues, and group dynamics. Tape recording is of obvious value to furnish verbatim data and for post interview fact-checking; this is especially important if no note-taker is available. However, groups may not want to be recorded or recording may be inadvisable if it influences responses.

Homogeneous Groups

A focus group is usually selected to be homogeneous on certain characteristics – not on attitudes and beliefs, but on characteristics like job type, socio-economic stratum, race, or gender. Group composition depends on the purpose of the interviews. For instance, if a school leader wants to learn middle school girls' views on pursuing advanced science and

---

[44] Search for "Survey and Program Areas" at the National Center for Education Statistics.

[45] For more on focus group methodology, see Edmunds (1999), Harrell and Bradley (2009), Krueger and Casey (2000), Latess (2008), or Patton (2002).

math in high school, the focus group's composition will be homogenous with respect to gender (girls) and grade level (7th and 8th graders).

Series of Focus Group Sessions

Usually moderators conduct multiple focus group sessions to interview different types of people in the population and to broaden the sample. The more groups interviewed, the more learned (up to a point), and the more robust the results.

Focus groups are samples of a target population. Generally, the more diverse the target population, the larger number of focus groups needed. If the target population of interest is elderly adults in the community, the size and diversity of this population likely necessitates multiple focus groups to capture the diversity of beliefs and attitudes.

Identify and Invite Respondents

Although a focus group's composition is homogeneous on certain chosen characteristics (see above), group members will have different views on the subject of the focus group. When selecting specific respondents, consider selecting people varying on other characteristics to avoid a sample that is too homogeneous. If, for example, a focus group consists of novice elementary teachers in the probationary portion of their contract, members should vary on characteristics like age, gender, subject specialization (if any), grade level, and job site.

Sometimes input from key individuals is important: the head of the PTA if a problem or potential decision affects school parents; the Chamber of Commerce director if a potential decision has implications for local business. Not only are certain individuals more knowledgeable than others, their input can cultivate their support, or at least minimize resistance (i.e., strategic intelligence).[46] Appendix 4-B provides a sample invitation letter.

Planning and Conducting Interviews

It is useful to write out the purpose for the focus group sessions. Here is an example: *To learn whether teachers think the screening assessment used for reading groups works well for grouping purposes, whether they think it provides useful instructional information, and whether an alternative instrument should be considered.* Here is another example: *Do Hispanic parents in the community feel adequately informed about their*

---

[46] See the discussion of stakeholder analysis in Chapter 3. For written cases of education administrators using focus groups, see Latess, Curtin, and Leck (2006), Wagner (1997), and Winand (2007). Reutzel, Fawson, & Smith (2007) used focus groups as part of an evaluation of phonics-based early elementary reading program. Shaver, Cuevas, and Lee (2007) used focus groups to understand urban elementary teachers' perceptions of impacts of state mandated science instruction and testing policies on ELL students. For other examples of improvement-oriented projects using focus groups, see Muzaffar, Castelli, Goss, Schere and Chapman-Novakofski (2011) and Rodriquez-Campos, Berson, Bellara, Owens and Walker-Egea (2010).

child's schoolwork and school policies and are they adequately informed about high priority expectations, policies, and participation opportunities?

In a GAPPSI project, the purpose for doing a focus group derives from a problem statement. The first purpose statement in the preceding paragraph means that the screening assessment is under review. This would not occur in the absence of concerns about the screening assessment and a need for information.

Each interview question must be justified. Think: how will responses to this question help? How do I use this information? If I did not know this, would it matter? If answers to these questions are not obvious, chances are your problem statement and purposes are murky.

There is no set number of questions to ask – it can range from one or two to upwards of six. Your interview guide should write out your questions and probes. Table 4.1 shows a portion of an interview guide – two questions to illustrate the format. The interview is about factors influencing teachers' instruction and curriculum planning.

Table 4.1
Excerpt From Interview Guide Showing Format

Topic	Question	Probes
State test influence	Does the grade 5 state test influence your science teaching?	topic choices, sequencing, pacing; instructional strategies; curriculum materials; homework assignments
Curriculum guide influence	How do you use the district's curriculum guide in your science teaching?	topic choices, sequencing, pacing; instructional strategies; curriculum materials; homework assignments

Do not try to cover too much; you risk getting superficial or even inaccurate information. Since some of the focus group time will inevitably be "off topic" (e.g., introduction; respondents wandering off point), you should take this into consideration in planning your allocation of time. If, say, an hour is planned, maybe 45 minutes will produce useful data.

Set ground rules at the beginning. Ask participants to refrain from side conversations, interruptions, or criticism of others' statements. If there will be difficult or controversial topics, begin with easier "ice-breaker" questions to encourage talking.

You may need to redirect or politely interrupt to keep responses on point or to encourage closure. At the same time, people must be allowed to talk freely; sometimes you do not know until several minutes have elapsed whether the answer will be informative or whether the person has lost track of the question.

Be aware of nonverbal communications. People in interviews can be nervous, so present a relaxed demeanor. Interviews are different from social conversation; in conversations we generally do not ask short questions and follow up with prompts for more information. In conversations we may interrupt someone, or interject an opinion, or scowl or nod approval, but in a focus group interview the moderator is a question asker and listener. Avoid signaling approval or disapproval and be prepared to follow a question with an additional prompt for elaboration, examples, and reasons.

Tape-recording is useful. If you are confident people will speak freely being recorded, there is no disadvantage to recording – you have the information to review if you want it. Also, taping makes it less imperative to have a note-taker.

Logistics

Pay attention to detail in planning to avoid foul-ups.

- Be clear in your directions about the focus group location, public transportation availability, parking, room location, and starting and ending times.
- Choose a comfortable room and seating; make sure there is enough seating; consider offering refreshments.
- Have a sign-in sheet, ask for contact information, and provide name tags.
- Create thank you notes or some other way to recognize the participants' contributions. If appropriate, tell them how they can contribute further input into the planning process.

Analysis and Reporting of Interviews

The goal of your analysis is to answer your questions. Your "raw" interview data will either be in the form of (a) written notes summarizing respondents' comments and including selected quotes; (b) fully recorded and transcribed responses;[47] or (c) a combination – which is to say, you have written notes as well as recorded responses, but the recorded responses are not entirely transcribed; they are used as back up (you mostly use your notes, but listen to the recorded material for details and key quotes).

Your analysis seeks the gist of the respondents' views on each of the questions. Your questions are the framework for analyzing your data. For each question you ask: What recurring ideas or sentiments are expressed by multiple respondents? Are statements by respondents on a particular subject largely the same – they generally express the same view – or are there important differences in the views expressed in the statements? For each focus group question, your task is to summarize the content of the answers and to represent whether the group's views are uniform, largely uniform, somewhat divided, or heavily divided.

Focus group interviews are decision-oriented. They seek information with clear implication for decisions. Above I presented a purpose statement for a focus group analysis: *To learn whether teachers think the screening assessment used for reading groups works well for grouping purposes, whether they think it provides useful instructional information, and whether an alternative instrument should be considered.* Your data analysis might lead to a conclusion like this: Teachers for the most part thought the assessment instrument accurately placed students into ability-based reading groups. The instrument was viewed as most accurate for students reading at a low level, and somewhat less accurate in distinguishing high level from middle level readers. Respondents found

---

[47] For an example of this, see Latess (2008).

little value in the instrument for instructional planning; with very few exceptions they said the instrument did not aid in designing individualized lessons to differentiate instruction among the reading groups.

Interviews conducted for program or policy evaluations are also decision-oriented, but generally will have a broader scope than for a GAPPSI paper. Usually, the purpose is not to arrive at a single over-arching conclusion, but to understand better how a program or policy operates and if there are improvement needs. For example, Appendix 4-C excerpts from a published evaluation identifying strengths, weaknesses, and outcomes of a family literacy program. The appendix excerpts from a larger set of results discussed in detail in the article. The authors report respondents' views on a range of dimensions bearing on the program (e.g., Easy to Use, Amount of Time, Interest and Engagement, Consistency of Use, Parent Enjoyment, Training) and present quotes illustrating both positive and negative sentiments on these program dimensions. Their analysis educates readers about the program's operation and effects and about ways the family literacy program could improve.

There is no single, prescribed format for reporting results from interview-based studies.[48] A graduate course paper, a policy brief, an executive summary, a 5 minute presentation, a memo – all are different vehicles with different audiences. One principle is invariant: you must always explain your sample, questions, and methods because your audience wants to know this – that is one way people weigh the validity and generalizability of conclusions. However, beyond this, as Sandelowski (1998, p 376) points out, "there is no one style for reporting the findings from qualitative research. Qualitative researchers must choose not only what 'story' they will tell, but also how they will tell it (Wolcott, 1990, p. 18). Qualitative researchers must select from an array of representational styles, formats, and 'language(s) of disclosure' (Thornton, 1987, p. 27) those that best fit their research purposes, methods, and data (Knafl & Howard, 1984). As Tierney (1995, p. 389) noted, 'one narrative size does not fit all'."

Survey-Interview Hybrids:
Delphi Technique

Purpose and Overview

The Delphi Technique is like a guided brainstorming session and a little like using a blog.[49] Its purpose is to generate, impartially evaluate, and select ideas from a group. The Delphi Technique combines features of both surveys and interviews. It can be done "live" and face-to-face, or entirely online.

The process must be directed by someone – a coordinator. The coordinator gives participants one or more specific, open-ended questions. The participants write 10 - 25

---

[48] Excellent discussions of reporting can be found in chapters 11 and 1 of Krueger (1998) and Sandelowski's (1998) "Writing a good read." Also, see Edmunds (1999), Patton (2002), or Wolcott (1990).

[49] For literature on the Delphi method see Adler & Ziglio (1996), Alexander (2004), Delbeq et al. (1975), or Rowe and Wright (1999).

word answers to each question and return their responses. The coordinator compiles and organizes the responses and re-sends a revised list and the process repeats itself so everyone has another input opportunity and has exhausted their ideas. A third round can be done if people are willing.

Example

Imagine legislators in your state are advocating stronger education accountability and want districts to develop systems of performance incentives for schools and teachers. Legislators are concerned about weak extrinsic incentives for high performance in schools and among teachers. Districts are mandated to submit plans for strengthening extrinsic performance incentives. Assume you are coordinating an effort to develop ideas for this plan. Here is how a Delphi process would work.

1) Enlist and Instruct Participants

Enlist a cross-section of teachers and administrators and explain the process and the objectives. People will want to know how the information will be used (e.g., reported to a district steering committee), what the ultimate decision-making process will be, and whether their participation is anonymous. Get responses from enough participants to feel confident you fully tapped the pool of ideas.

2) Send the Questionnaire to Participants

At the top of the questionnaire, summarize the issue; following your summary, instruct participants as follows:

> Generate 2-5 ideas for performance incentives. State each idea briefly, in a sentence or two. Your ideas need not be fully developed and avoid thinking at this point about constraints. You do not need to evaluate or justify ideas at this time. Your ideas will be anonymous.

Anonymous participation is likely to produce more ideas and less self-filtering. Participants should not have to worry about peer pressure or other concerns related to being identified. Give the participants a deadline.

3) Compile and Return: Round Two

Collect, review, and compile all the responses. Create a new organized list that is a compilation of the responses. Edit for clarity. Table 4.2 (top section) shows "round two" of the Delphi method – a compiled list returned to the participants and requesting additional ideas.

4) Compile and Return: Round Three

Repeating the process – a third round – enables participants to see the list and, if people are interested, to further elaborate, comment, or refine. An excerpt from "round three" is shown in the bottom section of Table 4.2 (at "A four day work week for one month"). In the "round three" excerpt below, the "round two" idea is in **bold** followed by round three comments. For a more complete set of round three results, see Appendix 4-D.

Table 4.2
Delphi Technique: Examples from Rounds Two and Three

Round Two Of Delphi On Performance Incentives

Below is the list of ideas compiled from the first round of idea-generation. The initial list had two or three times as many ideas as listed below, but many were redundant. The list below represents a consolidated list, organized so that similar ideas are grouped together.

There is space between each idea on the list where you can write additional comments. First review the entire list. Then elaborate on a few of the suggestions listed. This can be done by providing more details, or more specific recommendations, or examples, or "how to start" ideas. If you think of a new idea, add it to the list. Also, you can write specific strengths or weaknesses of any ideas.

\>>Do research to identify why some teachers are not high achievers and how to motivate them.

\>>Improve the status of the profession of "teacher." One way might be by changing the name of teachers to "educators."

\>>Develop a definition of a "high performance" or "low performance" teacher. Need to figure out how differences are measured.

\>>Evaluate teachers based on student achievement as one of a set of performance indicators.

\>>Compare pre- and post- test results of assessments administered at the start and end of each academic year.

\>>Use a nomination system to help identify high-performing teachers based on nominations from peers, students, parents, etc. Exemplary behaviors must be described. A committee of peers could evaluate submissions and hold public celebration(s) throughout school year.

\>>Share more standardized student achievement data with teachers. Much student achievement data is generated but comparatively little is communicated to teachers.

\>>Revise the standard evaluation process to include teacher portfolios so that high-performing teachers can be more readily identified.

\>>Give high performing teachers the option of assuming leadership roles (ex. master teacher, mentor teacher) with additional compensation for assuming additional responsibilities.

\>>Differentiated treatment of teachers must begin with an understanding from within the teaching ranks that some are in need of help to improve.

\>> Give high-performing teachers a one-year mentoring position to assist other teachers in the school or in other school districts through classroom visitations, instructional demonstrations, etc.

\>> Give high-performing teachers a our day work week for one month.

\>> Give high-performing teachers a access to grant money to promote experimentation in classroom instructional and learning strategies.

5) *Rating the Ideas*

What to do at this point depends on the plan established at the outset by the coordinator and group (see, above, step #1). One approach to idea evaluation is described in the next section on *Nominal Group Technique*: the ideas are whittled to a manageable number and systematically rated – again, in a group process.

Other people, not just the participants, can be invited to rate or comment on the ideas. For instance, the ideas can be converted into survey questions with scales. A broader group, then, could respond to the survey. Consider, however, that the original group will feel some ownership of the ideas generated and will have developed knowledge of the ideas and so their judgment may be of greater value.

Survey-Interview Hybrids:
Nominal Group Technique (NGT)

Purpose

The Nominal Group Technique (NGT) uses a group to generate ideas for decisions, to discuss the ideas, to prioritize the ideas, and to build consensus. Nominal Group and Delphi have similar purposes, but the Delphi Technique takes longer and is more work for the person directing the process because it generates a larger volume of ideas. Like Delphi, NGT can be done in a face-to-face meeting or online. The following description assumes face-to-face with a flipchart.

The NGT coordinator (who can be a participant too) leads the process. (1) The coordinator presents the topic, explains the purpose and the process, and asks for ideas. (2) Participants are then given about 5 - 10 minutes to write down, individually and privately, a list of responses. (3) Then, in round-robin fashion, the participants state one idea on their list, with the coordinator recording these ideas, one at a time, on a flipchart (or whatever is technology is used). The coordinator does not write down duplicate ideas, but if there is doubt that an idea is a duplicate or not, it should be added to the flipchart. The coordinator also at this time clarifies vague ideas. (4) This process continues until all ideas are exhausted. Participants should not comment on ideas during the process (similar to brainstorming). Participants may come up with additional ideas as the process is underway. (This process may need to be done in a way that the participants' ideas and ratings are anonymous. See the discussion on this below.)

When a final list is created, the ideas are assigned a letter (A, B, C, etc.). Then the group rates the ideas. This can be done in more than one way. Every participant is given a sheet (e.g., a score card) with two columns, one column to list their top three to five ideas, and the other column to assign a numerical rating. The rating can be done as a rank order or based on a scale.

Rank Ordering the Ideas: Method #1

Rank ordering requires each participant to put their choices in order. For instance, assume the group collectively has generated 9 ideas, labeled A – I. Each person is allowed to list their three top choices, with the top choice getting a score of 1, the next choice a 2, and the last choice a 3. Joe favors ideas B, D, and A. His rating sheet is shown in Table 4.3.

Table 4.3
Example of Joe's Rating Sheet (rank order)

Idea	Score
B	1
D	2
A	3

Scale-based Ratings of Ideas: Method #2

Scale-based scoring requires each participant to rate each idea (or a designated number, e.g., 3) using a pre-defined scale. Any scale can be used. A 1 to 10 scale is familiar.

Sue's score sheet is shown in Table 4.4, filled in with her ratings. In this example, each participant could rate their top five choices on a 1 to 10 scale. Sue has given the same ratings to several items (e.g., A and G). In the scale method, this is OK.

Table 4.4
Example of Sue's Rating Sheet (rating scale)

Idea	Score
A	2
B	7
C	1
D	5
E	3
F	1
G	2
H	9
I	1

Compiling and Presenting the Results

To compile the results, a spreadsheet is useful. A spreadsheet facilitates analysis and makes it easy to save the information for future use or documentation.

Table 4.5 shows an Excel spreadsheet compiling the information from the *rank order* score sheets (Table 4.3, above). The numbers in the column, "Total Score," are the sums of each row. The sum of the rankings for idea "B" is 10, and for idea "H" is 7. The column "Frequency in top 3" shows how many times each idea made it into the top 3. Again, idea B came out on top, five times being in the top 3.

Table 4.5
Nominal Group Technique Results Compiled Based on Rankings

Idea	Sue	Bob	Joe	Pam	Phil	Chris	Total Score	Frequency in top 3
A	0	0	3	0	0	0	3	1
B	2	3	1	0	1	3	10	5
C	0	0	0	3	0	0	3	1
D	3	0	2	0	3	1	9	4
E	0	1	0	0	0	0	1	1
F	0	0	0	0	0	0	0	0
G	0	0	0	0	0	0	0	0
H	1	0	0	2	2	2	7	4
I	0	2	0	1	0	0	3	2

Table 4.6 shows the information compiled from the *scale-based* ratings of the ideas (see Table 4.4). The numbers in the column, "Ave. Score," are the averages of each row. The average of the ratings for idea "B" is 8.0; for idea "H," it is 7.0. Idea B has the highest average score.

Table 4.6
Nominal Group Technique Results Compiled Based on Average Ratings

Idea	Sue	Bob	Joe	Pam	Phil	Chris	Ave. Score
A	2	3	5	4	1	4	3.2
B	7	4	10	8	9	10	8.0
C	1	1	2	2	1	2	1.5
D	5	4	7	5	4	9	5.7
E	3	6	4	5	8	7	5.5
F	1	2	5	1	3	1	2.2
G	2	1	2	1	3	2	1.8
H	9	7	6	5	6	9	7.0
I	1	5	1	4	2	3	2.7

Protecting Anonymity

The coordinator and the group should decide at the outset whether the NGT process, or parts of it, should be done with anonymity preserved. Clearly the flipchart approach describe above is not anonymous, but it can be made so. Either or both the idea-production phase or the idea-evaluation phase can be anonymous. If NGT participants have strong, differing feelings about ideas generated, then participants are likely to prefer anonymity.

In the anonymous approach, each individual would write their ideas privately on a sheet. Then the coordinator collects the sheets and compiles and displays the master list.

At this point, there may be a need for a group discussion to clarify the ideas on the list so the group develops a common understanding of each idea.

Reporting Results: Internal and Public Audiences

The coordinator (Delphi or Nominal Group) must organize and report final results. How to do this depends on how the results are being used. If the results are only for the participants in the process for planning discussions, a memo or presentation is appropriate – the audience and the participants are the same people so little explanation is needed.

On the other hand, the results may be for a broader audience. If so, the results must be presented properly in tables or other graphical formats, summarized, and interpreted. (See section below, "Quantitative Results Reported in Tables and Figures.") Chapter 5 goes into more depth on writing, reporting, and structuring communications. Next, I discuss collecting and using information in statistical formats – from quantitative databases.

PART 3
INFORMATION FROM ORGANIZATIONAL DATA

"Organizational data" is a third broad and mixed category of data sources for a GAPPSI project. All school systems collect data on students, parents, personnel, courses, programs, budgets, and facilities. Test scores, marking period grades, personnel records, demographic information, and financial records are examples. Some of the data, after processing and aggregation, goes also to state, federal, and other agencies. As an example, a parent registers in a school and fills out a form to qualify a child for free-lunch. This information is stored in district, state, and federal data systems. I also include in this section supplementary data you might collect on your own since it is sometimes necessary and feasible to do special data collections.

If you intend to use data from an organizational data system, be informed about "Federal Rights and Privacy" regulations (FERPA). FERPA specifies restrictions on access to *individual level* education records to protect the privacy of students and their families (aggregate data is almost always readily accessible). FERPA does *not* prohibit data access by authorized users, namely school, district, or state agency officials, as well as by people authorized by district or state official such as consultants, vendors, or researchers assisting with data management and analysis.

Using Public Data Tables and Reports for Descriptive Information

One category of quantitative information for papers and reports is called "descriptive statistics." Table 4.7 is an example. This form of information gives the reader context, like an opening scene in a movie showing a setting. A table like 4.8 is useful background.

Descriptive statistics can also help substantiate TLO/TMO claims as discussed in Chapter 2. Table 4.7 would support a problem statement from someone in Grove school concerned about having unusually high numbers of special education students relative to other schools in the district.

Table 4.7
Selected Demographic Figures: Five Elementary Schools in Dale School District

School	Enroll-ment	% free lunch	% ELL	% special education
Grove	322	22	19	19
Jones	433	15	7	12
Smith	545	44	15	9
Orchard	211	35	42	11
Bane	555	62	9	10

Some descriptive statistics are referred to as "indicators" because they reflect key aspects of an organization's inputs, conditions or performance.[50] Well known economic indicators include the GNP, unemployment rate, or stock market indexes (e.g., Dow Jones). You may be familiar with annual "school profile" reports – these are collections of statistical indicators. These profiles usually cover student, staff, and financial variables; some places also report results from annual surveys. Here are a few examples of statistical indicators:

- suspensions (% of high school students receiving 1 or more suspensions by semester)
- retention (annual % of students retained in grade)
- average daily attendance (ave. % of total school enrollment in attendance)
- academic attainment (annual % of students scoring at standard)
- annual expenditure per pupil (total $ allocation to a school per year divided by enrollment)
- absenteeism (ave. daily % of staff missing work per month)
- average annual salary
- annual professional development expenditure per teacher

An indicator derives meaning through comparison. Recall the three types of comparisons discussed in Chapter 2: with others, or over time, or with expectations. One of these frames of reference makes the indicator meaningful. Another feature of indicators is that they are built on a numerator and denominator, and the denominator is usually a unit of time or a per capita unit (e.g., per student).

There are many sources of education data. All states and districts make some forms of school data publicly accessible; however, depending on the state or district, access may be difficult or easy – everything from "available only by request" to well designed "point and click" websites with many reports and downloadable data sets.

---

[50] For more on indicators, see Chester (2005), Dinkes, Forrest, and Lin-Kelly (2007), National Forum on Education Statistics (2005), or Pincus (2006).

There are also data sources accessible from federal agencies. The websites below have web-tools to enter state, city, or school district names to generate indicator reports and download data on a variety of indicators, variables, and measures of state, school district, and community characteristics (e.g., poverty, occupations, employment, health, educational attainment, etc.).

- The U.S. Department of Education's National Center for Education Statistics makes available many forms of data for downloading (enrollment, assessment, staffing, financial, survey, and other variables). NCES website tools provide data at the district level, including comparative information among districts. One of the data tools, the "Common Core of Data" provides school level information.[51]
- U.S. Census Bureau (census.gov) has on-line tools to create tables of user-specified census-based information at the national, state, city, and school district level.
- University of Michigan's Inter-University Consortium for Political and Social Science Research (ICPSR) is the world's largest archive of digital social science data. ICPSR maintains dozens of large databases. For example, with "censusscope" you can produce state and county-level rankings by population growth, race, educational attainment, language, gender, and more.[52]
- Kids Count Data Center is a searchable database with national, state, and city data for over 100 measures of child well-being.[53]
- The Child Trends Database is a searchable website presenting hundreds of indicators of conditions and trends related to children's health, safety, fitness, social experiences, and academic development. This website compiles data from numerous federal agencies and nongovernmental organizations.[54]

Descriptive Studies:
Examining Relationships Among Multiple Variables

Introduction

As described above, descriptive statistics and indicators are like quantitative snapshots of organizational inputs, conditions, and performance. They summarize resource conditions, selected operations and practices, and aspects of climate and performance. However, summary statistics have limited explanatory power. They don't explain causes; they don't predict consequences.

---

[51]See, http://nces.ed.gov/datatools/

[52] See, www.icpsr.umich.edu/

[53]See, http://datacenter.kidscount.org/

[54]See, http://www.childtrendsdatabank.org/

For insights into causes and consequences, you examine relationships *among* variables. Doing this with organizational data can illuminate connections among inputs, organizational conditions and practices, and performance outcomes. Following are some key concepts and guidelines.

Correlations

"Correlation," in statistics terminology, refers to the strength of the relationship between two numerical variables. Imagine, for instance, you want to know the relationship between students' academic achievement and how much they like school.

Rating	GPA
9	4.0
8	3.2
8	3.1
7	2.7
7	3.9
7	2.5
6	3.6
6	2.6
6	3.4
5	2.4
5	3.7
5	2.2
4	3.7
4	2.8
3	1.5
3	1.9
2	0.2
2	1.0
1	0.7

Table 4.8 Student GPA & "Like School" Survey Rating

Table 4.8 shows a relationship for 21 students between their grade point average (GPA) and their rating from a survey about how much they like school. (The data have been sorted by the "Rating" variable to make the relationship between the two variables easier to see.) Figure 4.1 shows a scatter plot of that same data. You can conclude there is a statistical (positive) correlation between these two variables: on average students with higher GPAs express greater liking for school. This is not a perfect correlation. There are some students with lower GPAs who like school more than students with higher GPAs. But, overall, the pattern – a positive correlation – is clear.

Figure 4.1
Scatterplot of GPA and "Like School" Survey Rating

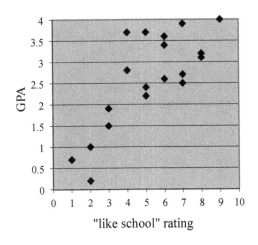

A negative correlation is when on the values on one variable get larger as the values on the other variable get smaller. For instance, if the other variable was "how many hours a week do you watch TV," instead of the "I like school" survey rating, chances are the correlation would be negative, because on average higher achieving students watch less TV.

Usually, we don't want to know just "is there a correlation?," but, "how strong is it?" The correlation statistic (abbreviated as "r") gives us a measure of the *strength* (magnitude) of the correlation. This statistic ranges from -1.0 to +1.0: the closer to -1.0 or +1.0, the stronger the relationship between the two variables; the closer to 0.0, the weaker the relationship. The correlation between GPA and "like school" in the above table is .78. That's a strong correlation.

The spreadsheet software, Excel, makes it easy to examine correlations and compute the statistic. The best way is to put the two numerical variables side by side as in

Table 4.8. The correlation calculator can be found in the "Data Analysis" tab.[55] Use the "Insert" tab and go to "charts" to create a scatterplot.

Nothing about causality is proven by a correlation. One variable *might* cause the other, but a correlation only shows a relationship. This is helpful to know, but don't infer causality without more information.

Crosstabulations

Problem statements often derive from comparisons among demographic groups (race, ethnicity, gender, class) or between special education and regular education students. These we know as "achievement gap" problem statements. The tables below are "cross-tabulations" (also see Table 4.7 above – "Selected Demographic Figures.")

Excel and other statistical software do crosstabulations easily. Table 4.9 shows three successive levels of disaggregation of test score data revealing, (#1), comparisons by grade level, (#2), then by grade level and classroom, and (#3), by grade level, class-room, and gender (#3). This is also known as "drilling down."

Table 4.9
Three Crosstabulation Tables Showing "Drilling Down"

(#1) Ave. Reading Scores By Grade Level in Orchard School		(#2) Ave. Reading Scores By Grade Level and Room in Orchard School			(#3) Ave. Reading Scores By Grade Level, Room, and Gender in Orchard School			
Grade	*Ave.*	*Grade*	*Room*	*Ave.*	*Grade*	*Room*	*Gender*	*Ave.*
3	54	3	A	57	3	A	F	62
4	59		B	51			M	53
5	57	4	C	60		B	F	52
6	52		D	58			M	51
Overall Ave.	55	5	E	65	4	C	F	62
			F	44			M	58
		6	G	54		D	F	58
			H	50			M	59
		Overall Ave.		55	5	Z	F	67
							M	63
						F	F	44
							M	44
					6	G	F	57
							M	53
						H	F	55
							M	45
					Overall Ave.			55

---

[55] For help on this, go to the web and search Excel help. The "Analysis ToolPak" – an Excel "Add in" must be installed to get all the statistical tools activated.

Another example is Table 4.10. Assume the concern in a school district is with girls seeming to avoid upper level science courses. One question is, "Are both girls and boys with good grades in middle school science equally likely to enroll in advanced science in high school?" Table 4.10 compares the proportion of girls and boys in high school AP science courses who, in middle school, got either an "A" or a "B." It would also be helpful to know if comparable percentages of girls and boys got good grades in middle school. If they did, and girls are still less likely to end up in advanced high school science courses, then there is evidence that girls' lower enrollments are not from lower prior achievement, but, rather, from something else, perhaps attitudes, or their parents, or guidance decisions. This is another example of "drilling down" with crosstabulations.[56]

Table 4.10
Boy v. Girl Participation in High School AP Science

	% enrolled in HS AP Chemistry		% enrolled in HS AP Physics	
Of boys & girls in 8th grade who got an A in science….	Boys: 40%	Girls: 25%	Boys: 50%	Girls: 20%
Of boys &girls in 8th grade who got a B in science….	Boys: 20%	Girls: 15%	Boys: 40%	Girls: 12%

Comparisons using crosstabulations do not prove causes, but clarify the problem by providing factual information about relationships among variables and by sometimes allowing you to *rule out* causes. Table 4.10 shows that girls with the same grades as boys in middle school science are *still* less likely to end up in AP Chemistry, so we should not attribute girls' under-enrollment to lower grades.

Further inquiries about causes may follow. You could ask girls and boys about what caused them to enroll in AP courses and ask other students with high grades who are not enrolled in AP courses, if they know about the AP courses or ever received encouragement to enroll. This provides information beyond the numbers to assist decision making.

Causes, Consequences, and Experimental Research Design

The above *descriptive* statistics reveal relationships among variables. They illuminate patterns among measureable aspects of behavior, organizational conditions, or performance. To understand whether "A causes B," however, requires more controlled observation and measurement. I discuss first features of an *ideal* analysis because understanding the ideal gives perspective on the strengths and weaknesses of more typical analyses.

The Ideal: Comparisons Based on Random Assignment

Let's say your school district is considering a middle school tutoring program for reading. Before committing to an expensive district-wide implementation, you want to know how

---

[56] Excel's "Pivot Tables" tool is excellent for doing crosstabulations.

effective it is. You could review effectiveness research on the particular tutoring program contemplated.[57] In addition, you could do a small experiment, measure the results, and learn from the trial.

From the entire roster of one middle school's sixth graders, you randomly select 30 for your experiment and they receive tutoring for six months. You have reading achievement scores for all sixth graders before and after the experiment. If you are confident in the validity of your outcome measure (reading test scores) and that the tutoring was done as designed, then you've got good evidence of the short term effectiveness of the program as measured by your test.

A guide from the U.S. Department of Education (CEP, 2003, p. 1)[58] gives this example:

 For example, suppose you want to test, in a randomized controlled trial, whether a new math curriculum for third-graders is more effective than your school's existing math curriculum for third-graders. You would randomly assign a large number of third-grade students to either an intervention [treatment] group, which uses the new curriculum, or to a control group, which uses the existing curriculum. You would then measure the math achievement of both groups over time. The difference in math achievement between the two groups would represent the effect of the new curriculum compared to the existing curriculum.

Figure 4.2
Key Design Features of Typical Experimental Study

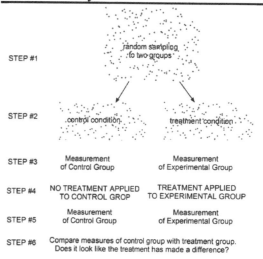

STEP #1	random sampling to two groups	
STEP #2	control condition	treatment condition
STEP #3	Measurement of Control Group	Measurement of Experimental Group
STEP #4	NO TREATMENT APPLIED TO CONTROL GROP	TREATMENT APPLIED TO EXPERIMENTAL GROUP
STEP #5	Measurement of Control Group	Measurement of Experimental Group
STEP #6	Compare measures of control group with treatment group. Does it look like the treatment has made a difference?	

Figure 4.2 shows graphically an experimental design. There are variants of this model, but all designs require random assignment. Most studies compare two groups, but a study could be designed with a control group and several treatment groups. Figure 4.2 shows measurements before the treatment (Step #3) and after the treatment (Step #5). These are called pre-measurement and post-measurement.

The Difficulties of Doing Experimental Studies in School Settings

Doing an experimental study in a school usually raises practical and ethical issues. First, parents *must* give prior, informed approval. This not only takes time, but can raise questions and concerns among parents and others. "You're doing this tutoring program? I

---

[57] See the section above "Literature To Substantiate Predictions."

[58] *Identifying and implementing educational practices supported by rigorous evidence: A user friendly guide*. Prepared by the Institute for Education Sciences, U.S. Department of Education, by the Coalition for Evidence-Based Policy, a project sponsored by the Council for Excellence in Government, 1301 K Street, NW, Suite 450 West, Washington, DC 20005.

want my child in that." "You are offering this new after-school study group and my daughter has an 80% chance of not getting randomly selected?" The public relations problems these questions create are obvious. Without random assignment, you don't have an experimental study (and therefore don't get conclusive evidence), but attempting random assignment raises question like these that *have* to be addressed and properly managed. Contemplating the time consumed and the potential human relations problems – for most educators it's not worth the trouble.

Randomized comparisons are more feasible in one situation: when students are *supposed* to be randomly assigned. Districts have done this when students are picked by lottery to get into a program or a certain school (e.g., a charter or magnet school). There are situations where a program or school has fewer available seats than there are applicants (e.g., 200 apply, but only 60 can be admitted). Parents accept this as being fair (even though they may wish the program to be larger). This situation creates an opportunity for a natural experiment. The students getting in are a random sample of those who have applied. Those getting in can then be compared on achievement or other measures with those who applied but did not get in.

Here is another example: some elementary schools have policies prohibiting parents from choosing teachers. When students are assigned to teachers, the policy requires that this is done randomly. If the school has standardized achievement tests and a way to measure academic growth during the year, then achievement growth differences among classrooms are most likely to result from differences among the teachers. However, *always* consider alternative explanations and intervening factors. Suppose teacher Smith had 25% more student turnover during the school year than other teachers. His classroom's growth scores are lower, but is this his fault? Or suppose, two months into the school year he experienced serious health or family problems affecting his work for several months. This year his classroom growth scores were lower, but if we looked at his growth scores for the previous three years, they were consistently above average. The point: be thoughtful in drawing conclusions from evidence and inferences about causality.

Causal Comparative Analyses

Do English Language Learners who have testing accommodations (e.g., someone reading questions to them) do better than those who read the questions themselves? Is the new "Algebra For All" policy producing higher math achievement by the end of 11th grade? Are the classroom aides deployed in 3 of the district's 8 elementary schools making a difference in attendance or discipline? These are typical questions inviting study. You can explore questions like these usefully with carefully controlled comparisons (sometimes called "quasi" experimental design).

"Controlled comparison" means the compared groups should be alike as possible in all ways except for the variable you are examining – the intervention. It is best to have "before-treatment" scores (or whatever measures you are using) for everyone involved in the comparison. Then you can determine more precisely the effects of the intervention, because you know if the two groups were initially the same or different.

Comparing Groups at the Same Time

Table 4.11 shows a simple example. The question is: does math achievement improve when students do at-home math drills for 4 nights a week, 15 minutes a night? In this made-up example, teachers in four classrooms administered a math test in September. The average scores for the two groups are shown. If they did not have these "pre" scores (Sept), and only had the results from the final test in November, they would incorrectly infer that the homework made no difference because the November average scores for both groups are the same. Actually, the homework group outgained the other group by 5 points.

Table 4.11
A Comparison Of Two Groups: Math Homework V. No Math Homework

	September Math Score Average	Intervention for two months	November Math Score Average
Group 1 – two classrooms (50 kids)	50	Assigned 15 minutes nightly math drills at home	58
Group 2 – two other classrooms (50 kids)	55	No assigned at-home math drills	58

The teachers cannot be certain that homework (assigned math drills) was the only cause of the greater gain in the homework group. What if one of the teachers in Group 1 was popular and picked by many parents who were strong homework supporters? It could be that Group 1's parents were part of the cause of Group 1's greater grains. (In other words, in the absence of these demanding parents, the drill assignment would prove less effective.) Without random assignment it is harder to rule out these kinds of "contaminating" factors. Nonetheless, studies like this can be very informative, but always consider multiple explanations in drawing conclusions.

Comparing Groups at Different Times

You can measure the effects of a new program by comparing the students in it to similar types of students before the program's inception. A high school starts a policy requiring all incoming freshmen with low 8th grade math achievement to take an extended Algebra course in 9th grade (5 periods a week). Fifty students are in extended Algebra. The rest of the students are in the regular 3 periods/week Algebra. Is this extended Algebra effective?

One useful analysis is this. Compare the 10th grade math test scores of the students in extended Algebra to the 10th grade math test scores of *the same types of students* from several prior years. The school has academic profile information on all 8th grade incoming cohorts for many prior years. So you compare the 10th grade math test scores of the 50 students in extended Algebra to 150 students from, say, the previous three incoming cohorts of 9th graders: 50 students from each prior year cohort who are just like the extended Algebra students in 8th grade math achievement and demographic characteristics. In other words, you compare the current group to prior groups who would have been selected for the extended Algebra if it had existed. If the current group has higher

10th grade math test scores than the prior groups, you have some evidence that the extended math is effective in this way. You don't have proof that it is better, but do have persuasive evidence.

The above examples are about academic achievement, but any variable of importance can be studied with appropriate measures. You might be interested in determining if a bullying-reduction program reduces bullying in your school or whether a drug education program changes attitudes about smoking and other drugs. You might be interested in determining if the behavior of students improves following a new discipline policy.

Quantitative Results Reported in Tables and Figures

Empirical results must be communicated (e.g., memo, report, presentation, brief, or website). Following are guidelines for presenting empirical results in a paper, presentation, or formal brief.

Quantitative data can be summarized in two formats: tables and charts. Tables report statistics *numerically*, as in Table 4.12. (Note, *text* reported in a tabular form is also referred to as a table, at least in American Psychological Association [APA] style.)

Table 4.12
Percentage of Students Scoring At or Above "Proficiency" in Reading on SMSA (2007)

School	Grade 3	Grade 5
Lakeview	52.9%	66.7%
Beech	59.2%	82.9%
Hilltop	66.9%	79.2%

Charts display quantitative information graphically as in bar graphs, histograms, scatterplots, and line graphs.

APA style uses the terms "tables" and "figures." A chart is referred to as a figure. Photographs and drawings are also figures, but these are not charts.

Following are three guidelines on making tables and figures clear and informative.

1) Titles Must Be Informative

Tables and figures must be clear, well-organized, and as much as possible, self-explanatory. Informative titles are essential; statistics within tables and figures should have appropriate labels. While some tables and figures cannot be completely self-explanatory, aid the reader with informative titles, headings, and descriptors.

2) Appropriate Terminology

Data analysis produces "results" (or "findings"). Data[59] are the raw information – the numbers, text characters, and codes in your database or data set. *Qualitative* data are verbal statements from people or anecdotal descriptions of behaviors and events. These "raw" data must be coded into categories, themes, or ratings before they can be systemat-

---

[59] Academics usually use "data" as a plural noun (datum is singular), but it is now common and acceptable to use "data" as a singular or plural.

ically analyzed. *Quantitative* data are numerical – test scores, survey ratings, marking period grades, discipline records, demographic information, census data, financial records, and personnel records are examples.

Generally speaking, you do not report "data." Rather, "results" or "findings" are reported as in, "The results show...." Or "Table 1 shows..."

Active voice. Use active voice whenever possible. It is clearer. In most contexts you can use the table or figure as the subject of your sentence – especially in the first sentence that introduces the table or figure. Here are a few examples:

- "Table 1 shows the mean scores on the job satisfaction survey items."
- "Figure 1 shows a scatterplot of student grades and test scores."

3) Explain Complex Tables and Figures

Complexity increases when tables and figures depict relationships among multiple variables (e.g., a correlation or regression analysis), especially if the statistics themselves are more complicated. For instance, suppose we want to compare states on the "degree of funding inequality among districts." A simple measure would be the difference in expenditures between the highest spending and the lowest spending district in each state. Most people are familiar with "per pupil expenditure" – it is a simple statistic: the amount spent in a district divided by the enrollment. The difference between the highest and lowest spending district is also simple – subtraction. The math is familiar; only a few variables are involved. Compare this with another measure of finance inequality, the coefficient of variation, computed by dividing the standard deviation of adjusted spending per weighted pupil by the state's average spending per pupil (Park & Skinner, 2003). Now we have less familiar statistics (standard deviation, adjusted spending, and the formula), more variables, and more abstract variables. The reader will need a more detailed explanation of the measure.

For example, look at Table 4.13, reporting test scores in a school district. Table 4.13 is complicated.

Table 4.13

Counts and (Percentages) of Students Staying At Same Performance Level (PL) or Changing Performance Levels From Grade 3 to Grade 5 on State Test in Three Elementary Schools

		Grade 5 Performance Levels (PL)					
		PL 1	PL 2	PL 3	PL 4	PL 5	Row Totals
Grade 3 Performance Levels (PL)	PL 5			6 (13)	18 (38)	23 (49)	47
	PL 4		1 (2)	16 (27)	29 (49)	13 (22)	59
	PL 3	7 (4)	22 (13)	91 (54)	39 (23)	8 (5)	167
	PL 2	10 (16)	21 (33)	30 (47)	3 (5)		64
	PL 1	15 (41)	13 (35)	9 (24)			37
Column Totals:		32	57	152	89	44	**374**

97

Table 4.13 does *not* present familiar statistics and it requires processing multiple pieces of information. While the title might be enough for some readers and calling it a cross-tabulation would help others, most would want a paragraph like this:

Table 4.13 reports PL scores in reading for a cohort of students from three elementary schools. Each student is tested in 3rd grade and again in 5th grade. The table shows how many students score at the same level in 5th as in 3rd grade, how many go up in PL, and how many go down. For instance, out 64 students (row total) who scored at PL 2 in 3rd grade, by 5th grade, 10 dropped to PL 1, 21 remained at PL 2, 30 increased to PL 3, and 3 increased to PL 4. (The percentages are in parentheses).

Your knowledge of your audience is your guide for how much explanation is needed. How much explanation is needed depends entirely on the target audiences' quantitative literacy; since readers vary, aim for the average and err on the side of providing more explanation rather than less. This aids the less knowledgeable reader. There is little point in presenting tables and figures readers cannot understand. More knowledgeable readers will not mind reading a few extra sentences of explanation; less knowledgeable readers will appreciate the help, and you lower the chance of frustrating and losing readers from struggling through complex tables and figures.

Distinctions Between Results and Conclusions

Reporting Results versus Drawing Conclusions

Reporting is describing, concluding is like interpreting. Reporting is "low inference" – you explain directly the figure's or table's information. Reporting is writing, "Enrollment in AP courses has increased 12% in five years." Conclusions are what you make of the information – its significance.

There is both theoretical and practical significance. *Theoretical* means the information's value in helping someone understand something better (how staff turnover affects curriculum planning); *practical* significance refers to the information's value in improving problem solving and planning.

When reporting results, highlight only the important information. Do not repeat in your narrative all the information in a table or figure. For example in Table 4.13 above, what is most illuminating is how many students increase in PL, how many stay the same, and how many decrease (and the percentages). Other information in the table is subordinate to this summary finding. Readers can browse a table or figure for additional details.

For lengthy reports with many tables and figures, place conclusions close to the reporting of results. Do not present table after table without stating the information's significance. No reader wants to slog through a dozen tables and wonder – what does all this mean? The reader must know the significance of the information presented.

Conclusions' Value for GAPPSI

Conclusions drawn from results are usually (a) propositions or inferences about causal processes, (b) judgments of degrees of success or failure of a method, program, or intervention, or (c) statements advocating a course of action. In GAPPSI, the significance of conclusions is related to their value in informing decisions. In scholarly research, a conclusion *is* the goal. In GAPPSI, a conclusion is a means toward a goal of organizational improvement.

SUMMARY AND CONCLUDING COMMENTS

This chapter covered systematic information-gathering – collecting information for a GAPPSI project and paper. Information sources discussed include published literature, focus group interviews, surveys, survey-interview hybrids, and organizational databases and studies. The goal is evidence to clarify problems, answer questions, and guide solutions.

As discussed in Part 1, you can educate yourself with literature related to your problem and contemplated solutions. Literature is useful:

- as a source of terms & definitions
- to establish that a problem is important
- as a source of examples
- to illustrate a principle or make a point
- to organize an argument or analysis
- to substantiate predictions

Literature by itself is not enough to fully understand local conditions or determine what to do; you need local data. Part 2 discussed information from people – surveys, focus groups, and survey-interview hybrids – and Part 3 discussed sources and uses of quantitative data from your organization as well as from government and foundation-supported centers that provide web-based access to education data.

These forms of information are necessary to make a GAPPSI paper or project evidence-based. This increases the odds that your analyses and decisions are correct. Effective use of evidence also strengthens your message's capacity to persuade and influence. Another important variable in your message's capacity to influence is how well you communicate. Chapter 5 turns to this subject.

REFERENCES

AIR (2007). *Moving forward: A guide for implementing comprehensive school reform and improvement strategies.* Washington, DC: The Comprehensive School Reform Quality Center at American Institutes for Research.

Adler, M. & Ziglio. E. (1996). *Gazing into the oracle: The Delphi Method and its application to social policy and public health.* London: Jessica Kingsley Publishers.

Albarracin, D., Johnson, B., & Zanna, M. (Eds.) (2005). *The handbook of attitudes.* Mahwah, N.J.: Lawrence Erlbaum Associates Publishers.

Alexander, K., Entwisle, D., & Olson, L., (2001). Schools, achievement, and inequality: A seasonal perspective. *Educational Evaluation and Policy Analysis, 23*(2), 171-191.

Alexander, D. C. (2004). A Delphi study of the trends or events that will influence the future of California charter schools. *Digital Abstracts International, 65*(10), 3629. (UMI No. 3150304).

Andrade, H, Buff, C., Terry, J., Erano, M., & Paolino, S. (2009). Assessment-driven improvements in middle school students' writing. *Middle School Journal, 40*(4), March, 4-12.

Boudett, K., City, E., & Murnane, R. (Eds.) (2005). *Data wise: A step-by-step guide to using assessment results to improve teaching and learning.* Cambridge, MA: Harvard Education Press.

Bradburn, S., Sudman, S., & Wansink, B. (2004). *Asking questions: The definitive guide to questionnaire design.* San Fransisco: Jossey-Bass.

Briggs, A. & Coleman, M. (Eds.) (2007). *Research methods in educational leadership and management.* Los Angeles, CA: Sage Publications

Buyukdamgaci, G. (2003). Process of organizational problem definition: How to evaluate and how to improve. *Omega, 31*(4), August, 327-239.

CEP (2003). Identifying and implementing educational practices supported by rigorous evidence: A user friendly guide. Prepared by the Institute for Education Sciences, U.S. Department of Education, by the Coalition for Evidence-Based Policy, a project sponsored by the Council for Excellence in Government, 1301 K Street, NW, Suite 450 West, Washington, DC 20005.

Collins, J. (2005). *Good to great and the social sectors.* Boulder, CO: Jim Collins.

Cox, J., & Cox, K. (2007). *Your opinion, please! How to build the best questionnaires in the field of education.* Thousand Oaks, CA: Corwin.

Creighton, T. (2007). *Schools and data: The educator's guide for using data to improve decision making* (2nd ed.). Thousand Oaks, CA: Corwin Press.

Delbeq, A., Van de Ven, A., & Gustafson, D. H. (1975). *Group techniques for program planning: A guide to nominal group and Delphi processes.* Glenview, USA: Scott, Foresman and Company.

Dinkes, R., Forrest, E., & Lin-Kelly, W. (2007). *Indicators of school crime and safety: 2007.* Washington, DC: National Center for Education Statistics, U.S. Department of Education.

Diperna, J. (2006). Academic Enablers and Student Achievement: Implications for Assessment and Intervention in the Schools. *Psychology in the Schools, 43*(1), 7-17.

Edmunds, H. (1999). *The focus group research handbook.* Lincolnwood, IL: NTC Business Books.

Furlong, M. Greif, J. Bates, M., Whipple, A., Jimenez, T., & Morrison, R. (2005). Development of the California school climate and safety survey-short form. *Psychology in the Schools,*

Gall, M., Gall, J., & Borg, W. (2003). *Educational research: An introduction* (7th ed.). Boston, MA: Allyn & Bacon.

Hammond, J., Keeney, R., & Raiffa, H. (1998). The hidden traps in decision making. *Harvard Business Review, 76*(5), Sep - Oct, 47-58.

Hampel, R. (1995). The micropolitics of RE: Learning. *Journal of School Leadership, 5*(6), November, 597--616.

Harrell, M. & Bradley, M. (2009). *Data collection methods: Semi-structured interviews and focus groups.* Santa Monica, CA: RAND.

Helwig, A., & Avitable, N. (2004). School children's responses on a semantic differential over a 10-year span. *Psychological Reports 95*(1), August, 345 - 355.

Herman, J. (1993). Strategic planning for school success. *NASSP Bulletin, 77*(557), December, 85 - 92.

Himmelfarb, S. (1993). The measurement of attitudes. In A. H. Eagly & S. Chaiken (Eds.), *The psychology of attitudes* (pp. 23-87). Fort Worth, TX: Harcourt Brace Jovanovich.

Knafl, K., & Howard, M. (1984). Interpreting and reporting qualitative research. *Research in Nursing & Health, 7,* 17–24.

Krueger, R. & Casey, M. (2000). *Focus groups. A practical guide for applied research* (3rd Edition). Thousand Oaks, CA: Sage Publications

Latess, J., Curtin, S., Leck, G. (2006). Breaking the silence. *Principal Leadership, 6*(8), April, 38-42.

Latess, J. (2008). *Focus-group research for school improvement: What are they thinking?* Lanham, MD: Rowman & Littlefield.

Leithwood, K. A., Leonard, L. J., & Sharratt, L. (1998). Conditions fostering organizational learning in schools. *Educational Administration Quarterly, 34*(2), 243-276.

Lewis, C., Perry, R., Hurd, J., & O'Connell, P. (2006). Lesson study comes of age in North America. *Phi Delta Kappan, 88*(4), December, 273-281.

Means, B., Padilla, C., & Gallagher, L. (2010). *Use of education data at the local level: From accountability to instructional improvement.* Washington, D.C.: U.S. Department of Education, Office of Planning, Evaluation, and Policy Development.

Muzaffar, H., Castelli, D., Goss, D., Scherer, J., & Chapman-Novakofski, K. (2011). Middle school students want more than games for health education on the internet. *Creative Education, 2*(4), 393-397.

NASDSE and CASE (2006). *Response to Intervention: NASDSE and CASE white paper on RtI.* Retrieved from: http://www.nasdse.org/Portals/0/Documents/Download%20Publications/RTIAnAdministratorsPerspective1-06.pdf

NCRTI (2010). *Essential components of RTI – A closer look at response to intervention.* Washington, D.C.: U.S. Department of Education, Office of Special Education Programs, National Center on Response to Intervention.

National Forum on Education Statistics. (2005). Forum Guide to Education Indicators (NFES 2005–802). U.S. Department of Education. Washington, DC: National Center for Education Statistics.

Newcomb, A. (2003). Peter Senge on organizational learning [interview]. *School Administrator, 60(* 5), May, 20-25

Newmann, F. and Associates. (1996). *Authentic achievement : Restructuring schools for intellectual quality.* San Francisco: Jossey Bass.

Orcher, L. (2007). *Conducting a survey.* Glendale, CA. Pyrczak Publishing.

Ostrom, T., Bond, C., Krosnick, J., & Sedikides, C. (1994). Attitude scales: How we measure the unmeasurable. In S. Shavitt & T. C. Brock (Eds.), *Persuasion: Psychological insights and perspectives* (pp. 15-42). Boston: Allyn & Bacon.

Park, J. & Skinner, R. (2003). Court-mandated change: An evaluation of the efficacy of state adequacy and equity indicators. In W. Fowler (Ed.) *Developments in school finance, 2003: Fiscal proceedings from the annual state data conference of July 2003, (NCES 2004–325)* (pp. 71-92). U.S. Department of Education, National Center for Education Statistics, Washington, DC: Government Printing Office.

Patton, M. (2002). *Qualitative research and evaluation methods.* Thousand Oaks, CA: Sage Publications.

Pincus, L. (2006). Who's counted? Who's counting: Understanding high school graduation rates. Washington, DC: *Alliance for Excellent Education.*

Public Agenda. (2007). A mission from the heart: Leaders in high-needs districts talk about what it takes to transform a school. NY: Wallace Foundation.

Reutzel, D., Fawson, P., & Smith, J. (2006). "Words to Go!": Evaluating a first-grade parent involvement program for "making" words at home. *Reading Research and Instruction*, 45(2), Winter, 119-59.

Rochefort, D. & Cobb, D. (1994). (Eds.) *The politics of problem definition: Shaping the policy agenda.* Lawrence, KA: University Press of Kansas.

Rodriquez-Campos, L., Berson, M., Bellara, A., Owens, C., & Walker-Egea, C. (2010). Enhancing evaluation of a large scale civic education initiative with community-based focus groups. *Studies in Learning, Evaluation, Innovation & Development,* 7(3), 87-100.

Rowe, G. & Wright, G. (1999). The Delphi technique as a forecasting tool: Issues and analysis. *International Journal of Forecasting, 15*(4), 353 - 375.

Sandelowski, M. (1998). Writing a good read: Strategies for re-presenting qualitative data. *Research in Nursing and Health, 21*(4), 375-382.

Schechter, C. (2008). Organizational learning mechanisms: The meaning, measure, and implications for school improvement. *Educational Administration Quarterly, 44*(2), 155-186.

Shaver, A., Cuevas, P., & Lee, O. (2007). Teachers' perceptions of policy influences on science instruction with culturally and linguistically diverse elementary students. *Journal of Research in Science Teaching, 44*(5), May, 725-46.

Silins, H. C., Mulford, W. R., & Zarins, S. (2002). Organizational learning and school change. *Educational Administration Quarterly, 38*, 613-642.

Smith G. F. (1989). Defining managerial problems: A framework for prescriptive theorizing. *Management Science, 35*(8), 963 81.

Thomas, S. (2004). *Using web and paper questionnaires for data-based decision making: From design to interpretation of the results.* Thousand Oaks, CA: Corwin.

Thornton, S. (1987). Artistic and scientific qualitative approaches: Influence on aims, conduct, and outcome. *Education and Urban Society, 20,* 25–34.

Tierney, W. (1995). (Re)Presentation and voice. *Qualitative Inquiry, 1,* 379–390.

Tversky, A. & Kahneman, D. (2000). Judgment under uncertainty: Heuristics and biases. In Connolly, T., Arkes, H. & K. Hammond (Eds.), *Judgment and decision making: An interdisciplinary reader* (pp. 35-52). Cambridge: Cambridge University Press.

Vadasy, P., Jenkins, J. & Pool, K. (2000). Effects of tutoring in phonological and early reading skills on students at risk for reading disabilities. *Journal of Learning Disabilities*, *33*(4), July/August, 579-590.

Vogt, P. (2007). *Quantitative research methods for professionals in education and other fields*. Upper Saddle River, N.J.: Prentice Hall.

Wagner, T. (1997). The new village commons – improving schools together. *Educational Leadership*, 54, February, 25-8.

Willis, G. (2005). *Cognitive interviewing: A tool for improving questionnaire design*. Thousand Oaks, CA: Sage.

Wolcott, H. (1990). *Writing up qualitative research*. Newbury Park, CA: Sage.

CHAPTER 5

GUIDELINES FOR CLARITY AND PERSUASIVENESS IN COMMUNICATING PROBLEMS, PLANS, AND SOLUTIONS

INTRODUCTION

Just prior to the 2010 national census, the US Census Bureau scrapped plans for census takers to use specially designed hand-held computers in the 2010 census count. The hand-helds were intended to make the census count more efficient and more accurate – just as hand-helds have revolutionized the package shipping industry and other services. The census project was plagued by poor communications between the census bureau and the computer contractor: unclear technical reports, conflicting messages, vague specifications, ineffective training, confusing memos, and so on. The initiative was abandoned, and the bureau scrambled to hire and train 600,000 additional collectors to do manual paper and pencil counts. The new cost: about 2 billion dollars above original projections.

You can have the best intentions and ideas, but they amount to little if they are communicated poorly. Whatever your form of communication – a memo, proposal, position paper, website – good intentions are not enough. Your audience cannot read your mind.

Writing and presenting well matters a lot. Ideas and plans can only be realized through actions, and actions depend on communications. These elements of communication are discussed in the following sections:[60]

Part 1: The purpose statement: state it quickly and clearly
Part 2: Structural organizers and conceptual chunking for comprehension and recall
Part 3: Paragraphs: focus and coherence
Part 4: Sentences: clarity, concision, continuity
Part 5: Word choices: precision, consistency, and impact

---

[60] This chapter focuses mainly on written communications – composing effective professional prose for a report, proposal, brief, memo, or paper. Similar principles apply for developing oral presentations, but the principles must be adapted for a listening audience. Here are some good books on writing: Lanham (2006); Pearsall (2009); Williams (2007). There are also many university-based websites with free materials for writing support. Munter (2012) and Rotondo & Rotondo (2002) offer guidance on oral presentations, with special attention to using PowerPoint.

PART 1
STATE YOUR PURPOSE CLEARLY AND QUICKLY

Three Key Points

Here are three key points about stating your purpose.

1) Ask yourself, what do I want to accomplish with my message? What, *specifically*, do I want my audience to believe or do because of my message? Ideally, focus on the "doing." That is a more stringent test of the specificity and clarity of your purposes. Then, strive to *express your purpose clearly in one sentence.*

2) Your purpose sentence should be *at the beginning or the end of a paragraph – not buried* in the middle. The first or last sentence of the paragraph gets attention.

Usually, we expect main ideas in lead-off sentences. We expect the remainder of the paragraph to elaborate. Busy readers often skim after the opening sentence. You do not want people skimming over critical points.

The last sentence also matters. Sometimes a paragraph will build to the concluding sentence and express the main point at the end. What works best depends on the narrative context and rhetorical purposes.

3) Get to your point quickly. What is your main idea? What do you want your readers to know, believe, or do? Your reader should understand this within the first 30 seconds of your message.

> *Exception #1: "Blurbs."* The 30 second rule does not apply to one or two paragraph communiqués. This rule is for longer memos, reports, proposals, briefs, white papers, and so forth. If the memo is only a paragraph or two, the 30 second rule is irrelevant. (Point #1 and #2 above still apply, however.)

> *Exception #2: "Openings."* An opening refers to starting with a compelling story, example, or set of facts. Done well, this arouses interest and attention, taking the reader to your thesis statement – the announcement of your purpose. An opening delays this announcement, but can create anticipation and deliver the main idea with more impact.

> An opening must be appropriately proportional to the length of your message. A 200 word memo does not need a 100 word opening. A full length paper, presentation, or report benefits from a stimulating opening. This chapter begins with an anecdote. Another example is in Appendix 5-A.

Purpose Statements: Some Examples

Example #1: a principal's opening statement at a district forum on attendance zone redistricting. (In grey highlight are key purpose sentences.)

> I urge you to oppose the proposed attendance-area redistricting plan. It will increase racial segregation and shift resources away from the neediest students in our district. Let me describe three problems with the proposed plan and suggest an alternative approach.

Example #2: A principal's memo to the faculty of an elementary school.

> Over the last two years bullying incidents have increased and we need to respond. Dan Smith chaired a committee to study the problem and develop recommendations. This memo provides background on the problem and presents the committee's recommendations:

- a system to monitor bullying
- incentives for students to report bullying
- policies to establish penalties for bullying behavior

At the next faculty meeting (October 15th) I would like to get your input on the feasibility of these recommendations.

Example #3:   From a teacher to the high school curriculum coordination committee.

FROM: Susan Jones
TO: Cameron High School Curriculum Coordination Committee
RE: Proposed agenda item: Do we have a misalignment between instruction and testing in 10th grade?

For that last three years our 10th grade scores on the state social studies test have fallen short of grade level standards. This drop in scores followed our implementation of block scheduling. I'm concerned the block scheduling system may have contributed to this.

Much of the content of the 10th grade state test is covered in 9th grade and the first semester of 10th grade, but hardly at all in the second semester of 10th grade in the months before the state test in April. The gap in instruction on tested content may contribute to the lower scores. We should examine whether our master schedule creates a "timing" misalignment between instruction and testing.

There is no single formula for stating the purpose – the main principle is *get to the point quickly, make it succinct, and give it a prominent position*. Don't hide it.

The Overview (for longer messages)

Longer messages may need an overview after a purpose statement. This shows the structure (organization) of the message. This is like stating the agenda at the beginning of a meeting or presenting an abstract for a grant proposal or journal article. An overview statement is like a roadmap, giving the big picture, the context. Here are two examples.

(1) If you are about to state several reasons in support of a position, announce this. Then, follow with the reasons. For example, you might write, "Following are three reasons we should …" and then bullet the three reasons. Then explain each reason.

(2) Here is another example of overview and structure.

The proposed program has five components:

1) a prescribed weekly reading list
2) monthly formative assessment
3) small group tutoring for at-risk students
4) a parent support liaison
5) a parent resource room

Following, I describe each component. The last section explains costs and first steps for implementation.

Purpose Statements Graphically Represented

The following figures show purpose statements graphically as a proportion of a larger narrative. The purpose statements are identified in dark grey. These examples are typical.

Figure 5.1
First Page of 10 Page Paper

Purpose statement in Abstract; elaboration of purpose at end of Introduction section.

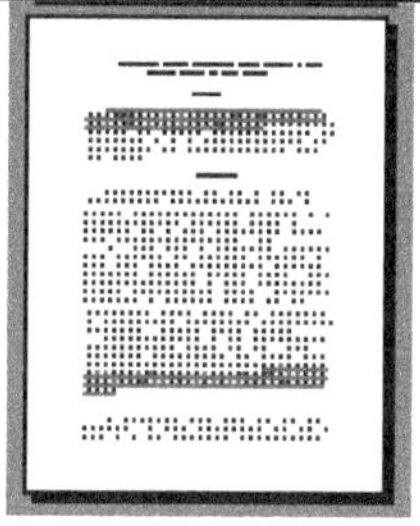

Figure 5.2
One Page Memo

Purpose statement at beginning and end

Figure 5.3
Purpose Statements in 1300 Word Grant Proposal

Starts with overview section, including a 50 word purpose statement; the purpose is reiterated at the end of "Problem Statement" on page 2. Next section, "Project Plan," is divided into three sections, each beginning with objectives. Altogether, there are five forms of purpose statements, starting general, getting progressively more specific.

PART 2
STRUCTURAL ORGANIZERS AND CONCEPTUAL CHUNKING: AIDS TO COMPREHENSION AND MEMORY

Have you ever read a proposal or paper and after a minute or two wonder, "where this is going?" Just as good novels and movies conform to conventions of plot and character, good expository prose adheres to principles of structure. In reading a novel or watching a movie, you know the rules – what characters do, what motivates them, how and why they get into conflicts, how they get out of them, when events should happen and why, and how the plot resolves. Violating understood rules usually creates confusion and dissatisfaction.

Making a message clear and comprehensible should not be hard. This is what must be clear to the reader or listener:

- The message's purpose
- The sequence of main ideas
- The logical connection among the main ideas

Structural organizers and *conceptual chunking* are devices to improve clarity and comprehensibility. Structural organizers include bullets, headings,[61] enumeration, layout, underlined text, and bold text. They draw the reader's attention to key ideas, reveal logical sequences of ideas, and show relationships among ideas.

Conceptual chunking refers to a single idea tying together a larger number of smaller units of information. The human brain can only retain in working memory a relatively small number of disparate pieces of information.

Can you retain six random numbers told to you (199 620)? Yes. Can you remember fifteen (199 620 062 016 202 6)? No. But what if those fifteen numbers are organized differently, like this: 1996 2006 2016 2026? The second configuration puts the numbers in four groups instead of six, but more important, we recognize the groupings of four as years; each year in the sequence is ten more than the previous one. This is a contrived example, but it shows that *information is more easily understood and remembered when disparate items of information are organized in ways that capitalize on the receiver's prior knowledge.*

Another simple illustration of chunking is the paragraph. A paragraph may contain six sentences, each expressing a different specific idea. But, if the paragraph is well constructed, all six sentences connect to each other and to the paragraph's main idea. When you read a well composed paragraph, you don't remember each sentence, but you do remember the main idea. You can say in a few words what the paragraph is about.

Another example of chunking is condensing lists into categories. Imagine a list of 13 agenda items for a committee meeting. As a random list, this information is hard to process; grouped in labeled categories (e.g., funding, staffing, public relations) you understand it. It makes sense. These are ways chunking organizes a message and aids comprehension and recall.

Structural Organizers and Conceptual Chunking - Example #1: Bullying Memo/Report

Following are additional guidelines and examples showing message organizing strategies. Figure 5.4 shows a logical organization for an extended memo or short report on bullying. (This is abridged; actual length, detail, and content would be dictated by the message's context and purposes.) You can quickly and easily identify its structure and main points.

---

[61] See Appendix 5-B for an illustration of a three-level heading system.

Figure 5.4
Extended Example #1: Bullying Memo

TO: Orchard Lane School faculty and staff   October 15
FROM: Principal Henrietta Stone
RE: Reducing "bullying" in Orchard Lane School

Over the last two years bullying incidents have increased and we need to respond. Dan Smith is chairing a committee to study the problem and develop recommendations. This memo reports their work to date and initial recommendations to be discussed by the faculty:
  • survey students on bullying
  • develop a system to monitor bullying
  • encourage students to report bullying
  • clarify bullying in our code of conduct policy
  • develop procedures for counseling and discipline for bullies

At the next faculty meeting (October 20th) we will discuss the bullying situation and what we can do to address it.

Bullying defined. Let me begin by defining bullying. ......

     [paragraph defining bullying; could draw on definitions from academic literature]

Bullying is increasing. It is clear that bullying in our school has increased. Observations by teachers and reported incidents by students show this. ......

     [paragraph establishing that bullying has increased]

Why bullying is a problem. Bullying is a problem for a number of reasons.
  • bullied children are hurt emotionally
  • may hurt academic achievement as well
  • perpetrators endanger others and themselves if they don't get help
  • adversely affects school climate
  • adversely affects PR for school

Developing an action plan. At the next meeting Dan will review the committee's work and recommendations, and then we will discuss the recommendations and solicit ideas and participation for next steps.

Structural Organizers and Conceptual Chunking - Example #2:
Diagramming a Literacy-improvement Initiative

"A picture is worth a thousand words"

In an influential study on visual memory, Standing, Conezio, and Haber (1970) showed participants 2,500 images, one by one (a few seconds per image). Three days later, the people viewed these same images again, but this time mixed in with several thousand other new images. The people were able to identify the images they had seen with over 90% accuracy.

     Verbal and visual information are processed in different parts of the brain. Images go into long term memory. When verbal information is supplemented with well designed images, recall and comprehension improve – *understanding*   (Bransford,

Brown, & Cocking, 1999; Buckner, Raichle, Miezin, & Petersen, 1996; Grady, McIntosh, Rajah, & Craik, 1998; Jensen, 2005; Joffe, Cain, & Maric, 2007; Larkin & Simon, 1987).

Diagrams help the message creator and the receiver (audience). A good diagram succinctly identifies key ideas and conveys relationships among them. Diagrams put the message into distinct, easy-to-communicate chunks.

Diagrams and chunking are under-utilized tools in leadership communications (e.g., drafting a proposal, presenting to a board, group planning). Diagrams won't replace words, but used well, they are very effective.

Figure 5.5 is part of a problem statement from a school's grant proposal to strengthen reading and writing instruction (summarized as "literacy" in the proposal).

Figure 5.5
__Key Barriers to Student Literacy__

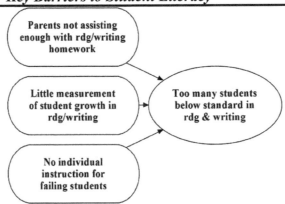

This diagram reflects decisions by the proposal writers about how to frame the problem. They considered a larger number of causal factors including low self-esteem, inadequate incentives to read more, insufficient planning time during school day, and large class sizes. (See Chapter 3's discussion of analyzing causes.) The grant proposal settled on the problem formulation in Figure 5.5. While other causes might operate, they fall outside the scope of the project as communicated in the proposal. As an audience, we just see the end product, and it looks simple and clear.

How many causes to identify: Three to five elements (e.g, causal factors) are easy to comprehend and remember. Avoid overloading graphics with too many elements and too much information. If it gets too complex you defeat the purpose of the graphic; on the other hand, provide enough information so the graphic makes sense by itself.

How to label the causes: (a) The label should clearly state the deficiency – the causal variable that needs to change. Ask yourself: if this variable were to change in the desired way, would it reduce the core problem? Would it positively affect the outcome variable? If the answer is not clear, then rethink your label. (b) The label should describe a controllable condition – a variable under some control by your planned program. Unemployment may be a cause, but beyond your control. (c) The label should be short and memorable. Ideally, you should be able to state it in a few words. Try for short labels for key elements in a diagram; the narrative can elaborate.

Put causal variables on the left and consequences on the right. We read from left to right and expect graphical representations of causal chains to start at the left and proceed to the right (top to bottom also suffices if page-space dictates). You can confuse by violating readers' ingrained expectations about spatial relations and directions of causality. You want the reader to "get it" – not think, "Why are the causes on the wrong side?"

Use arrows to show causality, not just lines. The arrows show your theory about the direction of causal influences. Your theory, needless to say, should be plausible.

Figure 5.5 ("Barriers...") serves another important purpose: It sets up proposed solutions. The problem definition in Figure 5.5 creates a rationale for the proposed solutions in Figure 5.6 aimed at the goal: higher literacy achievement.

Figure 5.6
Planned Initiatives to Improve Literacy

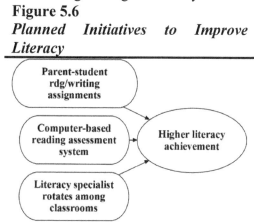

Diagramming causes and solutions this way helps both the message creator and the message receiver. It forces the message creator to think about the causal variables to identify, how they should be labeled, and their logical relationships to the core problem.

Diagrams also help structure the narrative. The narrative fills in the explanations. The narrative explains, for instance, what is meant by "little measurement of student growth." The narrative would explain that:

> Scores from annual state testing arrive too late to be useful and lack sufficient diagnostic information. Teachers' quarterly marking period grades in reading help identify low achieving students, but grades have limitations. Grades do not reflect uniform standards across teachers, are not based on standardized assessments, and do not provide reliable measures of growth over time. Thus, our existing assessment information is of limited value for monitoring student literacy growth, for reliably identifying students falling behind, and for determining specific instructional interventions.

Used appropriately, a good diagram enables the reader to visualize key ideas and their logical relationships. Using graphics to supplement words makes complex verbal information more understandable and easier to remember.

Structural Organizers and Conceptual Chunking - Example #3:

Other useful diagrams include flow charts, management charts, and timelines. Figure 5.7 is a flow chart showing a sequence of decisions and steps in an emergency response plan. Management charts show how a program is managed; timelines state a schedule of objectives.

Figure 5.7
School Emergency Planning: Lockdown, Evacuation, or Relocation Decisions

Source: Practical Information on Crisis Planning: A Guide for Schools and Communities. U.S. Department of Education, Office of Safe and Drug-Free, Washington, D.C., 2003.

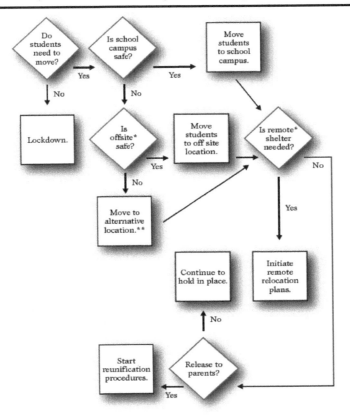

* "Offsite" means off the school campus but in vicinity.
   "Remote" means a location further from the school than offsite location.
** Be sure to prepare primary and secondary evacuation routes in advance.

Summary: Structural Organizers, Conceptual Chunking, and Diagrams

Purpose statements, overviews, conceptual diagrams, headings, and other organizers communicate the logical structure of your message. These organizers help make clear to the reader the parts of your message and logical relationships among the parts.

Diagrams help readers *see* the key pieces of information and organize them conceptually (Larkin & Simon, 1987; Robinson, 1998). This is important. When people can put facts and concepts into a larger structure they retain the information longer and understand it better (Bransford et al., 1999; Mayer, Heiser, & Lonn, 2001; Nesbit & Olusola, 2006; Robinson, 1998). Diagrams simplify and summarize key logical relationships and give message receivers a structure to understand and remember.

Creating diagrams takes time, but usually it is worth it. Diagrams can save you time by reducing the amount of narrative needed. Also, diagrams can decrease the

112

chance your audience misses or misinterprets portions of a message – and this can save time in the long run.[62]

We turn now to smaller chunks of narrative information: the paragraph. The paragraph is the building block of the message.

PART 3
PARAGRAPHS: FOCUS AND COHERENCE

A paragraph is a unit of information. It should convey a single idea as denoted by words like "focus" and "coherence." The reader should be able to summarize in a few words the paragraph's central idea – its message, its point. Experienced writers help the reader do this with clear, short lead sentences, and often reiterate the main idea in the last sentence.

Making Paragraphs Coherent

Paragraphs can lack coherence for many reasons. Here are some typical examples of coherence problems.

Paragraphs With Coherence Problems: Example #1

Some paragraphs open with one point and then meander. In the paragraph below, the principal is concerned about high teacher turnover in his school and in the district as a whole.

> Teachers are faced with declining public prestige and many often burn out or end up leaving the profession after only a few years on the job. To compound the problem, many times teachers use their own resources to purchase materials and supplies needed for the classroom. The average teacher spends more than $500 a year on various teacher-related expenses. Worst of all, it is usually the lowest paid first year teacher that spends the most time and money purchasing items and trying to prepare their classrooms to help students succeed.

Notice that the first sentence introduces two ideas – *declining prestige* and *teacher burn out* – but that the rest of the paragraph is mainly about *low pay*. These are three different ideas. The paragraph is not clearly about *one* idea.

Paragraphs With Coherence Problems: Example #2

This paragraph is from a leader advocating policies to support data-based decision making in the district.

> Another necessary element of the process of school improvement through data collection and analysis to be designed through this project is the ability to outlast the tenure of the person who

---

[62] To find graphics software, search the web with terms like flow chart tools or flow chart software. Some leading programs include SmartDraw, Inspiration, and Wizflo. Powerpoint has an "organization chart" slide, as well as other options.

develops it. The proposal to be developed as a result of this project will include recommendations to our school district leadership to embed elements of data collection and analysis in policy and regulation. Not only will this add permanence to the process of data-driven curricular and instructional improvement at Orchard Middle School, it will allow the process to spread across all schools in our district.

It takes multiple readings to decipher the main idea. The paragraph has several comprehension impediments – long sentences, multiple abstractions, and many prepositions and passive verbs. The first sentence is 33 words; you read 14 words before getting to the passive verb "to be designed." (We do not know who the designers are.) The reference to "the ability" in the first sentence is confusing – it appears that someone will design an element of a process and this element will be an "ability" to outlast a person.

Following are some revisions. In these examples, I make assumptions about the authors' intentions. As a reader you have no choice. You cannot mind-read; you only have the words on the page.

Improving The Paragraphs With Coherence Problems

On the left is the original (Table 5.1); on the right, a revision with additional comments. I use grey highlight to identify disparate ideas that create coherence problems.

Table 5.1
Toward More Coherent Paragraphs: Examples #1 and #2

ORIGINAL 90 word paragraph with coherence problems	REVISION [67 words] Shorter lead sentence with main idea: "why teachers leave the profession." Material removed: "declining prestige of the occupation" and "the lowest paid first year teacher that spends the most time and money." These important ideas deserve their own paragraphs.
Teachers are faced with declining public prestige and many often burn out or end up leaving the profession after only a few years on the job. To compound the problem, many times teachers use their own resources to purchase materials and supplies needed for the classroom. The average teacher spends more than $500 a year on various teacher-related expenses. Worst of all, it is usually the lowest paid first year teacher that spends the most time and money purchasing items and trying to prepare their classrooms to help students succeed.	Many teachers leave the profession after only a few years on the job. One reason is lack of resource support on the job. Teachers often spend their own time and money getting classroom supplies. The average teacher spends more than $500 a year on various teacher-related expenses. With so little support, many teachers leave. Another reason teachers leave the profession is declining public prestige. +++++++++++++++++ Here is a shorter, "punchier" version of the first sentence: Many teachers quit after working only a few years. One reason is...
ORIGINAL 97 word paragraph with coherence problems	REVISION [78 words] The first sentence presents a main idea. The remaining sentences express concerns motivating the proposed policy.
Another necessary element of the process of school improvement through data collection and analysis to be designed through this project is the ability to outlast the tenure of the person who develops it. The proposal to be developed as a result of this project will include recommendations to	We need a policy requiring data-driven school improvement planning. Otherwise we will continue to see wide variation in approaches to school improvement planning: some schools' plans being data-driven, others based on hunches and personal preferences. A district policy will make data-driven improvement

our school district leadership to embed elements of data collection and analysis in policy and regulation. Not only will this add permanence to the process of data-driven curricular and instructional improvement at Orchard Valley Middle School, it will allow the process to spread across all schools in our district.

planning an expected responsibility of school leadership.

Use Bullets or Enumeration to Organize Paragraphs With Multiple Related Ideas

If you need to present a series of parallel ideas (e.g., five things that went wrong; four characteristics of success; etc.), consider structuring the paragraph with enumeration – ideas in a list. Present the ideas succinctly, in parallel form. Table 5.2 show two examples.

Table 5.2
Toward More Coherent Paragraphs: Examples #3 and #4

ORIGINAL: 225 word communication to high school staff recounting problems with a prior mentoring initiative.	REVISION (98 words) Shortened first sentence; removal of extraneous material; list of key problems.
Last year we attempted to institute a mentoring program at the high school for at-risk students. Although the vision was there, the lack of structure in the program led to a great variety in the amount of time individual teachers put into their roles and thus a great variety in the level of individualized services and attention that students received. Data collection was random and based on logs that were maintained by the mentors. Certainly some students were probably better served and more successful because of this program. However, the design relied solely on teachers to utilize their planning time to meet with students and collaborate with their colleagues. No training was provided and mentors grew frustrated when students didn't respond to their efforts. Another difficulty arose as students who clearly needed additional guidance and support were not provided a mentor because they did not meet the initial selection criteria. A mechanism to keep up with a large part of the student body was not part of the initial program. While these drawbacks should not paralyze a program, the mentor initiative at the high school has not been continued. One major goal of the 9th grade campus is to keep interest and staff input high enough to encourage everyone to work continuously on improving our current practice and developing ways to improve for next year.	Last year we started a mentoring program for at-risk students. While we had a vision, implementation did not go well: • the program lacked structure - mentoring approaches and record-keeping varied among teachers • teachers had to give up personal planning time to mentor students and collaborate with colleagues • some teachers felt ill-prepared and became frustrated when students didn't respond to their efforts • many students needing mentoring didn't qualify because they did not meet the initial selection criteria. The mentor initiative has not been continued... +++++++++++++++++ (Here is another option for the opening.) We are discontinuing last year's mentoring program for at-risk students. The program had several problems:
ORIGINAL 351 word communication announcing new initiatives in a middle school.	REVISION (274 words) Starts with an overview of the initiatives in a topic sentence; removes extraneous material and creates a list.
This year we will pilot several programs, which include looping, full-inclusion, adding an addi-	This year we will pilot several programs: looping, full-inclusion, an additional course, and comput-

115

tional course and creative scheduling. We will also pilot a diagnostic assessment measuring student achievement growth, Assessment Systems for Measuring Growth. Our seventh (7th) and (8th) grade teams will loop in all content areas. The students receiving special education service will be provided instruction in a TAM class, so that they have access to the general curriculum and are challenged daily to meet the same content standards as their peers. Additionally, all students will have a course within their 7-period schedule called "Content II" which will focus on all four content areas in a four and a half (4 ½) block sessions. This course will be designed to meet the needs of students, preparing them for the State Assessment Program (SAP). This course will give each student a daily double–dose of content instruction. We have set up the schedule so that looping teams have common planning periods across the building. This will give you optimal planning opportunities with the teacher within your content/looping team. In these planning sessions you will have opportunities to discuss the students, the curriculum, and how you can better meet their needs on a daily basis. We have also planned for the schedule to rotate weekly. Doing so will give you the opportunity to reach and teach students at varying times of the day. The final component we have added to this school year is the pilot of an assessment tool, Assessment Systems for Measuring Growth. This tool is aligned to the State Content Standards, and can give us feedback on each student in as little as forty-eight (48) hours. We will use this assessment tool three (3) times this school year in order to measure academic progress. The test will be taken on the computer by every student in the areas of mathematics and reading. Once taken, teachers will receive instant scores and reports that immediately target the student's strength and weaknesses. It also allows for reports to be given to parents and other educational diagnosticians to help in meeting the needs of each individual student.

er-based testing.

Looping. Our seventh (7th) and (8th) grade teams will loop in all content areas. We have modified the master schedule so looping teams have common planning periods across the building. This creates planning time with colleagues in your content/looping team. These planning sessions should focus on ways to improve student academic work, learning, and conduct. The schedule rotates weekly creating opportunities to teach and assist students at varying times of the day.

Full-inclusion. Students in special education service will be in TAM classes, so that they have access to the general curriculum and are challenged daily to meet the same content standards as their peers.

An additional course. Additionally, all students will have a course within their 7-period schedule called "Content II" which will focus on all four content areas in 4 ½ block sessions. This course will strengthen student preparation for the State Assessment Program (SAP). Each student will get a daily "double–dose" of content instruction.

Computer-based testing measuring individual academic progress. We will pilot a computer-based testing system in mathematics and reading. This test is aligned with the State Content Standards. Students are tested 3 times a year. Individual and group scores are generated within 48 hours to track student growth. We will be able to target instruction at students' specific learning needs and provide reports of individual progress to parents.

Making Paragraphs Coherent:
Concluding Comments

In the examples above, the original paragraphs are long and disorganized – too many disparate ideas; too many long sentences; too much superfluous and distracting information. The paragraphs do not give the reader easy-to-remember "chunks" of information. The reader wants a paragraph that coheres around one main point.

PART 4
SENTENCES: THE MESSAGE'S BASIC UNIT
FIVE PRINCIPLES FOR CLEAR AND SUCCINCT SENTENCES

Introduction

Every sentence requires choices about words to use, verb forms, structure, and length. Experienced writers make sentence composition choices that aid comprehension; less experienced writers make composition choices that often impede comprehension. I refer to sentence composition choices as "comprehension facilitators" or "comprehension impediments." These are guidelines – general DOs and DON'Ts. I begin by discussing the value of active voice sentence construction.

Comprehension Facilitator: Active Verb Forms

Sentences can be constructed using active or passive verb forms as shown in Table 5.3. Usually, the active form is easier to understand because the sentence has a concrete actor doing something – an action. "The *committee*[actor] *designed*[action verb] the plan." This is easy to visualize. Active sentences reflect how we naturally think about causes and consequences. A cause happens *before* the consequence: an actor causes an action.

In passive construction, actors and actions are harder to discern. Instead of, "The committee designed the plan," the passive form is: "The plan *was designed by*[passive verb] the committee."[actor] The *consequence* of the committee's actions – "the plan" – comes first in the sentence, before we find out the actor. Some passive voice sentences omit the actor completely: "The plan has been[passive verb] designed." Notice that passive verbs are preceded by "state of being" verbs: is, am, were, was, are, be, being, been; helping verbs "have, has, and had" are also part of many passive sentences.

Readers prefer concrete actors and action verbs: plan, discuss, examine, promote, convince, persuade. Passive verb forms obscure the actions and the actors, and tend to be harder to understand.

Table 5.3
Passive Versus Active Sentence Structure

	Subject of the sentence	Verb	------------------
PASSIVE FORM	The lesson	was planned	by the teacher
ACTIVE FORM	The teacher	planned	the lesson

In the following pairs of sentences, notice how the active form is easier to read and understand.

[Passive] Observations were made by the investigator that...
[Active]   The investigator observed that...

[Passive] High levels of satisfaction were revealed among teachers in the study.
[Active] The study revealed teachers were highly satisfied.

[Passive] The coordination of professional development programs has received little planning.
[Active] We have not planned how to coordinate the professional development programs.

The above examples are short. Both sentences in each pair are pretty easy to understand (even though the active forms are better). However, string together a half dozen long, passive sentences and you end up with difficult-to-read prose. But I still want to emphasize, *passive voice is fine if used judiciously*. You can't write about ideas without ever using passive voice. Here are ways it is appropriate.

(1) Passive construction helps when we want to emphasize, not the subject, but the action affecting the subject.

Above, I wrote:
Sentences can be constructed using active or passive verb forms.
I did not write:
Writers construct sentences…
I want to emphasize "sentence construction," not "writers."

Suppose a principal wants to notify teachers about the results of a student survey:
Students in the ABC program were surveyed last week about their experiences. The results were positive.
The sentence could be (active voice):
Last week we surveyed the students in the ABC program about their experiences. The results were positive.
The second version emphasizes the subject "we;" the first version emphasizes the students being surveyed. Either is fine, but their emphases are a bit different.

(2) Passive construction can strengthen continuity between sentences (improved "flow"). Below, the second sentence below uses passive construction.

The School Improvement Council will review proposals for a new outdoor environmental learning site. The learning site will be designed to help integrate science and social studies. These subjects are disconnected in the school curriculum, but site-based environmental studies will show students linkages between science and social issues

Notice the second sentence is passive and without an actor. An active voice version would say who the designers are, but this is unimportant here. The paragraph is about the learning site and its function. If the second sentence had an actor, it might read like this:

Teachers working with environmental consultants will design the site to help integrate…..

But writing the second sentence this way puts the emphasis on the designers; it is more important to emphasize the learning site's role of integrating two curriculum subjects.
Notice also that the passive construction strengthens continuity between key ideas [in grey] of contiguous sentences.

The School Improvement Council will review proposals for a new outdoor environmental learning site. The learning site will be designed to help integrate science and social studies. These subjects are disconnected in the school curriculum, but site-based environmental studies will show students linkages between science and social issues

(3) Sometimes, as shown below, differences between active and passive construction are minor. Your purposes will determine what words and ideas to emphasize.

The students' progress is impressive. [emphasis on the *progress;* no actor]
We are impressed by the students' progress. [emphasis on actors' mental state of *being impressed*]

We have been distracted by the problems of a small number of students. [emphasis on *being distracted*]
The problems of a small number of students have been distracting. [emphasis on the *problems of students*]

The main point is this: other things equal, put actors and active verbs in your sentences. This helps clarity and readability. But there are contexts where passive construction helps you get your point across more effectively. The actor may not be important. Or you may want to deemphasize the do-er and emphasize what is being done. Passive construction is not only acceptable, but preferable if you recognize when passive voice achieves your purposes, if you do not overuse passives, if you do not inflict on your reader series of long-subject sentences, and if you eliminate wordiness. I discuss next these comprehension impediments and facilitators.

Comprehension Impediment: Long, Complex Subjects Before Getting To The Verb

The verb makes the sentence make sense. It is not until we get to the verb that we know what is going on, what the message is. Avoid sentences with long subjects before getting to the verb. Long subjects force the reader to process a lot of information before the verb. This taxes the reader's memory, impeding comprehension. It is like putting a heavy load on a computer's memory. The processing slows down. Here are examples:

Agencies that support adult and family literacy, technical training and school-to-work and job readiness programs are potential donors. [15 words before verb]

Common project related challenges such as scope creep, cost overruns, and failure to deliver on-time all cost the district money. [16 words before verb]

Among the parents of both professional backgrounds and blue-collar backgrounds and also among community leaders there is rising opposition to school board proposals that would implement the elimination of vocational courses in high school. [16 words before verb]

Cognitive processing slows when sentences have long, complex subjects before the verb. This impedes comprehension and recall.

The examples above are single sentences. When you read just one sentence with full attention, the sentence is reasonably clear. But imagine entire paragraphs full of lengthy sentences. Too often, we see prose like this:

> Providing everyone with time during the school day to work on district initiatives in a collegial matter is uncommon at the high school level. Yet, when we talk as a group about the things that we are in need of to implement greater interdisciplinary curriculum it is planning time that is always mentioned. Transitioning to an 8 period day and providing the opportunity to become involved in a professional learning community will assist us in our effort to collaborate by increasing available time. Creating common assessments, discussing curriculum, designing lessons, implementing instructional strategies and discussing classroom management are some of the collegial tasks and activities that will be facilitated as we develop productive professional learning communities. Implementing an 8 period day will also assist us in our implementation of other new initiatives: the 9th grade academy with its dual block schedule, elimination of low-level tracking, the creation of CP seminar courses, and using our grant funds for additional professional development.

The paragraph above takes effort to understand. It has coherence problems. Its sentences start with long, complex subjects before getting to the verb. In the first sentence, for instance, before you reach the verb you must hold in your head, "Providing everyone with time during the school day to work on district initiatives in a collegial matter." This is a big bundle of information. How much easier it is to understand this: "Under the current scheduling system, high school teachers have very little time during the day for collegial work."

Comprehension Facilitator: Short Subject, Active Verb

Here are examples of revisions to the four sentences and passages immediately above (Table 5.4). These revisions shorten the subject and use an active verb. The revisions use mostly the original vocabulary because I focus on rearranging the sentences. More substantive revisions would enhance the sentences' style and impact (you can think about these after reading this entire section).

Table 5.4
Four Examples – Original On The Left; Revision On The Right

ORIGINAL - long, complex subject	REVISION - shorter subject, active verb
Agencies that support adult and family literacy, technical training and school-to-work and job readiness programs are potential donors. [15 words before verb]	Potential donors are agencies that support adult and family literacy, technical training and school-to-work and job readiness programs. [2 words before verb]
Common project related challenges such as scope creep, cost overruns, and failure to deliver on-time all cost the district money. [16 words before verb]	The district loses money due to project related challenges such as scope creep, cost overruns, and failure to deliver on-time. [2 words before verb]
Among the parents of both professional backgrounds and blue-collar and among community leaders there is rising opposition to school board proposals that would implement the elimination of tracked courses in high school. [16 words before verb]	Community leaders and parents of all backgrounds increasingly oppose school board proposals to eliminate vocational courses in high school. [8 words before verb]

Providing everyone with time during the school day to work on district initiatives in a collegial matter is uncommon at the high school level. Yet, when we talk as a group about the things that we are in need of to implement greater interdisciplinary curriculum planning it is time that is always mentioned. Transitioning to an 8 period day and providing the opportunity to become involved in a professional learning community will assist us in our effort to collaborate by increasing available time. Creating common assessments, discussing curriculum, designing lessons, implementing instructional strategies and discussing classroom management are some of the collegial tasks and activities that will be facilitated as we develop productive professional learning communities. Implementing an 8 period day will also assist us in our implementation of other new initiatives: the 9th grade academy with its dual block schedule, elimination of low-level tracking, the creation of CP seminar courses, and using our grant funds for additional professional development. [160 words]

The district is implementing several new high school initiatives. These will fail if teachers lack common planning time.

Currently, high school teachers have little time during the day to work together. Changing to an 8 period schedule will create common planning time – time for designing interdisciplinary curriculum, creating common assessments, developing lessons, and discussing classroom management.

Common planning will also facilitate other district initiatives underway: designing the dual block schedule for 9th grade academy, eliminating tracking, creating CP seminar courses, and using our grant funds for additional professional development. [96 words]

Comprehension Impediment: Wordiness

Wordiness impedes comprehension. Each of the three main guidelines above leads to shorter, less wordy, sentences. Here are other contributors to wordiness.

Wordiness results from sentences with too many prepositions and articles (a, an, it, the, that, this). Prepositions are connectors (Table 5.5, left side). They describe a relationship between two or more words. Remove prepositions and articles whenever you can (e.g., see Table 5.5, right side on eliminating stock phrases).

Table 5.5 Wordiness Reduction: Prepositions

Common Prepositions			Eliminate Stock Phrases	
			Instead of...	*Use...*
about	during	of	due to the fact that	because
after	except	on	owing to the fact that	OR
around	for	over	for the reason that	since
at	from	since	on account of the fact that	
before	in	throughout	despite the fact that	although
beside	into	to	regardless of the fact that	OR
between	like	with		even though
by	near	without	at this point in time	now
			at the present time	
			on a daily basis	daily

Each of the sentences and passages revised above lost prepositions and articles in the revisions. Here are revisions of three more sentences with unnecessary prepositions and articles (Table 5.6).

Table 5.6 Weeding Out Prepositions and Articles

ORIGINAL Lots of prepositions	REVISION Few prepositions
It is a matter of utmost importance in the education of mathematics students that they receive instruction on topics that will insure vocational success in technological sectors. [27 words]	Mathematics instruction should prepare students for technology jobs. [8 words]
Because questions about the degree of implementation success of the drug program are emerging, formulation of multiple new strategies must be considered by the task force. [26 words]	The task force needs to consider new strategies, because the drug program was poorly implemented. [15 words]
The reason that there was a cost overrun was that unanticipated overhead charges were billed to the personnel account. [19 words]	Unanticipated overhead charges to the personnel account produced cost overruns. [10 words]

Imagine a chief executive writes an open memo about corporate values to middle management. The message is about risk-taking and learning from mistakes. The CEO writes:

> In the corporate world, disavowing responsibility or assigning blame for negative-impact decisions and initiatives is too often the response among organizational leaders and managers when a mistake has been made.
>
> While it is of importance that successful decisions and initiatives are acknowledged and rewarded, it is of equivalent importance that decisions and initiatives producing unexpected costs and other negative consequences are examined for their potential benefits for organizational learning.
>
> It is my position that under some conditions blame should not be assigned to business managers and leaders when they produce unexpected costs or other adverse consequence. The desired practice for our organization should be to collectively examine negative-impact decisions or initiatives to identify the positive learning outcomes that may accrue and to not be preoccupied with how to assign blame and accountability for the initial mistake.

The passage above is my rewrite of the opening paragraphs from "Mistakes" by Bill Gates. The passage above is what Lanham (2006) derisively refers to as "official style," common in the prose of government, bureaucratic, corporate, and academic writers. I rewrote the Gates paragraphs to make a point. Here is the original, in about 25% fewer words:

> In the corporate world, when someone makes a mistake everyone runs for cover. At Microsoft, I try to put an end to that kind of thinking.
>
> It's fine to celebrate success, but it is more important to heed the lessons of failure. How a company deals with mistakes suggests how well it will bring out the best ideas and talents of its people, and how effectively it will respond to change.
>
> The message I want a manager to communicate is, "I don't blame anybody in particular for this problem. What I care about is how well we rally around to come up with a new approach to resolve it."

Reducing Wordiness Example #1

Here is a sentence you just read: In the corporate world, disavowing responsibility or assigning blame for negative-impact decisions and initiatives is too often the response among organizational leaders and managers when a mistake has been made.

(1) Who/what is the actor? organizational leaders and managers

(2) What is the core action? disavowing responsibility or assigning blame

(3) Can the actor be put before the action? Yes:
    organizational leaders and managers disavow responsibility or assign blame

(4) What words and phrases can be removed?

    corporate world...organizational leaders and managers → corporate managers

    disavowing responsibility or assigning blame for negative-impact decisions and initiatives → mistake is made... blame others or disavow responsibility

(5) Can you write more concise versions of the sentence?

- When a mistake is made in the corporate world, managers too often blame others or disavow responsibility. [fewer words but still passive voice ("is made")]
- Corporate managers sometimes blame others or disavow responsibility when bad decisions are made.
- In the corporate world, when someone makes a mistake everyone runs for cover. [Original Gates version.]

Additional comments on example #1. The three revised versions are different, but each is better than the passive and wordy original. Two of the revisions use "manager" and formal language (e.g. "disavow responsibility"); Gates' original refers to "someone" and "everyone" and uses an informal, vivid expression ("runs for cover"). Each of the three sentences improves the original, but each conveys a different tone. The author must decide which is best, based on his/her rhetorical aims.

Reducing Wordiness Example #2

Here is another sentence: It is the function of this program to provide ongoing and systematic professional development in support of technology integration in the classroom.

(1) Who/what is the actor? this program

(2) What is the core action? provide ongoing and systematic professional development

(3) Can the actor be put before the action? Yes:
    This program provides ongoing and systematic professional development

(4) What words and phrases can be removed?
    It is the function of this program to provide → This program provides
    ongoing and systematic professional development → training for teachers

123

in support of technology integration in the classroom → to integrate technology into instruction

(5) Can you write more concise versions of the sentence?
- This program provides training for teachers to integrate technology into instruction.
- This program trains teachers to integrate technology into instruction.
- This program's purpose is to train teachers to integrate technology into instruction.
- This program trains teachers to use technology for instruction.

Additional comments on example #2. I removed "ongoing and systematic." Writers often add unnecessary filler words like these. If these words are essential (without a context here, we cannot determine this), then the next sentence can explain that the training is "ongoing and systematic." Writers often over-estimate the contribution of extra adjectives. Sometimes they add nuance and precision, but too often they add needless words and dilute the message.

Reducing Wordiness Example #3

Here is another sentence: Considerable fragmentation of the curriculum and inconsistency of instructional delivery have resulted from the absence of sufficient collegial planning opportunities during the school day.

(1) Who/what is the actor? The sentence has no concrete actor (passive form). Its subject is a concept:
> fragmentation of the curriculum and inconsistency of instructional delivery

(2) What is the core action? The action is passive, in the phrase: have resulted from

(3) Can an actor be put into the subject of the sentence and before the action? Yes, but this requires creating an actor ("our schedule") and an active verb ("prevents"):
> Our master schedule prevents collegial planning…

(4) What words and phrases can be removed?
> absence of sufficient collegial planning opportunities during the school day → Our master schedule prevents collegial planning…

> Considerable fragmentation of the curriculum and inconsistency of instructional delivery → fragmented curriculum and inconsistent instruction

(5) Can you write more concise versions of the sentence?

- Our master schedule prevents collegial planning, resulting in fragmented curriculum and inconsistent instruction.
- Because our master schedule prevents collegial planning, our curriculum is fragmented and instruction is inconsistent.
- Our teachers have no time for collegial planning; the result is fragmented curriculum and inconsistent instruction.
- Our teachers have no common planning time; consequently our curriculum is fragmented and instruction is inconsistent.

Additional comments on example #3. Avoid overloading sentences with abstractions. Too many abstract words in a sentence impede comprehension. The original sentence has *four* different key ideas: "master schedule," "collegial planning," "fragmented curriculum," and "inconsistent instruction." This is a lot for one sentence. Strung together these abstractions create a sentence impeding comprehension. If the sentence is followed by more overloaded sentences, the reader's cognitive processing gets bogged down.

Reducing Wordiness Example #4

Here are two sentences: The concern of declining physical activity in children must be addressed by every educator and educational institution. Physical activity interventions must be promoted that address this looming crisis of children's physical fitness.

(1) Who/what is the actor? "Educators" (mentioned in the first sentence) are the main actor in the above passage. The second sentence has no actor. The reader might infer an actor based on the prior sentence.

(2) What is the core action? There are several passive verb phrases.
    must be addressed
    must be promoted
    address this looming crisis

(3) Can the actor (subject) be put before the action? Here is the author's main message: The author *wants educators to promote more physical activity among schoolchildren*, but dilutes this message with passive verb phrases and wordiness.

(4) What words and phrases can be removed?
    educator and educational institution → educators OR schools OR we [if readers are educators]
    must be addressed/promoted → [delete]

(5) Can you write more concise versions of the sentence?

- Children's physical fitness has declined. Unless we strengthen physical education in schools, we will face a health crisis.

125

- Educators must promote more physical activity among children; if not, their fitness will suffer.
- Schools need more physical education programs to prevent a fitness crisis among today's youth.

Additional comments on example #4. Each revised sentence is clearer than the original. The first revised sentence emphasizes children's fitness decline; the second and third start with the need for, respectively, "educators" and "schools" to act. Note, also, that the first sentence uses "we," making author and readers part of the same community. The author must decide the appropriate version based on context and rhetorical aims.

Length and Variation of Sentences

Sentence Length

How long should sentences be?   On average, about 20-22 word sentences are found in more complex prose; shorter ones in simpler prose. "More complex" refers to policy arguments, position papers, grant proposals, analytical reports; "simpler" refers to descriptions of events and procedures.

Here are some sample sentence lengths:

- A 2200 word section from *Horace's Compromise* – 19 words/sentence.
- A 2500 word section from *Understanding By Design* – 20 words/sentence.
- An 1800 word section from a popular textbook on educational administration is 21 words/sentence.
- A 10,000 word feature article in *NY Times Magazine* is 24 words/sentence. (This article is written by an experienced book author.)
- A 1500 word *NY Times* article discussing recent brain research is 20 words/sentence.
- An 830 word *NY Times* editorial on the U.S. census is 24 words/sentence.
- A 450 word *NY Times* editorial on defense spending is 21 words/sentence.

Sentence Variation

Vary the length of your sentences to reduce monotony. Few reading experiences are more mind-numbing than reading one long sentence after another, especially if the sentences are complex, grammatically similar, and passively constructed.

Short, Punchy Sentences

Short sentences have more impact. They give punch to your prose. They grab the reader's attention. But don't overdo it.

It is not the writing is always better with shorter sentences. Any feature of style, over-used, loses effectiveness.

Analyze well written academic prose and you will see plenty of long sentences. What you will not see, for the most part, because experienced writers have learned to avoid the composition of sentences that are complicated in structure and protracted in length, are sentences that have lots of qualifiers, redundancies, dependent clauses, prepositional phrases, and nominalizations or other types of grammatical and lexical features that impede the reader's ability to comprehend and understand the meaning that they are intending to convey with their message. Whew! Don't write sentences like that. Long sentences are fine, if well constructed. But give the reader a break now and then. Add some short sentences.

PART 5
WORD CHOICES

Mark Twain wrote, "The difference between the almost right word and the right word is really a large matter – it's the difference between the lightning bug and the lightning." For most of us most of the time, our word choices lack consequences of the magnitude Twain implies, but word choices matter.

This section is about choosing and using *key words* carefully. Key words are the main ideas central to and repeated throughout a message. Should you call something an initiative, a project, or an innovation? Should you urge higher standards or greater rigor? Should you call attention to a personnel problem, a human resources issue, a productivity shortfall, substandard performance, a weak link, or something else?

When we communicate with others – conversing, presenting, writing – 95% of the words are automatic. But the remaining 5% are chosen words, and they can be pivotal, especially in professional interactions, and especially in leadership contexts. Choose these key words carefully. The 5% of words that are key have 95% of the impact. Be thoughtful and deliberate in your word choices, and expand your vocabulary. In this section I stress two principles: meaning and consistency.

Meanings and Connotations of Key Words:
Concepts, Labels, And Jargon

Education, like all fields, has its own professional lexicon. Consider the thousands of entries in the *Encyclopedia of American Education* (Unger, 2007). Table 5.7 has a few dozen examples. Words like these fill education discourse, but many of them lack precise meanings.

Table 5.7
Examples of Education Terminology

alignment	distributed leadership	multiple intelligences
at-risk student	exceptionalities	outcomes-based
authentic assessment	experiential learning	phonics
block scheduling	formative assessment	purpose-driven
community engagement	high stakes testing	remedial learning
competency-based instruction	inclusion	schemas
constructivist learning	learning community	spiral curriculum
cooperative learning	learning styles	standards based curriculum
curriculum integration	manipulatives	technology integration
differentiated instruction	mastery learning	whole language

Specialized terms are essential to define a community and enable communication, but they mean different things to different people. Remember that it is your audience's interpretation of words that matters. Here is an example of differing interpretations producing complications.

Several elementary schools were involved in a project to strengthen their science curriculum. "Formative assessments" were an integral part of the curriculum. These assessments came with a curriculum package, along with a variety of other instructional materials for students to conduct inquiries and experiments, do presentations, and write reports. Formative assessments are not tests in the conventional sense; they are more like diagnostic instruments to monitor student learning and design lessons so *all* students learn the intended science concepts (Black & Wiliam, 2004; Stiggins, 2004; Wiliam, 2006). This term is widely recognized and used in academic literature. Project leaders assumed most teachers understood the term as well.

A project like this creates communications challenges. Many people are involved, dispersed among different schools, and isolated in classrooms. The curriculum is unfamiliar and the teachers vary in experience, commitment to the project, and understanding of science.

The formative assessments ended up being used like tests by many of the teachers. They saw or heard the word "assessment" – and to them, that meant "test." Instead of using these formative assessments to reveal students' conceptual development and design instruction, many teachers used them as end-of-unit exams to assign grades and mark the completion of the unit. A central objective of the project was lost on many teachers.

As this case shows, if a group in a project does not have a common understanding of terms, miscommunication and misconceptions can create problems.

In organizational communications, people choose words to label complex ideas. Every chapter of this book, and the title itself, reflects word choices. In developing problem definitions, I use the word "gap." "Deviation" is another alternative. The material in Chapter 2 on "TLO/TMO" statements reflects other word choices. In writing or speaking contexts, think carefully about your audience in deciding the key words you choose.

Academic writers often try to coin terms calculated for effect. One notable example is "Shopping Mall High School," the 1985 book title by Powell, Farrar, and Cohen. The title speaks volumes and was memorable. The book was a highly influential best seller – not just because of the title, though. The argument was compelling and evidence based; the narrative, well crafted. But a great title helped immeasurably.

"Authentic assessment," coined in 1988 (Archbald & Newmann, 1988), defined a new category of assessment. The term is simple, catchy, and has favorable connotations. "Authentic testing" would not be as popular – many people have ambivalent feelings about the word "test." Authentic has connotations of real, genuine, and legitimate. By implication, other forms of assessment – namely standardized tests – are less authentic.

Authentic assessment as a concept was quickly embraced in the field of education. Authentic assessment projects sprung up in schools and districts throughout the country. The term helped educators think in new ways and more deeply about the goals and outcomes of instruction, about how to measure outcomes, and about the different purposes of assessment. Key words can inspire action, create a vision, label an initiative, and give meaning to participants.

Political communicators know this well. They give pleasant labels to policies and principles they favor and pejorative labels to those they oppose. Political opponents of inheritance taxes called them "death taxes" in press releases, speeches, and congressional deliberations. The coal industry, concerned about associations of coal burning with air pollution, now uses the term "clean coal" in advertising and public service announdements.

Key words combined into phrases – catch phrases – also can be influential if used well. Advertisers and political communicators rely heavily on catch phrases to inspire and motivate. Frank Luntz (2007), an author and political communications strategist, gives some examples:[63]

> **"If you remember only one thing..."** is the surest way to guarantee that voters will remember the one point that matters most to you. This is essential in complicated situations like the upcoming debt ceiling vote.
>
> **"Let's get to work"** was employed by Florida Governor Rick Scott in his successful campaign. No other end-of-speech rallying cry is more motivational to voters.
>
> **"Uncompromising integrity."** Of all the truthiness words, none is as powerful as "integrity," but in today's cynical environment, even that's not enough. People also need to feel that your integrity is absolute.
>
> **"No excuses."** Of all the messages used by America's business and political elite, no phrase better conveys accountability, responsibility and transparency. This phrase generates immediate respect and appreciation.

Word choices matter. Well-chosen words can enhance a message's appeal and make it stick.[64] But we are not just politicians and advertisers – words must mean something too. The term "authentic assessment" has been central to many change initiatives in schools, but not all successful. Why? Because the label itself is not enough – as the formative assessment case illustrates. In organizational leadership communications (unlike advertising and politics), if there is little substantive meaning behind the message then the communicator is mainly trafficking in slogans. You must be able to "walk the walk," not just "talk the talk."

Understand the meaning of the words you choose. You have to know what you are talking about. You have to know, as the expression goes, what it "looks like" in practice. Know the theory behind the word and the research behind the theory. You should be able to explain this to others. If you can't, you lose credibility and risk misunderstandings and miscommunication.

---

[63] http://www.huffingtonpost.com/frank-luntz/words-2011_b_829603.html

[64] Heath and Heath (2008) is an informative and readable text with many interesting examples.

Consistency and Repetition in Usage

Consistency is another important principle. When you choose key words, use them consistently. Inconsistent usage is confusing. If you call something "a project" in one portion of a message, don't call it "an initiative" a few plater.

Consider a proposal to develop online instruction. What should be the key term: web-based training? web-based courses? distance learning? technology utilization in education? online instruction? All are possibilities. If terms are inconsistent, the reader gets confused and the message gets diluted.

Imagine you are a high school educator. Your concern is with the number of students who are bored and listless in class. What do you call the problem? Different word choices have different meanings and connotations. Some terms are descriptive, focusing on the behavior without suggesting a cause, while other terms go further to suggest an underlying causal condition.

"Academic disengagement" is one choice. This term describes a condition, but does not suggest a cause. The term apathy is similar in this way. On the other hand, terms like "unmotivated" or "alienated" or "disillusioned" imply underlying causal states. The word to choose is the one that succinctly captures your concern, is memorable, and has the meanings you wish to convey.

Consider carefully your choices for key words. Use the literature as a guide. Decide on key words that label your problem, key causal variables, or key conditions and goal states. The more complicated a problem or initiative is and the more people involved, the greater the need for consistency in word usage.

If you are precise and consistent in your terminology, you increase the probability of achieving your objectives. On the other hand, you risk confusion and miscommunication when you misuse words, are inconsistent in usage (changing your terminology at different times, places, or portions of the message) or choose words that are vague and imprecise.

SUMMARY AND CONCLUDING COMMENTS

Seek first to understand, then to be understood.

Covey (1989)

Key Points

Most of this book is on the first part of Covey's adage – about understanding the problem. But when it is time for action, communicate to be understood.

Prose that is hard to understand undermines your purposes. Audiences cannot buy into your message if they have difficulty understanding it. Figure out exactly what your message is, organize your key ideas, and follow the principles and tools of effective communications.

- Remember the "first 30 seconds rule" – state your purpose quickly and prominently.
- Preview main ideas in introductions.

130

- Use structural and conceptual organizers; put your ideas into coherent, easy-to-discern chunks.
- Use graphics to represent ideas visually and to show connections among ideas.
- Avoid series of lengthy paragraphs.
- Avoid series of lengthy, complex sentences.
- Avoid sentences with long subjects before getting to the verb.
- Favor simplicity and directness.

If possible, use active voice. In writing and revising, ask yourself:

- Who/what is the actor?
- What is the core action?
- Can you put the actor before the action?
- Can you remove words and phrases?
- Can you write more concise versions of the sentence?

Words are powerful – politicians, advertisers know this; good leaders understand this. Good communicators:

- have a clear understanding of the objectives they want to achieve with their messages,
- understand the precise denotative and connotative meanings of words,
- develop an expansive and functional vocabulary,
- use words and craft sentences effectively to achieve their objectives.

Becoming a better writer requires recognizing your communications liabilities:

- You know what you want to say, but the reader does not.
- You know your own ideas and intentions; the reader has only the words you offer.
- You write slowly, mulling over your ideas and words and continually reinforcing your own understanding. The reader reads quickly with uneven attention.

Learning to write well takes time. You will not improve unless you reflect on and revise your writing. Reread your own material with a critical mindset; after a few days or weeks (depending on how much time you have), you can look at your own writing with more of a reader's perspective. Reread something you wrote a year or two ago. This can be eye-opening. Get feedback from other readers.

Being a critical reader helps you improve as a writer: don't just passively absorb the information you read. Reflect on the author's decisions of organization and style. These processes – reflection, revision, feedback, and critical reading – are essential to improve writing.

Over time, you will write better and faster. First drafts will need less revision. The guidelines of this chapter will help you improve immediately. How quickly you progress will depend on your starting point and how much you write. There is no end-point. Improvement is a life-long project.

Thinking, Writing, and Communicating

Chapters 1 through 4 addressed the analytical and empirical side of problem solving. I have concluded this book with a chapter on communications because writing helps your thinking and because action in organizations requires words and images.

Communications through writing disciplines your thinking. With just talk, vague ideas and fuzzy logic produce misunderstandings and bad decisions. In writing, fuzziness and vagueness are harder to hide. If you write your logic, your reasoning, your rationales and plans and get critical feedback from others, you will benefit. With time and experience the clarity and power of your ideas will improve; you will use language more effectively to inform and motivate. On this reciprocity between writing and thinking, George Orwell (1946, p.1) wrote:

> [The English language] …becomes ugly and inaccurate because our thoughts are foolish, but the slovenliness of our language makes it easier for us to have foolish thoughts.'

Problem solving and organizational improvement are group work. In real-life there is minimal separation between the "knowledge component" and the "communications component" when acting on problems and solutions. You may have deep and comprehensive knowledge about a situation, but unless you have 100% control over all aspects of problem solving – and ill-structured problems are nothing like this – you have to be able to communicate effectively with others and others with you. You cannot transmit your understanding directly into the minds of others. If your ideas are muddled, they lose power to motivate and guide.

Although there is literature aplenty on writing, graphics, and presenting, it is a "generic" literature. It does not reflect the language of education, leadership, and organizational problem solving. Thus, this chapter is a contribution to fill that gap.

REFERENCES

Archbald, D. & Newmann, F. (1988). *Beyond standardized testing: Assessing authentic academic achievement in the secondary school*. Reston VA: NASSP.

Black, P. & Wiliam, D. (2004). Classroom assessment is not (necessarily) formative assessment (and vice-versa). *Yearbook of the National Society for the Study of Education, 103*(2), 183-8.

Bransford, J., Brown, A., & Cocking, R. (1999). *How people learn: Brain, mind, experience, and school*. Washington, D.C.: National Academy Press

Buckner, R., Raichle, M., Miezin, F., & Petersen, S. (1996). Functional anatomic studies of memory retrieval for auditory words and visual pictures. *Journal of Neuroscience, 16*(19), 6219 – 6235.

Covey, S. (1989). *The 7 habits of highly effective people*. NY: Simon & Schuster.

Grady, C., McIntosh, A., Rajah, M., & Craik, F. (1998). Neural correlates of the episodic encoding of pictures and words. *Proceedings of the National Academy of Sciences, 95*(5), March, 2703-2708.

Heath,C. & Heath, D. (2008). *Made to stick: Why some ideas survive and others die.* NY : Random House.

Jensen, E. (2005). *Teaching with the brain in mind.* Alexandria, VA: ASCD.

Joffe, V., Cain, K., & Maric, N. (2007). Comprehension problems in children with specific language impairment: Does mental imagery training help? *International Journal of Language & Communication Disorders, 42*(6), November, 648-664.

Lanham, R. (2006). *Revising Prose* (5th Edition). Upper Saddle River, NJ: Prentice Hall.

Larkin, J. & Simon, H. (1987). Why a diagram is (sometimes) worth 10,000 words. *Cognitive Science, 11*, 65-100.

Luntz, F. (2007). *Words that work.* NY: Hyperion.

Mayer, R., Heiser, J., & Lonn, S. (2001). Cognitive constraints on multimedia learning: When presenting more material results in less understanding. *Journal of Educational Psychology, 93*(1), 187 – 198.

Munter, M. (2012). *Guide to managerial communication.* Upper Saddle River, NJ: Prentice Hall.

Nesbit, J. & Olusola, A. (2006). Learning with concept and knowledge maps: A meta-analysis. *Review of Educational Research, 76*(3), 413-448.

Orwell, G. (1946). Politics and the English language. *Horizon, 13*(76), April, 252-265.

Pearsall, T. (2009). *The elements of technical writing.* Boston: Pearson.

Powell, A., Farrar, E., & Cohen, D. (1985). *The shopping mall high school: Winners and losers in the educational marketplace.* Houghton Mifflin

Robinson, D. (1998). Graphic organizers as aids to text learning. *Reading Research and Instruction, 37*, Winter, 85-105.

Rotondo, J. & Rotondo, M. (2002). *Presentation skills for managers.* NY: McGraw-Hill.

Standing, L., Conezio, J., & Haber, R. N. (1970). Perception and memory for pictures: Single-trial learning of 2500 visual stimuli. *Psychonomic Science, 19*(2), 73-74.

Stiggins, R. J. (2004). *Classroom assessment for student learning: Doing it right, using it well.* Assessment Training Institute.

Unger, H. (2007). *Encyclopedia of American education (3rd edition).* NY: Facts On File.

Wiliam, D. (2006). Formative assessment: Getting the focus right. *Educational Assessment, 11*(3/4), 283-9.

Williams, J. (2007). *Style: Lessons in clarity and grace.* NY: Pearson Longman.

APPENDIX 2-A: EXAMPLE OF "ANECDOTAL EVIDENCE" (A DESCRIPTION OF INCONSISTENCY IN STANDARDS AND INSTRUCTION)

SOURCE: Page 9 from Smith, J., Lee, V., & Newmann, F. (2001). *Instruction and achievement in Chicago elementary schools.* Chicago: IL: Consortium for Chicago School Research.

It is 10:00 a.m. in a Chicago elementary school, time for language arts. In Classroom A, a third-grade teacher pronounces the vocabulary words for the day carefully and provides definitions for each word as she writes them on the board. After the students copy down the words and definitions, they turn to worksheets to practice using the new words in sentences. When the students have finished their worksheets, the teacher asks everyone to open their reading books to the same page, and the students take turns reading passages aloud. Toward the end of the lesson, the teacher draws students' attention to places in the story where the words are used, and asks yes/no questions to check comprehension.

In Classroom B, the teacher distributes lists of the same vocabulary words to her third graders. She divides the students into groups to undertake projects related to the words. One group uses the dictionary to locate definitions. Another group writes a story using the words. A third group develops a crossword puzzle, working up clues that will use the words as answers. When the groups complete these activities, they trade their results with one another, checking other students' work and critiquing the product. During the language arts period, the teacher moves from group to group, coordinating activities and providing assistance when students ask for help. Over the entire period, each group will be involved in each activity.

The content for these lessons is identical in both third-grade classrooms. That day's lesson plans for both teachers indicate that their classes are at exactly the same place in the year's progression of topics. The ways these lessons are taught in these two classrooms, however, differ dramatically. This comparison illustrates what has become a critical concern for school reform: how teachers should organize their lessons so that students will learn the knowledge and skills that the teachers wish to impart. The issue, in short, is how best to approach instruction to maximize student learning.

APPENDIX 2-B: OFFICIAL STATEMENTS OF "STANDARDS"

Below are links to "standards" documents in curriculum subjects and professional fields. The documents are developed by authoritative groups, prescribe best practices and desired learning outcomes, and can be useful for developing problem statements in papers and projects.

State Curriculum/Content/Achievement Standards are written expectations for student knowledge and achievement. Standards prescribe what students should know and be able to do by specified grade levels in each subject. See http://www.education-world.com/standards/state/index.shtml

National Educational Technology Standards (www.iste.org) describe model practices and proficiencies for uses of education technology in schools.

The National Staff Development Council has developed standards for professional development. Organized into 12 categories, they present a vision of the management, objectives, and resources required for an optimal professional development system within a school or district. (http://www.nsdc.org/standards/about/index.cfm).

National Board for Professional Teaching Standards are organized around five core propositions: commitment to student learning; mastery of subject matter knowledge; responsibility for managing and monitoring learning; systemic reflection on practice; participant in a learning community. (www.nbpts.org).

National Association for the Education of Young Children establishes standards and criteria for "best practices in the field and the benefits to stakeholders in early childhood education." http://www.naeyc.org/academy/primary/standardsintro

The National Association for Sports and Physical Education standards "define what a student should know and be able to do as result of a quality physical educa-tion program. These standards provide a framework for developing realistic and achievable expectations for student performance at every grade level." http://www.aahperd.org/naspe/standards/nationalstandards/

The Association of College and Research Libraries provides Information Literacy Competency Standards for Higher Education (http://www.ala.org/acrl/standards/informationliteracycompetency). In-formation literacy forms the basis for lifelong learning. It is common to all disciplines, to all learning environments, and to all levels of education. It en-ables learners to master content and extend their investigations, become more self-directed, and assume greater control over their own learning. An information literate individual is able to:

- Determine the extent of information needed
- Access the needed information effectively and efficiently
- Evaluate information and its sources critically
- Incorporate selected information into one's knowledge base
- Use information effectively to accomplish a specific purpose
- Understand the economic, legal, and social issues surrounding the use of information, and access and use information ethically and legally"

Title of Paper: **Implementing Formative Assessment in K-3 Science**
Problem: **We do not incorporate formative assessment enough in our science instruction**
Author: **Susan Jones**
Organizational Role: **Assistant Principal (former lead teacher), Clayton Elementary School**

Introduction and Problem Statement

Clayton Elementary School's teachers are trying to improve students' learning in science in the early elementary grades. Grades 3 and 5 achievement scores have been flat for five years. We believe scores can improve, but this will require curriculum modifications in the early grades.

We seek to improve our curriculum by collaborating to identify common grade level outcomes in science and by making instruction more individualized, less "whole class." A key means of doing this will be developing and using "formative assessments."

Formative assessment refers to student-level progress monitoring for the purpose of short term – next day or next week – instructional planning (Black, Harrison, Lee, Marshall, & Wiliam 2003; Borich & Tombari, 2004; Kennedy, Long & Camins, 2009). Formative assessment is especially focused on those students who lag behind their peers – students who are falling short of grade level achievement standards (Chapman & King, 2005; Goertz, Oláh & Riggan, 2009; Simpkins, Mastropieri & Scruggs, 2009).

We are all familiar with "summative" assessments – tests used to assign grades. Students take a test at the end of a unit and are awarded a grade. After the test, the class moves on to the next unit. This is assessment *of* learning and should be distinguished from assessment *for* learning as noted by Stiggins, Arter, Chappuis, and Chappuis (2004). These experts on assessment characterize assessment for learning by questions the learner asks him/herself and seven strategies as shown in Table 1.

Formative assessments are designed to provide *immediate* data to guide the teacher and student during the learning process. It is *during* the instruction and learning process that teachers need information to adapt and differentiate and individualize instruction and to improve learning, especially when they have a diverse classroom (Chapman & King, 2005).

Stiggins et al. (2004) give examples of formative assessment in ways that involve students in assessment *for* learning:

- Review anonymous work samples of strong and weak student work
- Elicit suggestions from students about criteria for work done well

Table 1
Formative Assessment: Questions and Strategies for the Learner

Where am I going?
1. Provide clear learning targets
2. Use examples of strong and weak student work

Where am I now?
3. Offer regular descriptive feedback
4. Teach students to self-assess and set goals

How can I close the gap?
5. Design lessons to focus on one aspect at a time.
6. Teach students focused revision
7. Engage students in self-reflection, and let them keep track of and share their learning

136

- Create scoring guides with clearly defined gradations of quality
- Give students numerous opportunities to practice scoring work with the scoring guide they created
- Revise anonymous work samples

In this kind of activity, as students gain experience in scoring work samples, they increase their ability to evaluate their own work. Then, revision allows students to go beyond evaluating work to actually using the criteria to improve quality and promote learning. This is an example of one kind of strategy we need to explore.

Some teachers are doing formative assessment already to some degree, but these efforts are not coordinated and there is inconsistency from one classroom to the next. I know this having been a teacher and I know this is not something most teachers routinely do – especially in the difficult subject of science. I know this also because of my years doing classroom observations here. Research shows this kind of variability among classrooms, though not uncommon in elementary schools, indicates a gap between models of standards-based curriculum and common practices at the classroom level (Corey, Phelps, Ball, Demonte, & Harrison, 2012; Rowan, Harrison, & Hayes, 2004).

In typical science instruction, assessment is in the form of periodic end-of-unit tests. Science instruction is usually done as whole-class instruction – reading, listening to the teacher, watching demonstrations, or doing seatwork, such as worksheets or silent reading (e.g., "friction" or "evaporation"). Occasionally, students do hands-on activities. After a 3 to 4 week unit, the students take a test, consisting of multiple choice questions, true-false, fill in the blank, or short answer questions. Then the class moves on to the next unit. Black and Wiliam (1998a) cite shortcomings with sole reliance on summative assessments:

> When the classroom culture focuses on rewards, "gold stars," grades, or class ranking, then pupils look for ways to obtain the best marks rather than to improve their learning. One reported consequence is that, when they have any choice, pupils avoid difficult tasks. They also spend time and energy looking for clues to the "right answer." Indeed, many become reluctant to ask questions out of a fear of failure. Pupils who encounter difficulties are led to believe that they lack ability, and this belief leads them to attribute their difficulties to a defect in themselves about which they cannot do a great deal (p.143).

Furthermore, we have not had a habit of collaborating on instructional improvement – particularly in the areas of testing and assessment. There has not been much discussion in the past on learning objectives, planning curriculum, and developing common assessments. Not surprisingly, as you might expect, curriculum and assessment practices vary a lot from classroom to classroom. Here are what I see as some specific gaps:

- We lack clear grade level science learning objectives. For the most part, instruction is driven by text materials, rather than by clear standards-based learning objectives. A few years ago, a district-supported audit reported that grade level academic objectives at the elementary level have not been clearly specified and there was little curriculum coordination between grades. This isn't good for building a coherent curriculum and giving all our students the prerequisite knowledge they need as they move from one grade and subject to the next.

- Some formative assessments have been provided, but so far not used much. We have been supplied with instructional kits in science, which include embedded instructional tasks and assessments, but these have not been used much, and, as I pointed out earlier, when they are used, it is variable from teacher to teacher – that is, not with joint planning or sharing of knowledge and practices.

- Finally, I have not seen much evidence of student self-assessment: Peer and student self-assessment is urged by leading experts, but has not been used systematically in Clayton (Leahy, 2005; Kennedy, Long, & Camins, 2009).

Purposes and Goals

This will be a multi-year process – developing common assessments, discussing outcomes, and strengthening our ability to differentiate and individualize instruction. This will improve our students' learning and development in science.

I believe we can achieve a 15 point increase in the percentage of students reaching grade level standards within two years. Research on formative assessment finds effect sizes ranging from .4 to .7 standard deviations suggesting that goal is attainable (Black & Wiliam, 1998b; White & Fredricksen, 1998). On our own curriculum-based assessments we do not have yet a baseline measure, but we can establish one to measure progress over the next several years.

I will work to make sure there is ample scheduled time for planning meetings and that you have access to help literature, training opportunities, and curriculum resources need to make this go forward.

Key Questions and Tasks

How clear, specific, shared, and standards-aligned are our grade level achievement objectives?

Tasks:
- review and identify effective curriculum mapping and alignment tools
- review state science standards
- compare standards with the curriculum plan for science in each classroom
- identify units and lessons that lack alignment
- choose units from instructional kits to use in each grade

Information sources:
- State Content Standards
- State Science Comprehensive Assessment Program
- Shepardson (2001); Wiggins & McTighe (2005)
- "Survey of Enacted Curriculum" web-based curriculum mapping tool

What models and methods of formative assessment are "best practices"?

We will review leading publications in formative assessment, including: Black, Harrison, Lee, Marshall, & Wiliam (2003); Buck & Trauth-Nare (2009); Enger & Yager (2001); Shepardson (2001); and Stiggins (2005).

How can we improve our use of available student data and reports to monitor student progress and plan instructional interventions?

Issue: most teachers not proficient with accessing and using current data systems. Student data is available electronically through web-accessible queries and reports.

Goal: teachers need to know how use these data systems more effectively.

Tasks: provide training/support; collect and analyze data from the formative assessments and develop a process to go from "results" to "action."

What is the best way to provide ongoing training and support for teachers?

Issue: How to use the time and resources we have to design an optimal system of support?

Three main resources we have: (a) regular planning time (collegial support), (b) periodic workshops in which district or outside trainers are used, and (c) web-based support through which we can organize and access our own information.

Tasks and information needed:
- identify web-based "group productivity" tools and as a group we will review these and select one to use.
- literature: Buck & Trauth-Nare (2009) and Shepardson (2001).

What should be the components of the system to manage and evaluate progress of our initiative?

- Develop a web-based project site to provide information, coordinate planning, schedule meetings, discuss issues
- Develop a timeline with objectives
- Develop a way to evaluate our progress based on (a) assessing progress in relation to project objectives and on (b) assessing student outcomes.
- Seek additional resources from within district or outside sources to support this initiative

Reference List

Black, P., Harrison, C., Lee, C., Marshall, B., & Wiliam, D. (2003) *Assessment for learning: putting it into practice.* New York, NY: McGraw-Hill.

Black, P. & Wiliam, D. (1998a). Inside the black box: Raising standards through classroom assessment. *Phi Delta Kappan, 80*(2) 139-147.

Black, P. & Wiliam, D (1998b). Assessment and classroom learning. *Assessment in Education, 5*(1), 7-71.

Borich, G. & Tombari, M. (2004) *Educational assessment for the elementary and middle school classroom.* Upper Saddle River, NJ: Prentice Hall.

Buck, G. & Trauth-Nare, A. (2009). Preparing teachers to make the formative assessment process integral to science teaching and learning. *Journal of Science Teacher Education 20*(5), October, 475-94.

Chapman, C. & King, R. (2005). *Differentiated assessment strategies: One tool doesn't fit all*. Thousand Oaks, CA: Corwin Press.

Corey, D., Phelps, G., Ball, D., Demonte, J., & Harrison, D. (2012). Explaining variation in instructional time: An application of quantile regression. *Educational Evaluation & Policy Analysis, 34*(2), 146-163.

Enger, S. &Yager, R. (2001) *Assessing student understanding in science*. Thousand Oaks, CA: Corwin Press

Goertz, M., Oláh, L., & Riggan , M. (2009). *Can interim assessments be used for instructional change?* (CPRE Policy Briefs, RB-51, available on-line).

Kennedy, C., Long, K., & Camins, A. (2009). The reflective assessment technique. *Science and Children 4(*4), December, 50-3.

Leahy, S., Lyon, C., Thompson, M. & Wiliam, D. (2005). Classroom assessment: Minute by minute, day by day. *Educational Leadership, (63)*3, 19-24.

Rowan, B., Harrison, D. & Hayes, H. (2004). Using instructional logs to study mathematics curriculum and teaching in the early grades. *Elementary School Journal, 105*(1), 103-127.

Shepardson, D (Ed.) (2001). *Assessment in science: A guide to professional development and classroom practice*. Boston: Kluwer Academic Publishers.

Simpkins, P. M., Mastropieri, M., Scruggs, T. (2009). Differentiated curriculum enhancements in inclusive fifth-grade science classes. *Remedial and Special Education, 30,*(5), 300-8.

Stiggins, R. (2005). *Student-involved assessment for learning*. Upper Saddle River, NJ: Prentice-Hall, Inc.

Stiggins, R., Arter, J., Chappuis, J. & Chappuis, S. (2004). *Classroom assessment for student learning: Doing it right – using it well*. Portland, OR: Pearson Assessment Training Institute, CD-ROM.

White, B. & Fredricksen, J. (1998). Inquiry, modeling, and metacognition: Making science accessible to all students. *Cognition and Instruction, 16*(1), 3-118.

Wiggins, G. & McTighe, J. (2005). Understanding by design. Upper Saddle River, NJ: Pearson.

Title of Paper: **Non-Graduating Seniors – A Problem at Marshall High School**
Problem: **Too many seniors fail to graduate**
Author: **Jane Reynolds**
Organizational Role: **Principal, Marshall High School**

Too Many Seniors Get Close To Graduating, But Don't

This year in early May, 310 seniors thought they would graduate in June from Marshall High School.   The 34 that didn't had received notification during May that they were ineligible to graduate due to various academic deficiencies.   Table 1 shows figures from that last four year – an average end-of-year loss of approximately 13% of the senior class.

Table 1
Non-Graduating Seniors: Last Four Years

School Year	# Eligible	# Graduated	# Loss	% Loss
This yr	310	276	34	11%
Last yr	295	254	41	14%
2 yrs ago	275	241	34	12%
3 yrs ago	314	268	46	15%

SOURCE: Marshall High School Guidance and Records Office

At Marshall, as it is with all high schools, not everyone who starts in 9th grade graduates. Some transfer and others drop out. For some students there is little the school can do to prevent their dropping out. Their personal problems or challenges are too great. However, it is very disappointing when students don't graduate despite being on track well into their senior year. Over the last four years, 155 Marshall students have reached 12th grade and not graduated.

This level of attrition is unacceptable. Families suffer and so does the community. While we need to tackle the full scope of issues related to dropping out, this paper and project focuses on a narrower problem – "senior non-graduation."

Project Purpose and Improvement Goal
Studying Senior Non-graduation and Possible Remedies

The improvement goal is to lower the yearly percentage of seniors who fail to graduate and to do this in a way that does not compromise our academic achievement standards. Research on dropout prevention programs and strategies will guide this initiative.

We should aim to reduce the percentage of nongraduating seniors by half. This goal is ambitious but I think reasonable given that well designed dropout prevention programs often produce 30% to 40% reductions of dropout rates. One review of dropout prevention programs concluded, "Using an average control group dropout rate of 21%, the mean odds ratio for the general programs translates into a dropout rate of 13% for the program groups" (Wilson, Tanner-Smith, Lipsey, Steinka-Fry, & Morrison, 2011, p. 49). This level of reduction in dropouts compares favorably with interventions reviewed by Prevatt and Kelly (2003) and by Cobb, Sample, Alwell, and Johns (2005). Since my focus here is on students *who have already become seniors*, it is reasonable to expect success rates better than those of typical dropout programs that deal with all students.

This project will investigate causes of and contributors to the seniors' academic struggles that prevent them from graduating. Based on this investigation we will develop plans to address this problem.

Causes of Non-Graduation

Before we can determine what to do, we need to explore the conditions or practices that may contribute to non-graduation. As a way to frame our investigation of this problem we can draw on research on dropping out and non-graduation. Even though the two problems may have somewhat different causes, they are not unrelated. Table 2 summarizes key findings from a recent study based on a survey and focus groups with a national sample of 16 – 25 year olds who had dropped out.

As Table 2 and other studies show (Alivernini & Lucidi, 2011; Bridgeland, Dilulio, & Morison, 2006; Menzer & Hampel, 2009), there are many reasons students drop out or fail to finish high school in four years. We will need to look at factors related to parental support, course curriculum, and in-school support from teachers and counselors. Also, we will need to review what more we can do to monitor student progress in academics, attendance, and other areas that may affect their likelihood of graduating or not graduating.

I will study this problem, enlist the participation and support of colleagues, and make recommendations. The recommendations will likely focus on having a better system to identify potential non-graduates and target appropriate support so that they get the help they need to graduate on time.

Table 2

Some Highlights from National Study of Dropouts

The dropouts in the study identified five major reasons for leaving school. They were bored with school (47 percent); had missed too many days and could not catch up (43 percent); spent time with people who were not interested in school (42 percent); had too much freedom and not enough rules in their lives (38 percent); and were failing (35 percent).

• A majority of students said that they were not motivated to work hard, but that they would have worked harder had their teachers demanded more. Seventy percent believed that they could have graduated if they had tried.

• Many students gave personal reasons for leaving school, which included the need to get a job, parenthood, or having to care for family members.

• Nearly half (45 percent) noted that earlier schooling had poorly prepared them for high school.

• Close to three-quarters of the students (71 percent) indicated that they started becoming disinterested in high school as early as 9th and 10th grades. Students noted that they would often go to school late, take long lunches, or skip classes or school entirely. Parents didn't oversee their child's attendance. Only one-fifth of parents were "very" involved in their child's schooling. Many [of the parents] were involved for discipline – and not instructional – purposes.

• Most students expressed regret for having dropped out of school. Eighty-one percent said that graduating from high school was important to success in life. Seventy-four percent said that if they could relive the experience, they would have stayed in school.

Source: Bridgeland, Dilulio, & Morison (2006).

Plan To Address the Problem of Non-Graduating Seniors:
Key Questions and Tasks

I propose the following inquiries and steps to work toward solutions to the nongraduation problem. This plan is preliminary and may evolve over time as we get more information and move forward with solutions.

Can we identify sooner and more accurately potential non-graduates?

The earlier we can identify students at risk for nongraduation, the earlier and more effectively we can provide help. Three sources of information will be useful: school data, people, and literature.

   School data. Based on school data from the past several years, I will explore developing a set of indicators (predictors) to identify seniors most at-risk of not graduating. I want to determine if we have data to create a reporting system to identify students at risk of not graduating. This will require technical assistance from district data specialists.

Table 3
Data Sources to Identify Predictors of Non-graduation

Data Source	Student and School Records Information
e-Data Sys	attendance, race, transcripts, current grades, school history, retention record
Data Center	test scores, discipline record
Cumulative File	activity participation, grades, educational testing results
Report Card	past teachers, class attendance, teacher comments
Guidance Office Records	student interventions, parent contacts
School Archives	guidance, intervention team, achievement team meeting minutes, free and reduce lunch status

   Table 3 lists the complete set of data sources to draw on. The electronic databases are reliable sources of student information because they are the school and district's primary reporting mechanism for federal and state school accountability measures. In addition are the data sources in school records with more information on students and programs.

   Two products will result from this initiative: (a) An assessment of our data system and its ability to give us actionable "early identification" information. (b) Recommendations to improve semester by semester monitoring of individual student progress toward graduation and to identify potential non-graduates.

   Consulting with teachers and students. I will talk with teachers and about six to eight students who were supposed graduate but failed to do so. We need to learn more about why some students falter toward the end of their high school program and don't graduate. The teacher interviews will be in a focus group format – three focus groups of 4 teachers apiece. The purpose of these discussions will be to ask "what happened?" and "what, if anything, could have been done differently so that they would have graduated?"

   Literature on high school drop outs. The first step of my literature search has identified the following papers to synthesize findings on predictors and the characteristics of delayed graduation and dropping out. Reviewing this literature will improve my understanding of this topic, help us know better what to look for in identifying at-risk students, and guide the design of interventions.

- Almedia, Johnson, & Steinberg (2006).
- Alivernini & Lucidi (2011).
- Bridgeland, Dilulio, & Morison (2006).
- Christle, Jolivette, & Nelson (2007).
- Legault, Green-Demers, & Pelletier (2006).
- Neild, Balfanz, & Herzog (2007).
- Rumberger (2004).
- Suh & Suh (2007).
- Swanson (2004).

How much are faculty aware of and concerned with non-graduation?

Reducing the numbers of non-graduates will require a team effort from teachers and guidance staff. Currently, it is not clear whether staff are aware of this problem. It is therefore important to assess staff views: What do they see as causes? What are their perceptions of the at-risk student? How do they assign responsibility for non-graduation and for efforts to prevent it? To what are they willing to commit time to address the problem given that affects a relatively small number of students.

I will develop a 10 minute online staff survey. Respondents will answer questions anonymously. The survey will ask respondents to identify their content area and seniority (in categories) to allow disaggregating results by these variables.

Several weeks after the survey information is obtained and analyzed, I will conduct an interactive presentation at a staff meeting. This will help raise awareness, assess attitudes, and gather more feedback. I will introduce the issue, present information, invite questions and comments, and ask for replies on index cards to a series of questions similar to those just described in the survey. The use of the index cards, collected at the end of the meeting, allows for open-ended statements of views and opinions.

How can we communicate to parents, students, and educators about the adverse consequences of not graduating?

When students in their senior year learn they are ineligible to graduate, it is a major setback and a shock to many students and parents. While some graduate eventually, others do not, and leave high school without a diploma.

When students fail to achieve a diploma, they lose out in many ways: economically, socially, and intellectually. Society also loses. "High school dropouts, on average, earn $9,200 less per year than high school graduates, and about $1 million less over a lifetime than college graduates. Students who drop out of high school are often unable to support themselves; high school dropouts were over three times more likely than college graduates to be unemployed in 2004. They are twice as likely as high school graduates to slip into poverty from one year to the next" (Bridgeland, Dilulio, & Morison, 2006, p. 2). One policy report estimates that dropouts from the Class of 2008 will cost the nation more than $319 billion in lost wages over the course of their lifetimes (AEE, 2008).

I will create a presentation and a parent letter communicating the serious consequences of not graduating for students. It will emphasize that students failing to earn a high school diploma are more likely to end up in lower-paying jobs, more likely to be unemployed, and less likely to become productive members of society. A program for at-risk students within the Chicago Public School system has parents sign a form acknowledging their understanding of consequences for students who do not graduate (see, "Use a form," 2004).

I will also create communications for the community to highlight negative consequences for the community and the community and the state, the purpose being to draw attention to the problem and create support for remedies.

We all have an interest in helping all our students graduate in four years, even if as individual staff members we do not feel a direct impact of dropouts. I will draw on the literature cited throughout this paper for support.

What specific interventions, incentives, or support systems have proven effective for keeping those at-risk of not graduating on a successful path to graduation? What evidence-based "best practices" are advocated in the literature?

I will review literature on student intervention models, drop-out prevention programs, and curriculum/instructional approaches related to improving high school graduation rates. Based on this I will produce a list of possible strategies to pursue.

The following literature will be consulted:

- Almedia, Johnson, & Steinberg (2006).
- Lehr, Clapper, & Thurlow (2005).
- Murphy, Beck, Crawford, Hodges, & McGaughy (2001).
- NASSP (2004).
- Powell, Farrar, & Cohen (1985).
- Sizer (2002).
- The Education Trust (2005).

Longer term planning concerning possible initiatives within the school to reduce the number of non-graduating seniors.

I will lead a planning committee to assess what is currently being done in the school and recommend ways to allocate appropriate resources and attention to the at-risk student. As a school we will need to implement some changes. To be effective, these changes will need appropriate resources and administrative support and may need to be formalized through policy changes. Solutions will likely involve a combination of early identification, strengthened incentives, and additional guidance and support for at-risk students. These will be the tasks of the planning committee.

Questions of interest are: What services and programs does Marshall offer seniors at-risk of not graduating? What could be key elements of a Marshall "senior graduation program?" How do the existing systems, programs, school culture and staff utilization need to change?

Reference List

AEE (2008). *The high cost of high school dropouts: What the nation pays for inadequate high schools.* Washington, DC: Alliance for Excellent Education.

Almedia, C., Johnson, C., & Steinberg, A. (2006). *Making good on a promise: What policymakers can do to support the educational persistence of dropouts.* Boston, MA: Jobs for the Future. [available online: www.jff.org/]

Alivernini, F., & Lucidi, F. (2011). Relationship between social context, self-efficacy, motivation, academic achievement, and intention to drop out of high school: A longitudinal study. *Journal of Educational Research, 104*(4), 241-252.

Bridgeland, J., Dilulio, J., & Morison, K. (2006). *The silent epidemic: Perspectives of high school dropouts.* A report by Civic Enterprises in association with Peter D. Hart Research Associates for the Bill & Melinda Gates Foundation. [available online: http://www.gatesfoundation.org]

Christle, C., Jolivette, K., & Nelson, C. (2007). School characteristics related to high school dropout rates. *Remedial and Special Education, 28*(6), November/December, 325-39.

Cobb, B., Sample, P., Alwell, M., & Johns, N. (2005). *Effective interventions in dropout prevention: A research synthesis. The effects of cognitive-behavioral interventions on dropout prevention for youth with disabilities.* Colorado State University, Fort Collins, CO: National Dropout Prevention Center for Students With Disabilities.

Lehr, C., Clapper, A, & Thurlow, M. (2005). *Graduation for all: A practical guide to decreasing school dropout.* Thousand Oaks, CA: Corwin Press.

Legault, L., Green-Demers, I., & Pelletier, L. (2006). Why do high school students lack motivation in the classroom? Toward an understanding of academic motivation and the role of social support. *Journal of Educational Psychology, 98*(3), August, 567-82.

Menzer, J. & Hampel, R. (2009). Lost at the last minute. *Phi Delta Kappan, 90*(9), 660-664.

Murphy, J., Beck, L., Crawford, M., Hodges, A. & McGaughy, C. (2001). *The productive high school: Creating personalized academic communities.* Thousand Oaks, CA: Corwin Press, Inc.

NASSP (2004). *Breaking ranks II: Strategies for leading high school reform.* Reston, VA: National Association of Secondary School Principals.

Neild, R., Balfanz, R., & Herzog, L. (2007). An early warning system. *Educational Leadership, 65*(2), 28-33.

Powell. A., Farrar, E. & Cohen, D. (1985). *The shopping mall high school: Winners and losers in the educational marketplace.* Boston, MA: Houghton Mifflin Company.

Prevatt, F., & Kelly, F. D. (2003). Dropping out of school: A review of intervention programs. *Journal of school psychology, 41*(5), 377-395.

Rumberger, R. (2004). Why students drop out of school. In *Dropouts in America: Confronting the graduation rate crisis* (pp. 131–155). Edited by G. Orfield. Cambridge, MA: Harvard Education Press.

Sizer, N. (2002). *Crossing the stage: Redesigning senior year.* Portsmouth, NH: Heinemann.

Suh, S., & Suh, J. (2007). Risk factors and levels of risk for high school dropouts. *Professional School Counseling, 10*(3), 297-306.

Swanson, C. (2004). *Who graduates? Who doesn't? A statistical portrait of public high school graduation, Class of 2001.* Washington, DC: The Urban Institute. [available online: www.urban.org/]

The Education Trust. (2005). *Gaining traction, gaining ground: How some high schools accelerate learning for struggling students.* [available online: www2.edtrust.org]

Use a form. (2004). Use a form that makes students think twice about dropping out. *Curriculum Review, 43*(9), 8-8.

Wilson, S., Tanner-Smith, E., Lipsey, M., Steinka-Fry, K., & Morrison, J. (2011). Dropout prevention and intervention programs: Effects on school completion and dropout among school-aged children and youth. *Campbell Systematic Reviews, 8.* [availale online: DOI: 10.4073/csr.2011.8]

Title of Paper: **Rising Suspension Rates: Investigating Causes and Remedies**
Problem: **Suspension rates have increased**
Author: **George Smith**
Organizational Role: **Principal, Valley High School**

Problem Statement

The first hints of a problem were when several teachers supervising the in-school suspension room commented that the room is too small and an assistant brought to my attention data indicating rising suspension rates over recent years. The teachers wanted a larger room or two different rooms so students couldn't sit too close and talk or disrupt each other. I knew from a previous year's report that suspensions had gone up.

I investigated with more data with help from a central office data specialist. I wanted figures from other schools in the district and per capita figures for more valid comparisons among different size schools and among year to year fluctuations. I decided on "suspensions per 100 students" computed as follows: "the number of incidents over the year resulting in a suspension" divided by the "total enrollment" multiplied by 100.

Table 1
Suspension Rates For VHS And Other High Schools

High School	2008	2009	2010	2011	2012
VHS*	16	17	24	26	30
Hamilton*	20	21	13	15	18
Jefferson*	18	19	15	18	24
Truman	8	6	8	12	10
Lincoln	16	22	14	20	16
Adams	10	13	15	13	11
All schools (ave. rate)	14.7	16.3	14.8	17.3	18.2

Cells show number of suspensions per 100 students (based on September 30 membership count). * Denotes demographically similar comparators.

Valley High School (VHS) referrals and suspension rates have indeed climbed over the last several years after a pattern of relative stability. The rates have trended upward in most schools, but our rates are higher and the increase over the last five years has been greater.

Our current annual suspension rate is 30 suspensions per 100 students. Two years ago it was 24 per 100; four years ago, 16. Rates seem to be trending upward in the district as a whole, but more at VHS. The three schools with asterisks are demographically similar.

Project Purpose

This project investigates causes of rising suspension rates in VHS and will provide recommendations for appropriate courses of action. Referral rates for suspensions have increased, but it is not clear why.

We need to determine whether student behavior has worsened, and if so, why; and whether teachers have a clear and accurate understanding of the school's discipline code and disciplinary referral procedures. We will also consider options including clarifying discipline procedures and implementing new supports and policies to improve student behavior.

Organizational Improvement Goal

The goal is to lower suspension referral rates significantly. Our target is at or below the average rate of suspension for schools in the district as shown in the table above.

Key Questions and Tasks

What are the statistics on VHS suspension rate trends and comparisons with other high schools?

We need to investigate our discipline data in more depth. Other analyses to be conducted include:
- percent of total VHS enrollment suspended at least once by year, for years 2008 - 2012;
- number of students (and percent of student body) with multiple suspension;
- among chronic offenders, what are their offenses?
- number of suspensions each week in VHS over the last three years;
- suspensions by category of offense (e.g., fighting, abusive language, trespassing, vandalism, theft, weapons possession, etc.);
- suspensions by categories of students (e.g., ethnic, gender, special education, free-lunch eligibility, achievement level);
- number/type of suspension referrals by referring teacher or administrator

What are causes of the rise in suspensions?

One explanation for rising referral rates is changes in student behavior. Possibly more students are committing more offenses meriting suspension. Another possibility is that the number of students committing offenses has not grown so much as the number of offenses has increased among those who commit offenses. Whether it is the former or the latter or some combination, this represents a worsening of student behavior that must be addressed because of its damaging effects on school climate, stuff time, the offending students, and those they affect. The high rates also adversely affect the entire school's reputation.

Another factor contributing to the rising rates may be an increasing propensity of teachers to issue referrals, which may occur even if student behavior has not materially worsened. It is possible teachers are simply more likely to refer students to the office for suspension based on the teachers' discretion and interpretation of the code of conduct rules. Behaviors among students that in the past may have been tolerated and not led to a referral perhaps are no longer tolerated; perhaps some teachers have become stricter. We do not know whether this is occurring but need to explore this. If teachers have inconsistent interpretations of code of conduct policies and reporting procedures, this inconsistency must be addressed, because it is important that rule are understood by all and consistently applied.

Key questions to explore include:

- Is VHS is enrolling more students who more frequently behave in ways that violate the school's code of conduct?
- Have conditions within the school changed in ways to cause more infractions of the code of conduct?
- Are staff members who make referrals following our policies (do we have clear, well understood policies)?
- Have teachers become less tolerant of disruptive behaviors?
- Are teachers more frequently referring students inappropriately for suspension (i.e., referrals for behaviors that are not really infractions of the rules)?

What literature can inform our deliberations on the suspension rate issue?

We will seek research-based guides for best practices for managing discipline at the high school level. Relevant questions and topics include prevention strategies, how to manage repeat offenders, tradeoffs between in-school and out-of-school suspension policies, staff training on conflict management, and legal issues connected with suspending students.[65]

What changes will be needed to lower the incidence of suspension referrals?

While we cannot yet determine what to do, we can assume some form of changes will be required, which are likely to be a combination of ways to alter the conditions that contribute to students' actions and ways we respond. It will be helpful to consider early one what some changes might be in order and the processes needed to design and implement changes.

References

Bonny, A., Britto, M., Klostermann, B., Hornung, R., & Slap, G. (2000). School disconnectedness: Identifying adolescents at risk. *Pediatrics, 106*(5), November, 1017-1021.

Copelan, R. (2006). Assessing the potential for violent behavior in children and adolescents. *Pediatrics in Review, 27*, e36-e41.

Skiba, R., Peterson, R., & Williams, T. (1997). Office referrals and suspension: Disciplinary intervention in middle schools. *Education and Treatment of Children 20*, August, 295-315.

---

[65] It is important for safety, public information, and for legal reasons to maintain accurate and up-to-date records on students and disciplinary actions, especially those exhibiting a propensity for threatening behavior (Bonny, Britto, Klostermann, Hornung, & Slap, 2000l ; Copelan, 2006; Skiba, Peterson, & Williams, 1997). This is necessary also to make sure school counselors are attempting to help these students.

APPENDIX 3-D: ANALYZING THE SUSPENSION PROBLEM – CAUSAL MAP OF FACTORS AND INTERRELATIONSHIPS

This causal map relates to the problem of rising suspension referral rates at Valley High School discussed in Chapter 3 and presented in Appendix 3-C, "Rising Suspension Rates: Investigating Causes and Remedies." Causal mapping is discussed in the Chapter 3 section, "Causal Analysis to Generate Questions (Conjectures)."

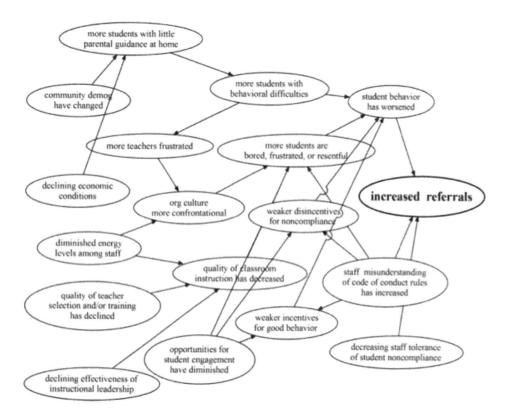

APPENDIX 3-E: PLANNING DISTRICTWIDE SUPPLEMENTAL MATH
INSTRUCTION TO ADDRESS LOW 8th GRADE MATHEMATICS ACHIEVEMENT
– SAMPLE DECISION CHARTS

The decision charts below are part of the problem statement of low mathematics achievement discussed in Chapter 3's section "Decision Charts." The charts show decision alternatives in both a centralized management approach versus a more decentralized implementation. The top chart shows the decentralized, "site-based" approach; the bottom one is the district managed implementation. In the charts are *decision alternatives* ("Alt" in the chart), *tradeoffs* ("pros" and "cons"), and *key uncertainties* associated with different alternatives ("unknowns").

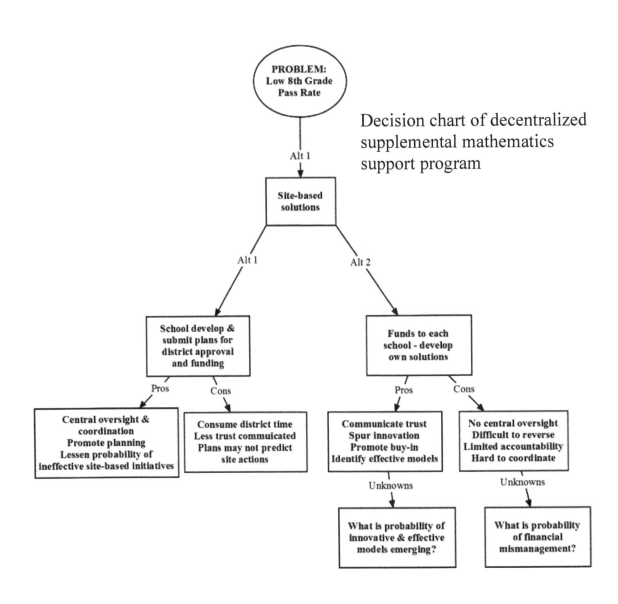

Decision chart of decentralized supplemental mathematics support program

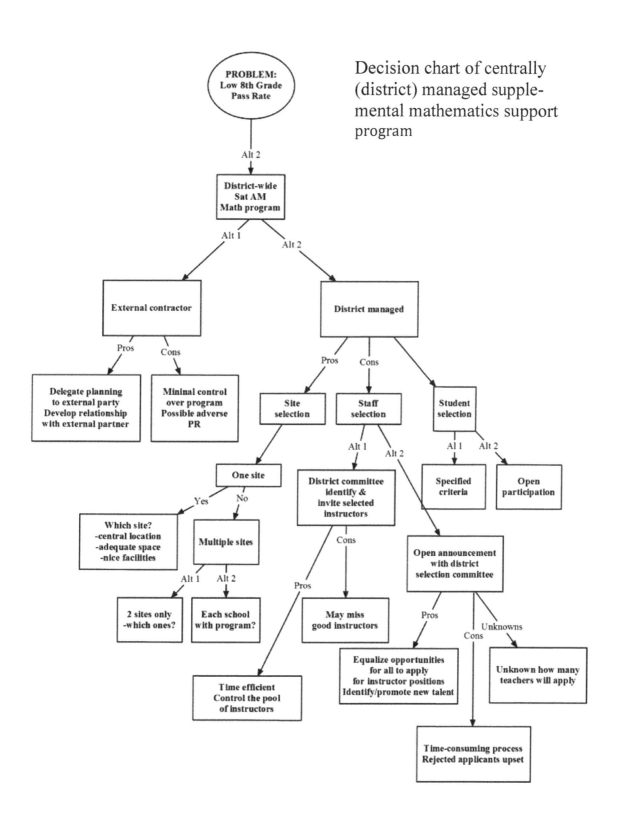

Decision chart of centrally (district) managed supplemental mathematics support program

PROBLEM: Low 8th Grade Pass Rate

Alt 2

District-wide Sat AM Math program

Alt 1 → External contractor
Alt 2 → District managed

External contractor
- Pros: Delegate planning to external party / Develop relationship with external partner
- Cons: Mininal control over program / Possible adverse PR

District managed
- Pros
- Cons

Site selection
Staff selection
Student selection

One site
- Yes: Which site? -central location -adequate space -nice facilities
- No: Multiple sites
  - Alt 1: 2 sites only -which ones?
  - Alt 2: Each school with program?

Time efficient / Control the pool of instructors

Staff selection
- Alt 1: District committee identify & invite selected instructors
  - Cons: May miss good instructors
  - Pros: Time efficient / Control the pool of instructors
- Alt 2: Open announcement with district selection committee
  - Pros: Equalize opportunities for all to apply for instructor positions / Identify/promote new talent
  - Cons: Time-consuming process / Rejected applicants upset
  - Unknowns: Unknown how many teachers will apply

Student selection
- Al 1: Specified criteria
- Alt 2: Open participation

153

APPENDIX 4-A: CHECKLIST OF QUESTIONS TO ASSESS A QUANTITATIVE STUDY'S QUALITY

Introduction and Problem/Purpose Statement
• Is the introduction/rationale section clear and organized? (The rationale is the reason for doing the study – why it is significant, why the information is important, what we will learn and how what we learn can be used.)
• Does the study ask clear and focused questions? Are the questions all presented in one place, near the beginning?
• Is it clear and logical how the questions follow from the rationale?
• Does the study define terms and concepts that are important in the analysis? Do the authors pose excessively broad questions or more questions than the study actually answers?

Sample
• Is the explanation of the study's sample clear? Do you understand it?
• Is the justification for the sample logical? Do we know why the people [or other units] in the sample were the ones chosen?
• Is the sample appropriate for the study? Does the sample draw on enough observations to allow trustworthy conclusions?
• Are subgroups (samples) that are *compared with each other* in the study appropriately equivalent (i.e., appropriate matched)? – or at least equivalent enough that observed differences between "control" group(s) and "treatment" group(s) are not likely to be caused by initial differences in the groups or other factors that may "contaminate" the study?

Instruments and Measures
• Are the study's instruments valid? What evidence or support is provided to show that the instruments measure what they claim to measure?

• Are the constructs that the instruments claim to measure (e.g., achievement, ability, skills, traits, attitudes, opinions) clearly defined and do the definitions make sense?

Comparisons
• Are the "control conditions" and the "treatment conditions" (or whatever comparisons are being done) well designed or well chosen to support inferences about their effects?
• Are the "control conditions" and the "treatment conditions" (or whatever comparisons are being done) truly different from each other?

Findings and Conclusions
• Do you trust the author's claims about the findings? That is, do you trust that the evidence really supports the study's conclusions? Do interpretations and/or conclusions go beyond the evidence?
• Are there other plausible explanations for the findings? What other possible causes may account for the observed findings? Are these considered? Are alternative causes and explanations likely?
• Does the author provide appropriate qualifications for his/her findings and conclusions (the author acknowledges possible unique characteristics of or biases within the sample or limitations of the instruments)?

Presentation & Style
• Are the tables clear and well organized, with all tables and variables within the tables meaningfully labeled?
• When you read a table, do you have all the information you need to understand the table?
• Are the descriptions and explanations of the findings clear and organized?
• Are the conclusions clearly presented?

APPENDIX 4-B: SAMPLE LETTER INVITING PARTICIPANTS TO A FOCUS GROUP

Date
Name
Address
Dear [Name],

[Name of school] is looking for ways to improve and needs your help.

We would like to cordially invite you to join us in a group discussion to talk about education issues in our community, specifically our plans to redesign our high school. We want to hear your opinions and ideas for creating a better school for our students and our community.

The group will consist of about seven other people like you and a moderator.

Thank you for considering being a part of this discussion. If you have any questions, please feel free to call me at [phone number].

Sincerely,

Name & Title

....

RSVP

Name: _____

Best telephone number or email address to contact me:

_____

___ Yes, I can participate in a research group discussion at [time] on [date]. I will see you at [location].

___ No, I cannot participate in this research group discussion. Please let me know if you have other dates and times available.

___ No, I am not interested in participating in any research group discussion.

** Please return RSVP in the self-address, stamped envelope included. **

(Source: www.smallschoolsproject.org – a Gates Foundation reform project, now defunct)

APPENDIX 4-C: EXAMPLE OF REPORTING INTERVIEW RESULTS

Parent Responses to Selected Focus Group Questions about the "Words to Go" Program

Theme Emerging From Questions	Selected Examples Of Positive Responses	Selected Examples Of Negative Responses
Easy to Use	"I'm the parent that goes I don't understand what your teacher is asking with this." This program is totally easy. The most explanatory that I have ever had." "What I thought was helpful was the page, the lesson that comes with it." "Well, even your child can do it on their [sic] own practically."	Grouping or sorting words I think is, I think that's harder for me than for the kids to understand. Sometimes we don't have enough letters to make all the words on the script.
Amount of Time	"I thought eight words per day were doable. We get all her homework done in 5 or 10 minutes except for her 15 minutes of reading time."	"My child really enjoys saying, 'okay mom, we need to do this now.' And so it does force me to take the time. Even if we do it in the car, and we've done that."
Interest and Engagement	Well we have a zip lock bag that each week we cut everything out, put everything in the zip lock bag, and then we work on it each night and put them back inside. On Thursday night we take all that and we trash it. She's so excited at the end of the week to put that in the trash.	He is one of the highest ones in the And so I think the program is working for some of them. He is a high achiever and so I think to him that was just a waste of time and boring.
Consistency of Use	I did eight every night because the teacher said making words – eight words every day – is important. And so I'm going to have her continue so she doesn't lose it during the summer. Just have her know that she has to work on that for a little while each day.	I noticed that when we very first got them, the first of the year, he was okay for about a week. And then it was, "This is boring. I don't want to do this anymore. This is dumb. Why do I have to do it?"

Source: Reutzel, D., Fawson, P., & Smith, J. (2006). "Words to Go!": Evaluating a first-grade parent involvement program for "making" words at home. *Reading Research and Instruction, 45*(2), Winter, 119-59.

APPENDIX 4-D: ROUND 3 LIST FROM DELPHI IDEA-GENERATION PROCESS FOCUSED ON STRENGTHENING PERFORMANCE INCENTIVES FOR TEACHERS AT THE BUILDING LEVEL

As discussed in Chapter 4, this list is an excerpt from two prior rounds of idea-generation. It is just an excerpt, showing 7 round two ideas (in bold) and the round three ideas that embellish the round two ideas. The complete list (not shown here) has 47 round two ideas and hundreds of round three ideas. For more details on the Delphi information-gathering process, see Chapter 4, "Delphi Technique" and references provided.

>>**Do research to identify why some teachers are not high achievers and how to motivate them.**
-Some teachers got into the profession for the money and not for the job. With the law and unions that teachers are involved in, my cause some teachers to strike and as result students may end up in loosing schools days.
-Sponsor a graduate thesis on this subject
-Conduct a survey with the teachers themselves to identify what would motivate them to do more or what obstacles they encounter that prevent them from achieving more in the classroom.
-Investigation of motivation factors is valuable, but can be difficult to obtain. Honest expression is required by each individual; this can be difficult if some individuals feel a threat from the activity. They may respond with what they believe is wanted; may be concerned about retribution by the administration.
-Research should examine what conditions are best for different teaching styles/approaches. In some situations, the teacher may not be in an environment that is most conducive to their teaching style.
-Research on motivation not necessary. Motivate teachers by providing rewards!
-Some indicators may be professional satisfaction, quality of resources, and relationship with the administrative staff. Motivation may be offered through financial incentives and advancement within a career path.

>>**Improve the status of the profession of "teacher." One way might be by changing the name of teachers to "educators."**
-Instead of educators- professors – like European status
-I think career ladder and promotional opportunities would do more to improve status than just calling teachers by another name.
-I do not believe that changing the name would have any impact. If teachers wish to be viewed as more professional, they may need to assimilate the professional attributes of those outside education to

be accepted by those outside education. One possible way is to work a "year round" schedule.
-Why not change it to coach and professional mediator? In many cases I don't think this would make much of a difference. It is the equivalent of changing stewardess to flight attendant. The duties are the same.
-It will take more than a name change to improve "status."

>>**Use a nomination system to help identify high-performing teachers based on nominations from peers, students, parents, etc.**
-Exemplary behaviors must be described. A committee of peers could evaluate submissions and hold public celebration(s) throughout school year.
-The exemplary behaviors must be operationally defined. Nominees must provide concrete examples of their practice from the definition. But nominations may become political. Also, apathy may prevent some worthy recipients from getting nominated.
-Similar to "Teacher of the Year," yet includes more than one teacher
-Good place to start, will have to consider professional jealousy, etc.
-Peer recognition is powerful. Team building and concepts such as Total Quality Management could be utilized to modify or reinforce peer behavior. Public awards, in many cases, have a more lasting affect than pure financial rewards.

>>**Revise the standard evaluation process to include teacher portfolios so that high-performing teachers can be more readily identified.**
-Would require complete overhaul of the current system
-Administration must have defined role in peer evaluation.
-The emphasis would be more on mentoring, and constructive criticism
-Display portfolios in teachers' lounge or main office.

-A comprehensive portfolio could add multiple perspectives in the evaluative process.

-Teachers may begin by including certificates of attendance to professional development sessions, performance evaluations, student comments (if teacher does evaluation for own edification)

-This is a very practical idea. Research shows portfolios are a successful means of evaluating student performance. Perhaps a trial period could take place. A district could implement different means of teacher evaluation and use feedback from the teachers to decide whether or not it was successful.

-Educators will need training to achieve this

>>**Give high performing teachers the option of assuming leadership roles (ex. master teacher, mentor teacher) with additional compensation for assuming additional responsibilities.**

-This could increase teachers' commitments to their jobs. Many teachers complain they are underpaid and unrecognized for their work. Giving better performing teachers leadership roles is consistent could strengthen professional accountability.

-One problem with promoting teachers to leadership positions based on merit in teaching is it pulls them from what they do well … teaching. I support instead additional compensation for high performance … give leadership roles based on leadership potential and skills.

-Excellent idea. Modeling is always a good concept….even if it is my title alone.

-Assign (informally and in non-threatening way), effective teachers to new or even experienced teachers. The pairs of teachers can use common time to discuss things such as management and content issues.

-This idea is embodied in most peer coaching approaches. A key is structuring peer experiences so they are non-threatening, and so that trust is built between partnered teachers. Teachers often work in relative isolation, so the peer coaching model helps promote talk about teaching strategies and techniques and forces teachers to leave their own classroom and see what is happening in other rooms.

-Creates teacher empowerment. Additional compensation rewards the most able – like merit pay. This recognizes and reward expertise in more substantive ways than intrinsic motivators.

-Feasible, probably, but could cause tension among staff.

-Will require careful negotiation, trust

-Requires a fund to support new opportunities for teacher leadership roles, like release-time to work with other teachers.

-Teachers assuming these roles could be considered the "elder states-people". Younger, less experienced teachers will relate to "master teachers;" may create incentives to model their behavior and careers.

>> **A one-year mentoring position to assist other teachers in the school or in other school districts through classroom visitations, instructional demonstrations, etc.**

-Excellent idea. Pride and recognition for the teacher doing the mentoring, but also s/he learns additional strategies through teaching others.

-Teachers receiving training feel less threatened when comes from peer rather than supervisor.

-Provide training to the teacher on effective mentoring skills. Provide guidelines for successful mentoring relationships.

-Similar to the cadre teachers in several districts, although their positions last for more than one year.

-Would there be a stipend or other type of compensation for this? It would be difficult to name a teacher who would be interested in doing this.

>> **A four day work week for one month.**

-This would be a great idea if laws didn't regulate the number of days which students needed to attend school. Reducing the work week would extend the school year into the summer.

-Fantastic idea – however with the shortage of substitute teachers it could potentially create staffing problems.

-Does this involve the district hiring substitutes? Good idea, but then a teacher would have to provide lesson plans, and there is already a shortage of subs.

-Idea sounds great, but has a drawback….you pull your best teacher out of the classroom for one day a week. Pull other duties off of their plate; keep them in the classroom.

-Logistics of this suggestion are a concern. Would this indicate a four-day workweek for students also, if a guest teacher were the instructor for the fifth day?

- Would the students be excused on that fifth day too? If not, would a substitute be hired? Often it is more work to have a substitute.

>> **Offer plaques, certificates, awards, "thank you" posters**

-Can encourage other teachers to follow suit

-Administrators may start with recognition of perfect attendance for a particular year

-Personal note may be better to avoid the competitive spirit of who gets the thank you poster.

-Have classroom children create poster thanking their teacher

-Add written notes to personnel file.

APPENDIX 5-A: OPENING WITH AN ANECDOTE TO ILLUSTRATE A PROBLEM

The Problem: Too Many Unrelated, Unsustained 'Improvement' Programs

SOURCE: Newmann, F., Smith,B., Allensworth, E. and Bryk, A. (2001). *School instructional program coherence: Benefits and challenges*. Chicago, IL: Consortium on Chicago School Research. (pp. 9 – 11)

A TV newscaster, on assignment to publicize progress in urban school reform, is explaining why he selected Travis Elementary School for his story:

> "There's so much happening. The teachers are a great group and their principal is always getting them new programs and equipment. The entryway has plaques, commendations, pictures and letters to show all the activities they are involved in. It lists all the school improvement initiatives, too. For reading alone they have Reading Recovery, SRA, Great Books, Accelerated Reader, Drop Everything and Read (DEAR), and Links to Literacy. The mathematics initiatives include Plato, The Algebra Project, Family Math, and a new textbook series. The school has programs with over a dozen social service partners and community groups. Lots of the faculty sponsor special programs for the kids, too. Gosh, I remember when I used to visit these urban schools and they seemed like graveyards where nothing was happening and few were trying."

The reporter's positive comments were appreciated, but people more familiar with Travis knew that, in spite of all the hard work and innovation, student scores in reading and mathematics remained far below the district's performance standards. The principal and teachers attended meetings and conferences to take advantage of new opportunities, but many staff members were tired and frustrated. One teacher said:

> "Some Saturday mornings I can't remember which workshop I'm supposed to go to. I know it's a bad weekend when I'm supposed to be at two at once. Or, when what they tell us to do at one workshop is the opposite of what was suggested at the last. In class, I just tryout bits of each as best I can."

Travis' principal respected her teachers and worked tirelessly to bring them new resources and ideas: "My teachers are doing their absolute best. They're trying terribly hard, most of them. There's so much out there to do. And I keep finding more, and asking them to do more. Sometimes I feel like we're juggling too many balls in the air, and either we're going to drop the balls, or we're going to be so tired, and pulled in so many directions, we're the ones who are going to drop."

> "My teachers are doing their absolute best. They're trying terribly hard, most of them. There's so much out there to do. And I keep finding more, and asking them to do more. Sometimes I feel like we're juggling too many balls in the air, and either we're going to drop the balls, or we're going to be so tired, and pulled in so many directions, we're the ones who are going to drop."

The story of Travis reflects a trend among many urban schools, including schools in Chicago. On the one hand, administrators and teachers want to adopt programs and materials that might help them teach more effectively. On the other, there are so many meetings and workshops, that staff express not only fatigue, but also professional frustration. They find themselves faced with a large and fragmented array of school improvement grants, programs, and partnerships that rarely afford them the time or support to adopt and master practices that may improve student learning.

Principals are caught in a bind. Some recognize that their faculty might be "juggling too many balls." On the other hand, they also know that they cannot expect their schools to improve if everything stays the same. Hooking up with multiple improvement initiatives often seems the only way to bring needed resources to a school and to promote the work and commitment of staff with very different interests or strengths. Moreover, the emotional and social needs of many of their students are enormous, far beyond what a school can address on its own. For this reason, partnerships with external organizations seem essential. Even when principals recognize that their teachers are stretched in too many directions, they seem unable to cut programs, believing strongly that they need all of these extra resources to help the children.

Research has documented the importance of school organizational factors such as a unity of purpose, a clear focus, and shared values for student learning. Research has also drawn attention to the problem of incoherent school programs, where diverse initiatives set up to serve important needs, but which lack the sustained attention of the majority of staff within the school, have no apparent effects on the core goal of improving student achievement. Earlier Consortium research focused specific attention on the problems of "Christmas tree" innovations; that is, change or improvement strategies that bring attention to a school through numerous program and equipment purchases but fail to build its capacity to improve teaching and learning. Other research has pointed out how cluttered and contradictory state and district policy environments also fragment school development efforts. All this implies the need for instructional program coherence.

APPENDIX 5-B: ILLUSTRATION OF A THREE-LEVEL HEADING SYSTEM

COMPARATIVE FRAMES OF REFERENCE FOR DEVELOPING A PROBLEM STATEMENT

The title is not considered a heading.

Introduction

A problem definition is an interpretation and an argument. [It ref]lects your perspective on a situation. It is an interpretation based on facts, l[...]

These are Level 1 headings.

Different Types of Comparisons in Problem Statements

To support your problem statement, you can answer the question "compared to what" in essentially three ways: other organizations, prior states in your organization, or goals and standards. Also, be clear in distinguishing whether your focus in [...] conditions, or performance. These topics are the focus of this section.

This is the first of four Level 2 headings on this page.

Comparison To Others

The "others" here refers to other similar organizations (or departments, offices, associations, professions). If the problem concerning you is X in some identifiable unit within your organization (or in your organization as a whole), present evidence showing X is worse in this unit than in other comparable units or organizations (e.g., morale is lower in this department than in most all other departments in the university).

Comparison To Past Conditions/Performance

A second type of comparison is to your organization's past. Changes for the worse in conditions or performance are persuasive in defining a problem. The drop-out rate in Springville HS has been increasing for the last five years. These are examples of the second type of comparison.

Comparison To Goals and Standards

A third type of comparison is to goals or standards presc[...] type of comparison, the performance gap is not between you and [...] between current performance and past performance. Rather, the [...] and a set of expectations derived from an authoritative source.

This Level 2 section has two subsections with Level 3 headings.

Distinguishing Among Inputs, Conditions, and Performance

Some problem statements focus on *inputs* or *conditions* in the organization, less on *performance*. Other problem definitions start with claims about performance deficiencies, and then analyze the conditions or inputs accounting for the performance deficiency. The next two sections explain in more detail these distinctions.

Defining organizational inputs, conditions, and performance. Performance is the degree to which an organization achieves its goals. Goals are the intentions; performance is what happens. It is important to understand that the word "performance" (as in "org[...]. A variable is a something that varies, that exists in greater or less[...]

These are Level 3 headings. There is a period at the end, and only the first word is capitalized.

Linking problems to goals. A problem definition re[...]ffect performance. To be persuasive, your problem definition must s[...] and performance. When arguing that conditions are a problem, your logic assumes that fixing these conditions will improve organizational performance. If this logic is not credible, the problem statement will not be persuasive. You make a problem significant in the minds of others by establishing its causal connection to performance.

161